CW01376489

ИЗДАНИЕ НА АНГЛИЙСКОМ И РУССКОМ ЯЗЫКАХ

Современный бестселлер: билингва

ХРОНИКИ НАРНИИ

Конь и его мальчик

КЛАЙВ С. ЛЬЮИС

THE CHRONICLES OF NARNIA

The Horse and His Boy

C.S. LEWIS

МОСКВА
2017

УДК 811.111(075.4)
ББК 81.2Англ-93
Л91

C.S. Lewis

THE HORSE AND HIS BOY

Перевод с английского *Н. Трауберг*

Составление упражнений *А. Логиновой*

Оформление *В. Безкровного*

Льюис, Клайв Стейплз.

Л91 Хроники Нарнии. Конь и его мальчик = The Chronicles of Narnia. The Horse and His Boy / Клайв С. Льюис ; [пер. с англ. Н. Трауберг]. — Москва : Эксмо, 2017. — 352 с. — (Современный бестселлер: билингва).

ISBN 978-5-699-84286-5

В этом издании читателям предлагаются неадаптированный оригинальный текст и классический перевод удивительной повести из волшебной эпопеи «Хроники Нарнии». Какой была Нарния в эпоху правления Питера, Сьюзен, Люси и Эдмунда? И какие приключения происходили с ними и с другими чудесными героями?

Чтение текста в оригинале позволит значительно усовершенствовать знание английского, а перевод на русский язык поможет разрешить возникающие по ходу чтения вопросы и трудности. Для углубления знаний английского и облегчения понимания текста предлагаются упражнения.

Книга будет интересна и полезна всем, кто знает и изучает английский язык с преподавателем или самостоятельно.

УДК 811.111(075.4)
ББК 81.2Англ-93

ISBN 978-5-699-84286-5

Contents

To David and Douglas Gresham

Chapter 1

HOW SHASTA SET OUT ON HIS TRAVELS

This is the story of an adventure that happened in Narnia and Calormen and the lands between, in the Golden Age when Peter was High King in Narnia and his brother and his two sisters were King and Queens under him.

In those days, far south in Calormen on a little creek of the sea, there lived a poor fisherman called Arsheesh, and with him there lived a boy who called him Father. The boy's name was Shasta. On most days Arsheesh went out in his boat to fish in the morning, and in the afternoon he harnessed his donkey to a cart and loaded the cart with fish and went a mile or so southward to the village to sell it. If it had sold well he would come home in a moderately good temper and say nothing to Shasta, but if it had sold badly he would find fault with him and perhaps beat him. There was always something to find fault with for Shasta had plenty of work to do, mending and washing the nets, cooking the supper, and cleaning the cottage in which they both lived.

Shasta was not at all interested in anything that lay south of his home because he had once or twice been to the village with Arsheesh and he knew that there was nothing very interesting there. In the village he only met other men who were just like his father — men with long, dirty robes, and wooden shoes turned up at the toe, and

Посвящается Дэвиду и Дугласу Грэшемам

Глава 1

ПОБЕГ

Это повесть о событиях, случившихся в Нарнии и к югу от неё тогда, когда ею правили король Питер и его брат и две сестры. В те дни далеко на юге, у моря, жил бедный рыбак по имени Аршиш, а с ним мальчик по имени Шаста, звавший его отцом. Утром Аршиш выходил в море ловить рыбу, а днём запрягал осла, клал рыбу в повозку и ехал в ближайшую деревню торговать. Если он выручал много, то возвращался в добром духе и Шасту не трогал; если выручал мало, придирался, как только мог, и даже бил мальчика. Придраться было не трудно, потому что Шаста делал всё по дому: стряпал и убирал, а также стирал и чинил сети.

Шаста никогда не думал о том, что лежит от них к югу. С Аршишем в деревне бывал, и ему там не нравилось. Он видел точно таких людей, как его отец, — в неопрятных длинных одеждах, сандалиях и тюрбанах, с грязными длинными бородами, медленно толковавших об очень скучных делах. Зато его

turbans on their heads, and beards, talking to one another very slowly about things that sounded dull. But he was very interested in everything that lay to the North because no one ever went that way and he was never allowed to go there himself. When he was sitting out of doors mending the nets, and all alone, he would often look eagerly to the North. One could see nothing but a grassy slope running up to a level ridge and beyond that the sky with perhaps a few birds in it.

Sometimes if Arsheesh was there Shasta would say, 'O my Father, what is there beyond that hill?' And then if the fisherman was in a bad temper he would box Shasta's ears and tell him to attend to his work. Or if he was in a peaceable mood he would say, 'O my son, do not allow your mind to be distracted by idle questions. For one of the poets has said, "Application to business is the root of prosperity, but those who ask questions that do not concern them are steering the ship of folly towards the rock of indigence."'

Shasta thought that beyond the hill there must be some delightful secret which his father wished to hide from him. In reality, however, the fisherman talked like this because he didn't know what lay to the North. Neither did he care. He had a very practical mind.

One day there came from the South a stranger who was unlike any man that Shasta had seen before. He rode upon a strong dappled horse with flowing mane and tail and his stirrups and bridle were inlaid with silver. The spike of a helmet projected from the middle of his silken turban and he wore a shirt of chain mail. By his side hung a curving scimitar, a round shield studded with bosses of brass hung at his back, and his right hand grasped a lance. His face was dark, but this did not surprise Shasta because all the people of Calormen are like that; what

живо занимало всё, что лежит к северу, но туда его не пускали. Сидя на пороге и занимаясь починкой сети, мальчик с тоской глядел на север, но видел только склон холма, небо и редких птиц.

Когда Аршиш бывал дома, Шаста спрашивал: «Отец, что там, за холмом?» Если Аршиш сердился, то драл его за уши, если же был спокоен, отвечал: «Сын мой, не думай о пустом. Как сказал мудрец, прилежание — корень успеха, а те, кто задаёт пустые вопросы, ведут корабль глупости на рифы неудачи».

Шасте казалось, что за холмом — какая-то дивная тайна, которую отец до поры скрывает от него. На самом же деле рыбак говорил так, ибо не знал, да и знать не хотел, какие земли лежат к северу. У него был практический ум.

Однажды с юга прибыл незнакомец, совсем иной, чем те, кого видел Шаста до сих пор. Он сидел на прекрасном коне, и седло его сверкало серебром. Сверкали и кольчуга, и острие шлема, торчащее над тюрбаном. На боку его висел ятаган, спину прикрывал медный щит, в руке было копьё. Незнакомец был тёмен лицом, но Шаста привык к темнолицым, а удивило его иное: борода, выкрашенная в алый цвет, вилась кольцами и лоснилась от благовоний. Аршиш понял, что это тархан, то есть вельможа, и склонился

did surprise him was the man's beard which was dyed crimson, and curled and gleaming with scented oil. But Arsheesh knew by the gold on the stranger's bare arm that he was a Tarkaan or great lord, and he bowed kneeling before him till his beard touched the earth and made signs to Shasta to kneel also.

The stranger demanded hospitality for the night which of course the fisherman dared not refuse. All the best they had was set before the Tarkaan for supper (and he didn't think much of it) and Shasta, as always happened when the fisherman had company, was given a hunk of bread and turned out of the cottage. On these occasions he usually slept with the donkey in its little thatched stable. But it was much too early to go to sleep yet, and Shasta, who had never learned that it is wrong to listen behind doors, sat down with his ear to a crack in the wooden wall of the cottage to hear what the grown-ups were talking about. And this is what he heard.

'And now, O my host,' said the Tarkaan, 'I have a mind to buy that boy of yours.'

'O my master,' replied the fisherman (and Shasta knew by the wheedling tone the greedy look that was probably coming into his face as he said it), 'what price could induce your servant, poor though he is, to sell into slavery his only child and his own flesh? Has not one of the poets said, "Natural affection is stronger than soup and offspring more precious than carbuncles?"'

'It is even so,' replied the guest dryly. 'But another poet has likewise said, "He who attempts to deceive the judicious is already baring his own back for the scourge." Do not load your aged mouth with falsehoods. This boy is manifestly no son of yours, for your cheek is as dark as mine but the boy is fair and white like the accursed but beautiful barbarians who inhabit the remote North.'

до земли, незаметно показывая Шасте, чтобы и тот преклонил колени.

Незнакомец попросил ночлега на одну ночь, и Аршиш не посмел отказать ему. Всё лучшее, что было в доме, хозяин поставил перед ним, а мальчику (так всегда бывало, когда приходили гости) дал кусок хлеба и выгнал во двор. В таких случаях Шаста спал с ослом, в стойле. Но поскольку было ещё рано и никто никогда не говорил ему, что подслушивать нельзя, он сел у самой стены.

— О, хозяин! — промолвил тархан. — Мне угодно купить у тебя этого мальчика.

— О, господин мой! — ответил рыбак, и Шаста угадал по его голосу, что глазки у него алчно блеснули. — Как же продам я, твой верный раб, своего собственного сына? Разве не сказал поэт: «Сильна, как смерть, отцовская любовь, а сыновняя дороже, чем алмазы»?

— Возможно, — сухо выговорил тархан, — но другой поэт говорил: «Кто хочет гостя обмануть — подлее, чем гиена». Не оскверняй ложью свои уста. Он тебе не сын, ибо ты тёмен лицом, а он светел и бел, как проклятые, но прекрасные нечестивцы с севера.

'How well it was said,' answered the fisherman, 'that Swords can be kept off with shields but the Eye of Wisdom pierces through every defence! Know then, O my formidable guest, that because of my extreme poverty I have never married and have no child. But in that same year in which the Tisroc (may he live for ever) began his august and beneficent reign, on a night when the moon was at her full, it pleased the gods to deprive me of my sleep. Therefore I arose from my bed in this hovel and went forth to the beach to refresh myself with looking upon the water and the moon and breathing the cool air. And presently I heard a noise as of oars coming to me across the water and then, as it were, a weak cry. And shortly after, the tide brought to the land a little boat in which there was nothing but a man lean with extreme hunger and thirst who seemed to have died but a few moments before (for he was still warm), and an empty water-skin, and a child, still living. 'Doubtless,' said I, 'these unfortunates have escaped from the wreck of a great ship, but by the admirable designs of the gods, the elder has starved himself to keep the child alive and has perished in sight of land.' Accordingly, remembering how the gods never fail to reward those who befriend the destitute, and being moved by compassion (for your servant is a man of tender heart) — '

'Leave out all these idle words in your own praise,' interrupted the Tarkaan. 'It is enough to know that you took the child — and have had ten times the worth of his daily bread out of him in labour, as anyone can see. And now tell me at once what price you put on him, for I am wearied with your loquacity.'

'You yourself have wisely said,' answered Arsheesh, 'that the boy's labour has been to me of inestimable value. This must be taken into account in fixing the price. For

— Дивно сказал кто-то, — парировал рыбак, — что око мудрости острее копья! Знай же, о мой высокородный гость, что я, по бедности своей, никогда не был женат. Но в год, когда Тисрок (да живёт он вечно) начал своё великое и благословенное царствование, в ночь полнолуния, боги лишили меня сна. Я встал с постели и вышел поглядеть на луну. Вдруг послышался плеск воды, словно кто-то грёб вёслами, и слабый крик. Немного позже прилив прибил к берегу маленькую лодку, в которой лежал иссушенный голодом человек. Должно быть, он только что умер, ибо ещё не остыл, а рядом с ним был пустой сосуд и живой младенец. Вспомнив о том, что боги не оставляют без награды доброе дело, я прослезился, ибо раб твой мягкосердечен, и...

— Не хвали себя, — прервал его тархан. — Ты взял младенца, и он отработал тебе вдесятеро твою скудную пищу. Теперь скажи мне цену, ибо я устал от твоего пусторечия.

— Ты мудро заметил, господин, — сказал рыбак, — что труд его выгоден мне. Если я продам этого отрока, то должен купить или нанять другого.

if I sell the boy I must undoubtedly either buy or hire another to do his work.'

'I'll give you fifteen crescents for him,' said the Tarkaan.

'Fifteen!' cried Arsheesh in a voice that was something between a whine and a scream. 'Fifteen! For the prop of my old age and the delight of my eyes! Do not mock my grey beard, Tarkaan though you be. My price is seventy.'

At this point Shasta got up and tiptoed away. He had heard all he wanted, for he had often listened when men were bargaining in the village and knew how it was done. He was quite certain that Arsheesh would sell him in the end for something much more than fifteen crescents and much less than seventy, but that he and the Tarkaan would take hours in getting to an agreement.

You must not imagine that Shasta felt at all as you and I would feel if we had just overheard our parents talking about selling us for slaves. For one thing, his life was already little better than slavery; for all he knew, the lordly stranger on the great horse might be kinder to him than Arsheesh. For another, the story about his own discovery in the boat had filled him with excitement and with a sense of relief. He had often been uneasy because, try as he might, he had never been able to love the fisherman, and he knew that a boy ought to love his father. And now, apparently, he was no relation to Arsheesh at all. That took a great weight off his mind. 'Why, I might be anyone!' he thought. 'I might be the son of a Tarkaan myself — or the son of the Tisroc (may he live for ever) or of a god!'

He was standing out in the grassy place before the cottage while he thought these things. Twilight was coming on apace and a star or two was already out, but the

— Даю тебе пятнадцать полумесяцев, — сказал тархан.

— Пятнадцать! — взвыл Аршиш. — Пятнадцать монет за усладу моих очей и опору моей старости! Не смейся надо мною, я сед. Моя цена — семьдесят полумесяцев.

Тут Шаста поднялся и тихо ушёл, потому что знал, как люди торгуются, а, стало быть, Аршиш выручит за него больше пятнадцати монет, но меньше семидесяти, и спор протянется не один час.

Не думайте, что Шаста чувствовал то же самое, что почувствовали бы вы, если бы ваши родители решили вас продать. Жизнь его была не лучше рабства, и тархан мог оказаться добрее, чем Аршиш. К тому же он очень обрадовался, узнав свою историю. Он часто сокрушался прежде, что не может любить рыбака, и когда понял, что тот ему чужой, с души его упало тяжкое бремя. «Наверное, я сын какого-нибудь тархана, — подумал мальчик, — или Тисрока (да живёт он вечно), а то и божества!»

Тем временем сумерки сгущались и редкие звёзды уже сверкали на небе, хотя у заднего края оно отливало багрянцем. Конь пришельца, привязанный

remains of the sunset could still be seen in the west. Not far away the stranger's horse, loosely tied to an iron ring in the wall of the donkey's stable, was grazing. Shasta strolled over to it and patted its neck. It went on tearing up the grass and took no notice of him.

Then another thought came into Shasta's mind. 'I wonder what sort of a man that Tarkaan is,' he said out loud. 'It would be splendid if he was kind. Some of the slaves in a great lord's house have next to nothing to do. They wear lovely clothes and eat meat every day. Perhaps he'd take me to the wars and I'd save his life in a battle and then he'd set me free and adopt me as his son and give me a palace and a chariot and a suit of armour. But then he might be a horrid cruel man. He might send me to work on the fields in chains. I wish I knew. How can I know? I bet this horse knows, if only he could tell me.'

The Horse had lifted its head. Shasta stroked its smooth-as-satin nose and said, 'I wish you could talk, old fellow.'

к столбу, мирно щипал траву. Шаста погладил его по холке, но конь никак не отреагировал на ласку, и мальчик подумал: «Кто его знает, какой он, этот тархан!»

— Хорошо, если добрый, — продолжил Шаста, не заметив, что размышляет вслух. — У некоторых тарханов рабы носят шёлковые одежды и каждый день едят мясо. Может быть, он возьмёт меня в поход, и я спасу ему жизнь, и он освободит меня, и усыновит, и подарит дворец... А вдруг он жестокий? Тогда закуёт меня в цепи. Как бы узнать? Конь-то знает, да не скажет.

Конь поднял голову, и Шаста, погладив его шёлковый нос, воскликнул:

— Ах, умел бы ты говорить!

And then for a second he thought he was dreaming, for quite distinctly, though in a low voice, the Horse said, 'But I can.'

Shasta stared into its great eyes and his own grew almost as big, with astonishment.

'How ever did *you* learn to talk?' he asked.

'Hush! Not so loud,' replied the Horse. 'Where I come from, nearly all the animals talk.'

'Wherever is that?' asked Shasta.

'Narnia,' answered the Horse. 'The happy land of Narnia — Narnia of the heathery mountains and the thymy downs, Narnia of the many rivers, the plashing glens, the mossy caverns and the deep forests ringing with the hammers of the Dwarfs. Oh the sweet air of Narnia! An hour's life there is better than a thousand years in Calormen.' It ended with a whinny that sounded very like a sigh.

'How did you get here?' said Shasta.

'Kidnapped,' said the Horse. 'Or stolen, or captured whichever you like to call it. I was only a foal at the time. My mother warned me not to range the Southern slopes, into Archenland and beyond, but I wouldn't heed her. And by the Lion's Mane I have paid for my folly. All these years I have been a slave to humans, hiding my true nature and pretending to be dumb and witless like their horses.'

'Why didn't you tell them who you were?'

'Not such a fool, that's why. If they'd once found out I could talk they would have made a show of me at fairs and guarded me more carefully than ever. My last chance of escape would have been gone.'

'And why — ' began Shasta, but the Horse interrupted him.

'Now look,' it said, 'we mustn't waste time on idle questions. You want to know about my master the

— Я умею, — тихо, но внятно ответил конь.

Думая, что это ему снится, Шаста всё-таки крикнул:

— Быть того не может!

— Тише! — сказал конь. — На моей родине есть говорящие животные.

— Где это? — спросил Шаста.

— В Нарнии.

И когда оба они успокоились, конь рассказал: Меня украли. Если хочешь, взяли в плен. В бытность мою жеребёнком мать запрещала мне убегать далеко к югу, но я не слушался. И поплатился за это, видит лев! Много лет я служу злым людям, притворяясь тупым и немым, как их кони.

— Почему же ты им не признаешься?

— Не такой я дурак! Они будут показывать меня на ярмарках и сторожить пуще прежнего. Но оставим пустые беседы. Ты хочешь знать, каков мой хозяин Анрадин. Он жесток. Со мной — не очень, кони дороги, а тебе, человеку, лучше умереть, чем быть рабом в его доме.

Tarkaan Anradin. Well, he's bad. Not too bad to me, for a war horse costs too much to be treated very badly. But you'd better be lying dead tonight than go to be a human slave in his house tomorrow.'

'Then I'd better run away,' said Shasta, turning very pale.

'Yes, you had,' said the Horse. 'But why not run away with me?'

'Are you going to run away too?' said Shasta.

'Yes, if you'll come with me,' answered the Horse. 'This is the chance for both of us. You see, if I run away without a rider, everyone who sees me will say "Stray horse" and be after me as quick as he can. With a rider I've a chance to get through. That's where you can help me. On the other hand, you can't get very far on those two silly legs of yours (what absurd legs humans have!) without being overtaken. But on me you can outdistance any other horse in this country. That's where I can help you. By the way, I suppose you know how to ride?'

'Oh yes, of course,' said Shasta. 'At least, I've ridden the donkey.'

'Ridden the *what*?' retorted the Horse with extreme contempt. (At least, that is what he meant. Actually it came out in a sort of neigh — 'Ridden the wha-ha-ha-ha-ha?' Talking horses always become more horsy in accent when they are angry.)

'In other words,' it continued, 'you *can't* ride. That's a drawback. I'll have to teach you as we go along. If you can't ride, can you fall?'

'I suppose anyone can fall,' said Shasta.

'1 mean can you fall and get up again without crying and mount again and fall again and yet not be afraid of falling?'

'I — I'll try,' said Shasta.

— Тогда я убегу, — сказал Шаста, сильно побледнев.

— Да, беги, — сказал конь. — Со мною вместе.

— Ты тоже убежишь?

— Да, если убежишь ты, — кивнул конь. — Тогда мы, может быть, и спасёмся. Понимаешь, если я буду без всадника, люди увидят меня, подумают: «У него нет хозяина», — и погонятся за мной. А с всадником другое дело... Вот и помоги мне. Ты ведь далеко не уйдёшь на этих дурацких ногах (ну и ноги у вас, людей!), тебя поймают. Умеешь ездить верхом?

— Конечно, — сказал Шаста. — Я часто езжу на осле.

— На *чём*? Ха-ха-ха! — презрительно усмехнулся конь (во всяком случае, хотел усмехнуться, а вышло скорей «го-го-го!..»; у говорящих коней лошадиный акцент сильнее, когда они не в духе). — Одним словом, не умеешь. А падать хотя бы?

— Падать умеет всякий, — ответил Шаста.

— Навряд ли, — сказал конь. — Ты умеешь падать, и вставать, и, не плача, садиться в седло, и снова падать, и не бояться?

— Я... постараюсь.

'Poor little beast,' said the Horse in a gentler tone. 'I forget you're only a foal. We'll make a fine rider of you in time. And now — we mustn't start until those two in the hut are asleep. Meantime we can make our plans. My Tarkaan is on his way North to the great city, to Tashbaan itself and the court of the Tisroc — '

'I say,' put in Shasta in rather a shocked voice, 'oughtn't you to say "May he live for ever"?'

'Why?' asked the Horse. 'I'm a free Narnian. And why should I talk slaves' and fools' talk? I don't want him to live for ever, and I know that he's not going to live for ever whether I want him to or not. And I can see you're from the free North too. No more of this Southern jargon between you and me! And now, back to our plans. As I said, my human was on his way North to Tashbaan.'

'Does that mean we'd better go to the South?'

'I think not,' said the Horse. 'You see, he thinks I'm dumb and witless like his other horses. Now if I really were, the moment I got loose I'd go back home to my stable and paddock; back to his palace which is two days' journey South. That's where he'll look for me. He'd never dream of my going on North on my own. And anyway he will probably think that someone in the last village who saw him ride through has followed us to here and stolen me.'

'Oh hurrah!' said Shasta. 'Then we'll go North. I've been longing to go to the North all my life.'

'Of course you have,' said the Horse. 'That's because of the blood that's in you. I'm sure you're true Northern stock. But not too loud. I should think they'd be asleep soon now.'

'I'd better creep back and see,' suggested Shasta.

'That's a good idea,' said the Horse. 'But take care you're not caught.'

— Бедный ты, бедный, — гораздо ласковей сказал конь, — всё забываю, что ты детёныш. Ну ничего, со мной научишься! Пока эти двое спорят, будем ждать, а заснут — тронемся в путь. Мой хозяин едет на север, в Ташбаан, ко двору Тисрока.

— Почему ты не прибавил «да живет он вечно»? — испугался Шаста.

— А зачем? Я свободный гражданин Нарнии. Мне не пристало говорить, как эти рабы и недоумки. Я не хочу, чтобы он вечно жил, и знаю, что он умрёт, чего бы ему ни желали. Да ведь и ты свободен, потому что с севера. Мы с тобой не будем говорить на их манер! Ну, давай обсуждать наши планы. Я уже сказал, что мой человек едет на север, в Ташбаан.

— Значит, нам надо ехать к югу?

— Нет. Если бы я был нем и глуп, как здешние лошади, то побежал бы домой, в своё стойло. Дворец наш — на юге, в двух днях пути. Там он и будет меня искать. Ему и не догадаться, что я двинусь к северу. Скорее всего, решит, что меня украли.

— Ура! — закричал Шаста. — На север! Я всегда хотел узнать, что там.

— Конечно, — сказал конь, — ты ведь оттуда и, я уверен, хорошего северного рода. Только не кричи. Скоро они заснут.

— Я лучше посмотрю, — сказал Шаста.

— Хорошо, только поосторожней.

It was a good deal darker now and very silent except for the sound of the waves on the beach, which Shasta hardly noticed because he had been hearing it day and night as long as he could remember. The cottage, as he approached it, showed no light. When he listened at the front there was no noise. When he went round to the only window, he could hear, after a second or two, the familiar noise of the old fisherman's squeaky snore. It was funny to think that if all went well he would never hear it again. Holding his breath and feeling a little bit sorry, but much less sorry than he was glad, Shasta glided away over the grass and went to the donkey's stable, groped along to a place he knew where the key was hidden, opened the door and found the Horse's saddle and bridle which had been locked up there for the night. He bent forward and kissed the donkey's nose. 'I'm sorry we can't take you,' he said.

'There you are at last,' said the Horse when he got back to it. 'I was beginning to wonder what had become of you.'

'I was getting your things out of the stable,' replied Shasta. 'And now, can you tell me how to put them on?'

For the next few minutes Shasta was at work, very cautiously to avoid jingling, while the Horse said things like, 'Get that girth a bit tighter,' or 'You'll find a buckle lower down,' or 'You'll need to shorten those stirrups a good bit.' When all was finished it said:

'Now; we've got to have reins for the look of the thing, but you won't be using them. Tie them to the saddle-bow: very slack so that I can do what I like with my head. And, remember — you are not to touch them.'

'What are they for, then?' asked Shasta.

'Ordinarily they are for directing me,' replied the Horse. 'But as I intend to do all the directing on this journey, you'll please keep your hands to yourself. And there's

Было совсем темно и очень тихо, одни лишь волны плескались о берег, но этого Шаста не замечал, потому что слышал их день и ночь, всю жизнь. Свет в хижине погасили. Он прислушался, ничего не услышал, подошёл к единственному окошку и различил секунды через две знакомый храп. Ему стало смешно: подумать только, если всё пойдёт как надо, он больше никогда этих звуков не услышит! Стараясь не дышать, он немножко устыдился, но радость была сильнее стыда. Тихо пошёл он по траве к стойлу, где был ослик — знал, где лежит ключ, — отпер дверь, отыскал седло и уздечку: их спрятали туда на ночь, — поцеловал ослика в нос и прошептал: «Прости, что мы тебя не берём».

— Пришёл наконец! — сказал конь, когда он вернулся. — Я уже гадал, что с тобой случилось.

— Доставал твои вещи из стойла, — ответил Шаста. — Не скажешь, как их приладить?

Потом довольно долго он возился с вещами, стараясь ничем не звякнуть, а конь давал указания: «Тут потуже. Нет, вот здесь. Подтяни ещё». Напоследок он сказал:

— Вот смотри: это поводья, — но ты их не трогай. Приспособь их посвободней к луке седла, чтобы я двигал головой как хотел. И главное, не трогай.

— Зачем же они тогда? — спросил Шаста.

— Чтобы меня направлять. Но сейчас выбирать дорогу буду я, тебе их трогать ни к чему. А ещё — не вцепляйся мне в гриву.

another thing. I'm not going to have you grabbing my mane.'

'But I say,' pleaded Shasta. 'If I'm not to hold on by the reins or by your mane, what *am* I to hold on by?'

'You hold on with your knees,' said the Horse. 'That's the secret of good riding. Grip my body between your knees as hard as you like; sit straight up, straight as a poker; keep your elbows in. And by the way, what did you do with the spurs?'

'Put them on my heels, of course,' said Shasta. 'I do know that much.'

'Then you can take them off and put them in the saddle-bag. We may be able to sell them when we get to Tashbaan. Ready? And now I think you can get up.'

'Ooh! You're a dreadful height,' gasped Shasta after his first, and unsuccessful, attempt.

'I'm a horse, that's all,' was the reply. 'Anyone would think I was a haystack from the way you're trying to climb up me! There, that's better. Now sit *up* and remember what I told you about your knees. Funny to think of me who has led cavalry charges and won races having a potato-sack like you in the saddle! However, off we go.' It chuckled, not unkindly.

And it certainly began their night journey with great caution. First of all it went just south of the fisherman's cottage to the little river which there ran into the sea, and took care to leave in the mud some very plain hoof-marks pointing South. But as soon as they were in the middle of the ford it turned upstream and waded till they were about a hundred yards farther inland than the cottage. Then it selected a nice gravelly bit of bank which would take no footprints and came out on the Northern side. Then, still at a walking pace, it went Northward till the cottage, the one tree, the donkey's stable, and the creek —

— За что же мне держаться? — удивился Шаста.

— Сжимай покрепче колени, — сказал конь. — Тогда и научишься хорошо ездить. Сжимай мне коленями бока сколько хочешь, а сам сиди прямо и локти не растопыривай. Что ты там делаешь со шпорами?

— Надеваю, конечно, — сказал Шаста. — Уж это я знаю.

— Сними их и положи в перемётную суму. Продадим в Ташбаане. Снял? Ну, садись в седло.

— Ох какой ты высокий! — с трудом выговорил Шаста после первой неудачной попытки.

— Я конь, что поделаешь. А ты на меня лезешь как на стог сена. Вот так получше! Теперь *распрямись* и помни насчёт коленей. Смешно, честное слово! На мне скакали в бой великие воины, и дожил я до такого мешка! Что ж, поехали. — И он засмеялся, но не сердито.

Конь превзошёл себя — так был осторожен. Сперва он пошёл на юг, старательно оставляя следы на глине, и начал переходить вброд речку, текущую в море, но на самой её середине повернул и пошёл против течения, а потом вышел на каменистый берег, где следов не остаётся, и долго двигался шагом, пока хижина, стойло, дерево — словом, всё, что знал Шаста, — не растворилось в серой мгле июльской ночи. Тогда мальчик понял, что они уже на вершине холма, отделявшего от него мир. Он не мог толком разобрать, что впереди — как будто

everything, in fact, that Shasta had ever known — had sunk out of sight in the grey summer-night darkness. They had been going uphill and now were at the top of the ridge — that ridge which had always been the boundary of Shasta's known world. He could not see what was ahead except that it was all open and grassy. It looked endless: wild and lonely and free.

'I say!' observed the Horse. 'What a place for a gallop, eh!'

'Oh don't let's,' said Shasta. 'Not yet. I don't know how to — please, Horse. I don't know your name.'

'Breehy-hinny-brinny-hooky-hah,' said the Horse.

'I'll never be able to say that,' said Shasta. 'Can I call you Bree?'

'Well, if it's the best you can do, I suppose you must,' said the Horse. 'And what shall I call you?'

'I'm called Shasta.'

'H'm,' said Bree. 'Well, now, there's a name that's *really* hard to pronounce. But now about this gallop. It's a good deal easier than trotting if you only knew, because you don't have to rise and fall. Grip with your knees and keep your eyes straight ahead between my ears. Don't look at the ground. If you think you're going to fall just grip harder and sit up straighter. Ready? Now: for Narnia and the North.'

и впрямь весь мир, очень большой, пустой, бесконечный.

— Ах, — обрадовался конь, — самое место для галопа!

— Ой, не надо! — сказал Шаста. — Я ещё не могу... пожалуйста, конь! Да, как тебя зовут?

— И-йо-го-го-га-га-га-а!..

— Мне не выговорить, — сказал Шаста. — Можно я буду звать тебя Игого?

— Что ж, зови, если иначе не можешь, — согласился конь. — А тебя как называть?

— Шаста.

— Да... Вот это и впрямь не выговоришь. А насчет галопа ты не бойся: он легче рыси, не надо подниматься-опускаться. Сожми меня коленями (это называется «шенкеля») и смотри прямо между ушами. Только не гляди вниз! Если покажется, что падаешь, сожми сильнее, выпрями спину. Готов? Ну, во имя Нарнии!..

Chapter 2

A WAYSIDE ADVENTURE

It was nearly noon on the following day when Shasta was wakened by something warm and soft moving over his face. He opened his eyes and found himself staring into the long face of a horse; its nose and lips were almost touching his. He remembered the exciting events of the previous night and sat up. But as he did so he groaned.

'Ow, Bree,' he gasped. 'I'm so sore. All over. I can hardly move.'

'Good morning, small one,' said Bree. 'I was afraid you might feel a bit stiff. It can't be the falls. You didn't have more than a dozen or so, and it was all lovely, soft springy turf that must have been almost a pleasure to fall on. And the only one that might have been nasty was broken by that gorse bush. No: it's the riding itself that comes hard at first. What about breakfast? I've had mine.'

'Oh, bother breakfast. Bother everything,' said Shasta. 'I tell you I can't move.' But the horse nuzzled at him with its nose and pawed him gently with a hoof till he had to get up. And then he looked about him and saw where they were. Behind them lay a little copse. Before them the turf, dotted with white flowers, sloped down to the brow of a cliff. Far below them, so that the sound of the breaking waves was very faint, lay the sea. Shasta had never seen it from such a height and never seen so much of it before, nor dreamed how many colours it had. On either hand the coast stretched away, headland after headland, and at the points you could see the white foam running

Глава 2

ПЕРВОЕ ПРИКЛЮЧЕНИЕ

Солнце стояло высоко, когда Шаста проснулся, ибо что-то тёплое и влажное прикоснулось к его щеке. Открыв глаза и увидев длинную конскую морду, он вспомнил вчерашние события, сел и, громко застонав, еле выговорил:

— Ой, всё у меня болит. Всё как есть.

— Здравствуй, маленький друг, — сказал конь. — Ты не бойся, это не от ушибов, ты и упал-то раз десять, и всё на траву. Даже приятно... Правда, один раз отлетел далеко, но угодил в куст. Словом, это не ушибы, так всегда бывает поначалу. Я уже позавтракал, давай и ты.

— Какой там завтрак: я двинуться не могу.

Но конь не отставал: трогал несчастного и копытом, и мордой, пока тот не поднялся на ноги, а поднявшись — не огляделся. Оттуда, где они ночевали, спускался пологий склон весь в белых цветочках. Далеко внизу лежало море — так далеко, что едва доносился всплеск волн. Шаста никогда не смотрел на него сверху и не представлял, какое оно большое и разноцветное. Берег уходил направо и налево, белая пена кипела у скал, день был ясный, солнце сверкало. Особенно поразил Шасту здешний воздух. Он долго не мог понять, чего же не хватает, пока не дога-

up the rocks but making no noise because it was so far off. There were gulls flying overhead and the heat shivered on the ground; it was a blazing day. But what Shasta chiefly noticed was the air. He couldn't think what was missing, until at last he realized that there was no smell of fish in it. For of course, neither in the cottage nor among the nets, had he ever been away from that smell in his life. And this new air was so delicious, and all his old life seemed so far away, that he forgot for a moment about his bruises and his aching muscles and said:

'I say, Bree, didn't you say something about breakfast?'

'Yes, I did,' answered Bree. 'I think you'll find something in the saddle-bags. They're over there on that tree where you hung them up last night — or early this morning, rather.'

They investigated the saddle-bags and the results were cheering — a meat pasty, only slightly stale, a lump of dried figs and another lump of green cheese, a little flask of wine, and some money; about forty crescents in all, which was more than Shasta had ever seen.

While Shasta sat down — painfully and cautiously — with his back against a tree and started on the pasty, Bree had a few more mouthfuls of grass to keep him company.

'Won't it be stealing to use the money?' asked Shasta.

'Oh,' said the Horse, looking up with its mouth full of grass, 'I never thought of that. A free horse and a talking horse mustn't steal, of course. But I think it's all right. We're prisoners and captives in enemy country. That money is booty, spoil. Besides, how are we to get any food for you without it? I suppose, like all humans, you won't eat natural food like grass and oats.'

'I can't.'

'Ever tried?'

дался, что нет главного — запаха рыбы. (Ведь там — и в хижине, и у сетей — рыбой пахло всегда, сколько он себя помнил.) Это ему очень понравилось, и прежняя жизнь показалась давним сном. От радости он забыл о том, как болит всё тело, и спросил:

— Ты что-то сказал насчет завтрака?

— Да, — ответил конь, — посмотри в сумках. Ты их повесил на дерево ночью... нет, скорей под утро.

Он посмотрел и нашёл много хорошего: совсем свежий пирог с мясом, кусок овечьего сыра, горстку сушёных фиг, плоский сосудец с вином и кошелёк с деньгами. Столько денег — сорок полумесяцев — он никогда ещё не видел.

Потом он осторожно сел у дерева, прислонился спиной к стволу и принялся за пирог; конь тем временем пощипывал травку.

— А мы можем взять эти деньги? — спросил Шаста. — Это не воровство?

— Как тебе сказать, — ответил конь, прожёвывая траву. — Конечно, свободные говорящие звери красть не должны, но это... Мы с тобой бежали из плена, мы — в чужой земле, деньги — наша добыча. И потом, без них не прокормишься. Насколько мне известно, вы, люди, не едите травы и овса.

— Не едим.

— А ты пробовал?

'Yes, I have. I can't get it down at all. You couldn't either if you were me.'

'You're rum little creatures, you humans,' remarked Bree.

When Shasta had finished his breakfast (which was by far the nicest he had ever eaten), Bree said, 'I think I'll have a nice roll before we put on that saddle again.' And he proceeded to do so. 'That's good. That's very good,' he said, rubbing his back on the turf and waving all four legs in the air. 'You ought to have one too, Shasta,' he snorted. 'It's most refreshing.'

But Shasta burst out laughing and said, You do look funny when you're on your back!'

'I look nothing of the sort,' said Bree. But then suddenly he rolled round on his side, raised his head and looked hard at Shasta, blowing a little.

'Does it really look funny?' he asked in an anxious voice.

'Yes, it does,' replied Shasta. 'But what does it matter?'

'You don't think, do you,' said Bree, 'that it might be a thing *talking* horses never do — a silly, clownish trick I've learned from the dumb ones? It would be dreadful to find, when I get back to Narnia, that I've picked up a lot of low, bad habits. What do you think, Shasta? Honestly, now. Don't spare my feelings. Should you think the real, free horses — the talking kind — do roll?'

'How should I know? Anyway I don't think I should bother about it if I were you. We've got to get there first. Do you know the way?'

'I know my way to Tashbaan. After that comes the desert. Oh, we'll manage the desert somehow, never fear. Why, we'll be in sight of the Northern mountains then. Think of it! To Narnia and the North! Nothing will stop us then. But I'd be glad to be past Tashbaan. You and I are safer away from cities.'

— Да, бывало. Нет, не могу. И ты бы не мог на моём месте.

— Странные вы твари, — заметил конь.

Пока Шаста доедал лучший завтрак в своей жизни, его друг завалился на землю и принялся кататься, приговаривая:

— Ах, хорошо! Спину почешешь, ногами помашешь. Покатайся и ты — сразу легче станет.

Но Шаста лишь рассмеялся:

— Какой ты смешной!

— Ничего подобного! — возразил было конь, но тут же лёг на бок и испуганно спросил: — Неужели смешной?

— Да, а что?

— А вдруг говорящие лошади так не делают? — перепугался конь. — Вдруг это глупая, *здешняя* привычка? Какой ужас! Прискачу в Нарнию, и окажется, что я не умею себя вести. Как ты думаешь, Шаста? Нет, честно. Я не обижусь. Настоящие, свободные кони... говорящие... они катаются?

— Откуда же мне знать? Да ты не бойся! Приедем — увидим. Ты знаешь дорогу?

— До Ташбаана — знаю. Потом дороги нет, там большая пустыня. Ничего, одолеем! Нам будут видны горы, ты подумай — северные горы! За ними Нарния! Только бы пройти Ташбаан! От остальных городов надо держаться подальше.

'Can't we avoid it?'

'Not without going along way inland, and that would take us into cultivated land and main roads; and I wouldn't know the way. No, we'll just have to creep along the coast. Up here on the downs we'll meet nothing but sheep and rabbits and gulls and a few shepherds. And by the way, what about starting?'

Shasta's legs ached terribly as he saddled Bree and climbed into the saddle, but the Horse was kindly to him and went at a soft pace all afternoon. When evening twilight came they dropped by steep tracks into a valley and found a village. Before they got into it Shasta dismounted and entered it on foot to buy a loaf and some onions and radishes. The Horse trotted round by the fields in the dusk and met Shasta at the far side. This became their regular plan every second night.

These were great days for Shasta, and every day better than the last as his muscles hardened and he fell less often. Even at the end of his training Bree still said he sat like a bag of flour in the saddle. 'And even if it was safe, young 'un, I'd be ashamed to be seen with you on the main road.' But in spite of his rude words Bree was a patient teacher. No one can teach riding so well as a horse. Shasta learned to trot, to canter, to jump, and to keep his seat even when Bree pulled up suddenly or swung unexpectedly to the left or the right — which, as Bree told him, was a thing you might have to do at any moment in a battle. And then of course Shasta begged to be told of the battles and wars in which Bree had carried the Tarkaan. And Bree would tell of forced marches and the fording of swift rivers, of charges and of fierce fights between cavalry and cavalry when the war horses fought as well as the men, being all fierce stallions, trained to bite and kick, and to rear at the right moment so that the

— Обойти его нельзя?

— Тогда придётся сильно кружить, боюсь заплутаться. В глубине страны — большие дороги, возделанные земли... Нет, пойдём вдоль берега. Тут никого нет, кроме овец, кроликов и чаек, разве что пастух-другой. Что ж, тронемся?

Шаста оседлал коня и с трудом забрался в седло: так болели ноги, — но Игого сжалился над ним и до самых сумерек шёл шагом. Когда уже смеркалось, они спустились по тропкам в долину и увидели селение. Шаста спешился и купил там хлеба, лука и редиски, а конь, обогнув селение, остановился дальше, в поле. Через два дня они снова так сделали, и через четыре — тоже.

Все эти дни Шаста блаженствовал. Ноги и руки болели всё меньше. Конь уверял, что в седле он сидит как мешок («Стыдно, если кто увидит!»), но учителем был терпеливым — никто не научит ездить верхом лучше, чем сама лошадь. Шаста уже не боялся рыси и не падал, когда конь останавливался с разбегу или неожиданно кидался в сторону (оказывается, так часто делают в битве). Конечно, Шаста просил, чтобы конь рассказал, как сражался вместе с тарханом, и тот рассказывал, как они переходили вброд реки, и долго шли без отдыха, и бились с вражьим войском. Боевые кони, самой лучшей крови, бьются не хуже воинов: кусаются, лягаются и умеют, когда надо, повернуться так, чтобы всадник получше ударил врага мечом или боевым топориком. Правда, рассказывал он реже, чем Шаста о том просил, чаще отнекивался: «Да ладно, чего там: сражался-то я по воле Тисрока, словно раб или немая лошадь. Вот в Нарнии, среди

horse's weight as well as the rider's would come down on an enemy's crest in the stroke of sword or battleaxe. But Bree did not want to talk about the wars as often as Shasta wanted to hear about them. 'Don't speak of them, youngster,' he would say. 'They were only the Tisroc's wars and I fought in them as a slave and a dumb beast. Give me the Narnian wars where I shall fight as a free Horse among my own people! Those will be wars worth talking about. Narnia and the North! Bra-ha-ha! Broo hoo!'

Shasta soon learned, when he heard Bree talking like that, to prepare for a gallop.

After they had travelled on for weeks and weeks past more bays and headlands and rivers and villages than Shasta could remember, there came a moonlit night when they started their journey at evening, having slept during the day. They had left the downs behind them and were crossing a wide plain with a forest about half a mile away on their left. The sea, hidden by low sandhills, was about the same distance on their right. They had jogged along for about an hour, sometimes trotting and sometimes walking, when Bree suddenly stopped.

'What's up?' said Shasta.

'S-s-ssh!' said Bree, craning his neck round and twitching his ears. 'Did you hear something? Listen.'

'It sounds like another horse — between us and the wood,' said Shasta after he had listened for about a minute.

'It *is* another horse,' said Bree. 'And that's what I don't like.'

'Isn't it probably just a farmer riding home late?' said Shasta with a yawn.

'Don't tell me!' said Bree. '*That's* not a farmer's riding. Nor a farmer's horse either. Can't you tell by the sound? That's quality, that horse is. And it's being ridden by a real horseman. I tell you what it is, Shasta. There's a Tarkaan

своих, я буду сражаться как свободный! За Нарнию! О-го-го-го-о!»

Вскоре Шаста понял, что после таких речей конь пускается в галоп.

Уже не одну неделю двигались они вдоль моря и видели больше бухточек, речек и селений, чем Шаста мог запомнить. Однажды в лунную ночь они не спали, ибо выспались днём, а в путь вышли под вечер. Оставив позади холмы, они пересекли равнину и слева, в полумиле, увидели лес. Море лежало справа, за низкой песчаной дюной. Конь то шёл шагом, то пускался рысью, но вдруг резко остановился.

— Что там? — спросил Шаста.

— Тшш! — Конь насторожил уши. — Ты ничего не слыхал? Слушай!

— Как будто лошадь, к лесу поближе, — сказал Шаста, послушав с минутку.

— Да, это лошадь. Ах как нехорошо!..

— Ну и что такого? Может, крестьянин едет!

— Крестьяне так не ездят, — возразил Игого, — и кони у них не такие. Это настоящий конь и настоящий тархан. Нет, не конь... слишком легко ступает... так-так... Это прекраснейшая кобыла.

under the edge of that wood. Not on his war horse — it's too light for that. On a fine blood mare, I should say.'

'Well, it's stopped now, whatever it is,' said Shasta.

'You're right,' said Bree. 'And why should he stop just when we do? Shasta, my boy, I do believe there's someone shadowing us at last.'

'What shall we do?' said Shasta in a lower whisper than before. 'Do you think he can see us as well as hear us?'

'Not in this light so long as we stay quite still,' answered Bree. 'But look! There's a cloud coming up. I'll wait till that gets over the moon. Then we'll get off to our right as quietly as we can, down to the shore. We can hide among the sandhills if the worst comes to the worst.'

They waited till the cloud covered the moon and then, first at a walking pace and afterwards at a gentle trot, made for the shore.

The cloud was bigger and thicker than it had looked at first and soon the night grew very dark. Just as Shasta was saying to himself, 'We must be nearly at those sandhills by now,' his heart leaped into his mouth because an appalling noise had suddenly risen up out of the darkness ahead; a long snarling roar, melancholy and utterly savage. Instantly Bree swerved round and began galloping inland again as fast as he could gallop.

'What is it?' gasped Shasta.

'Lions!' said Bree, without checking his pace or turning his head.

After that there was nothing but sheer galloping for some time. At last they splashed across a wide, shallow stream and Bree came to a stop on the far side. Shasta noticed that he was trembling and sweating all over.

— Похоже, сейчас она остановилась, — заметил Шаста.

— Верно. А почему? Потому что остановились и мы... Друг мой, кто-то выследил нас.

— Что же теперь делать? — испугался Шаста. — Как ты думаешь, они нас видят?

— Нет, слишком темно, к тому же тучи! Как только они закроют луну, можно двигаться к морю. Если что, песок скроет шаги.

Они подождали и сперва шагом, потом лёгкой рысью двинулись к берегу. Но странное дело: уже стало совсем темно, а море всё не показывалось. Только Шаста подумал: «Наверное, мы уже проехали дюны», — как вдруг сердце у него упало: оттуда, спереди, послышалось долгое, скорбное, жуткое рычание. В тот же миг конь повернул и понёсся во весь опор к лесу, от берега.

— Что это? — в ужасе выговорил Шаста.

— Львы! — на скаку бросил конь не оборачиваясь.

Пока перед ними не сверкнула вода, оба молчали. Перейдя вброд широкую мелкую речку, конь остановился. Он весь вспотел и сильно дрожал, а когда немного отдышался, сказал:

'That water may have thrown the brute off our scent,' panted Bree when he had partly got his breath again. 'We can walk for a bit now.'

As they walked Bree said, 'Shasta, I'm ashamed of myself. I'm just as frightened as a common, dumb Calormene horse. I am really. I don't feel like a Talking Horse at all. I don't mind swords and lances and arrows but I can't bear — those creatures. I think I'll trot for a bit.'

About a minute later, however, he broke into a gallop again, and no wonder. For the roar broke out again, this time on their left from the direction of the forest.

'Two of them,' moaned Bree.

When they had galloped for several minutes without any further noise from the lions Shasta said, 'I say! That other horse is galloping beside us now. Only a stone's throw away.'

'All the b-better,' panted Bree. 'Tarkaan on it — will have a sword — protect us all.'

'But, Bree!' said Shasta. 'We might just as well be killed by lions as caught. Or *I* might. They'll hang me for horsestealing.' He was feeling less frightened of lions than Bree because he had never met a lion; Bree had.

Bree only snorted in answer but he did sheer away to his right. Oddly enough the other horse seemed also to be sheering away to the left, so that in a few seconds the space between them had widened a good deal. But as soon as it did so there came two more lions' roars, immediately after one another, one on the right and the other on the left, the horses began drawing nearer together. So, apparently, did the lions. The roaring of the brutes on each side was horribly close and they seemed to be keeping up with the galloping horses quite easily. Then the

— Теперь не унюхают: вода отбивает запах. Пройдёмся немного.

Пока они шли по мелководью, Игого признался:

— Шаста, мне очень стыдно. Я перепугался, как немая тархистанская лошадь. Да, я недостоин называться говорящим конём. Я не боюсь мечей, и копий, и стрел, но *это... это...* Пройдусь-ка лучше рысью.

Только рысью шёл он недолго: уже через минуту пустился галопом, — что неудивительно, ибо совсем близко раздался глухой рёв, на сей раз — слева, из леса.

— Ещё один! — проговорил конь на бегу.

— Эй, слушай, — крикнул Шаста, — та лошадь тоже скачет!

— Ну и хо-хо-хорошо! У тархана меч... так что защитит нас.

— Да что ты заладил: львы да львы! — возмутился Шаста. — Нас могут поймать. Меня повесят за конокрадство!

Он меньше, чем конь, боялся львов, потому что никогда их не видел.

Конь только фыркнул в ответ и прянул вправо. Как ни странно, другая лошадь прянула влево, и вслед за этим кто-то зарычал — сначала справа, потом слева. Лошади кинулись друг к другу. Львы, видимо, тоже, поскольку рычали попеременно с обеих сторон, не отставая от скачущих лошадей. Наконец луна выплыла из-за туч, и в ярком свете Шаста увидел ясно, как днем, что лошади несутся морда к морде, словно на скачках. Игого потом говорил, что таких скачек в Тархистане отродясь не видывали.

cloud rolled away. The moonlight, astonishingly bright, showed up everything almost as if it were broad day. The two horses and two riders were galloping neck to neck and knee to knee just as if they were in a race. Indeed Bree said (afterwards) that a finer race had never been seen in Calormen.

Shasta now gave himself up for lost and began to wonder whether lions killed you quickly or played with you as a cat plays with a mouse and how much it would hurt. At the same time (one sometimes does this at the most frightful moments) he noticed everything. He saw that the other rider was a very small, slender person, mail-clad (the moon shone on the mail) and riding magnificently. He had no beard.

Something flat and shining was spread out before them. Before Shasta had time even to guess what it was there was a great splash and he found his mouth half full of salt water. The shining thing had been a long inlet of the sea. Both horses were swimming and the water was up to Shasta's knees. There was an angry roaring behind them and looking back Shasta saw a great, shaggy, and terrible shape crouched on the water's edge; but only one. 'We must have shaken off the other lion,' he thought.

The lion apparently did not think its prey worth a wetting; at any rate it made no attempt to take the water in pursuit. The two horses, side by side, were now well out into the middle of the creek and the opposite shore could be clearly seen. The Tarkaan had not yet spoken a word. 'But he will,' thought Shasta. 'As soon as we have landed. What am I to say? I must begin thinking out a story.'

Then, suddenly, two voices spoke at his side.

'Oh, I *am* so tired,' said the one.

Шаста уже ни на что не надеялся: думал лишь о том, как лев съедает жертву: сразу или сперва играет, как кошка с мышкой, и очень ли это больно. Думал он об этом, но видел всё (так бывает в очень страшные минуты), поэтому заметил, что другой всадник мал ростом, что кольчуга его ярко сверкает, в седле он сидит как нельзя лучше, а бороды у него нет.

Что-то блеснуло внизу перед ними, и прежде чем догадался, что это, Шаста услышал всплески и ощутил во рту вкус солёной воды. Они попали в узкий рукав, отходящий от моря. Обе лошади плыли, да и Шасте вода доходила до колен. Сзади слышалось сердитое рычание, и, оглянувшись, Шаста увидел у воды тёмную глыбу, но одну: другой лев, видимо, отстал.

Похоже, лев не собирался ради них лезть в воду. Кони наполовину переплыли узкий залив, уже был виден другой берег, а тархан не говорил ни слова. «Заговорит, — подумал Шаста. — Как только выйдем на берег. Что я ему скажу? Надо что-нибудь выдумать...»

И тут до него донеслись голоса:

— Ах как я устала!..

'Hold your tongue, Hwin, and don't be a fool,' said the other.

'I'm dreaming,' thought Shasta. 'I could have sworn that other horse spoke.'

Soon the horses were no longer swimming but walking and soon with a great sound of water running off their sides and tails and with a great crunching of pebbles under eight hoofs, they came out on the farther beach of the inlet. The Tarkaan, to Shasta's surprise, showed no wish to ask questions. He did not even look at Shasta but seemed anxious to urge his horse straight on. Bree, however, at once shouldered himself in the other horse's way.

'Broo-hoo-hah!' he snorted. 'Steady there! I *heard* you, I did. There's no good pretending, Ma'am. I heard you. You're a Talking Horse, a Narnian horse just like me.'

'What's it got to do with you if she is?' said the strange rider fiercely, laying hand on sword-hilt. But the voice in which the words were spoken had already told Shasta something.

'Why, it's only a girl!' he exclaimed.

'And what business is it of yours if I am *only* a girl?' snapped the stranger. 'You're probably only a boy: a rude, common little boy — a slave probably, who's stolen his master's horse.'

'That's all *you* know,' said Shasta.

'He's not a thief, little Tarkheena,' said Bree. 'At least, if there's been any stealing, you might just as well say I stole *him*. And as for its not being my business, you wouldn't expect me to pass a lady of my own race in this strange country without speaking to her? It's only natural I should.'

'I think it's very natural too,' said the mare.

'I wish you'd held your tongue, Hwin,' said the girl. 'Look at the trouble you've got us into.'

— Тише, Уинни! Придержи язычок!

«Это мне нравится, — подумал Шаста. — Честное слово, лошадь заговорила!»

Вскоре обе лошади уже не плыли, шли, а потом вылезли на берег. Вода струилась с них, камешки хрустели под копытами. Маленький всадник, как это ни странно, ни о чём не спрашивал, даже не глядел на Шасту, но Игого вплотную подошёл к другой лошади и громко фыркнул.

— Стой! Я тебя слышал. Меня не обманешь. Госпожа, ты ведь говорящая лошадь, тоже из Нарнии!

— Тебе какое дело? — воскликнул странный тархан и схватился за эфес, но голос выдал его с головой.

— Да это девочка! — догадался Шаста.

— И что с того? — возмутилась незнакомка. — Зато ты мальчишка! Грубый, глупый мальчишка! Наверное, раб и конокрад.

— Нет, маленькая госпожа, — вмешался конь. — Он меня не крал. Если уж на то пошло, то это я его украл. Что же до того, моё ли это дело, посуди сама: земляки непременно приветствуют друг друга на чужбине.

— Конечно, — поддержала его лошадь.

— Уж ты-то помолчи! — прикрикнула на неё девочка. — Видишь, в какую беду я из-за тебя попала!

'I don't know about trouble,' said Shasta. 'You can clear off as soon as you like. We shan't keep you.'

'No, you shan't,' said the girl.

'What quarrelsome creatures these humans are,' said Bree to the mare. 'They're as bad as mules. Let's try to talk a little sense. I take it, ma'am, your story is the same as mine? Captured in early youth — years of slavery among the Calormenes?'

'Too true, sir,' said the mare with a melancholy whinny.

'And now, perhaps — escape?'

'Tell him to mind his own business, Hwin,' said the girl.

'No, I won't, Aravis,' said the mare putting her ears back. 'This is my escape just as much as yours. And I'm sure a noble war-horse like this is not going to betray us. We are trying to escape, to get to Narnia.'

'And so, of course, are we,' said Bree. 'Of course you guessed that at once. A little boy in rags riding (or trying to ride) a war-horse at dead of night couldn't mean anything but an escape of some sort. And, if I may say so, a highborn Tarkheena riding alone at night — dressed up in her brother's armour — and very anxious for everyone to mind their own business and ask her no questions — well, if that's not fishy, call me a cob!'

'All right then,' said Aravis. 'You've guessed it. Hwin and I are running away. We are trying to get to Narnia. And now, what about it?'

'Why, in that case, what is to prevent us all going together?' said Bree. 'I trust, Madam Hwin, you will accept such assistance and protection as I may be able to give you on the journey?'

'Why do you keep talking to my horse instead of to me?' asked the girl.

— Никакой беды нет, — заметил Шаста. — Можете ехать куда ехали. Мы вас не держим.

— Ещё бы держали! — воскликнула всадница.

— Как трудно с людьми! — сказал кобыле конь. — Ну просто мулы... Давай мы с тобой разберёмся. Видимо, госпожа, тебя тоже взяли в плен, когда ты была жеребёнком?

— Да, мой господин, — печально ответила та. — Меня, кстати, Уинни зовут.

— А теперь ты сбежала?

— Скажи ему, чтобы не лез, когда не просят, — вставила всадница.

— Нет, Аравита, не скажу, — воспротивилась Уинни. — Я и впрямь бежала. Не только ты, но и я. Такой благородный конь нас не выдаст. Господин, мы держим путь в Нарнию.

— И мы тоже. Всякий поймёт, что оборвыш, едва сидящий в седле, откуда-то сбежал. Но не странно ли, что молодая тархина едет ночью, без свиты, в кольчуге своего брата, и боится чужих, и просит всех не лезть не в своё дело?

— Ну хорошо, — сказала девочка. — Ты угадал, мы с Уинни сбежали из дому и едем в Нарнию. Что же дальше?

— Дальше мы будем держаться вместе. Надеюсь, госпожа, ты не откажешься от моей защиты и помощи? — обратился конь к Уинни.

— Почему ты спрашиваешь мою лошадь, а не меня? — разгневалась Аравита.

'Excuse me, Tarkheena,' said Bree (with just the slightest backward tilt of his ears), 'but that's Calormene talk. We're free Narnians, Hwin and I, and I suppose, if you're running away to Narnia, you want to be one too. In that case Hwin isn't *your* horse any longer. One might just as well say you're *her* human.'

The girl opened her mouth to speak and then stopped. Obviously she had not quite seen it in that light before.

'Still,' she said after a moment's pause, 'I don't know that there's so much point in all going together. Aren't we more likely to be noticed?'

'Less,' said Bree; and the mare said, 'Oh do let's. I should feel much more comfortable. We're not even certain of the way. I'm sure a great charger like this knows far more than we do.'

'Oh come on, Bree,' said Shasta, 'and let them go their own way. Can't you see they don't want us?'

'We do,' said Hwin.

'Look here,' said the girl. 'I don't mind going with *you*, Mr War-Horse, but what about this boy? How do I know he's not a spy?'

'Why don't you say at once that you think I'm not good enough for you?' said Shasta.

'Be quiet, Shasta,' said Bree. 'The Tarkheena's question is quite reasonable. I'll vouch for the boy, Tarkheena. He's been true to me and a good friend. And he's certainly either a Narnian or an Archenlander.'

'All right, then. Let's go together.' But she didn't say anything to Shasta and it was obvious that she wanted Bree, not him.

— Прости, госпожа, — сказал конь, чуть-чуть прижимая уши, — у нас в Нарнии так не говорят. Мы с Уинни — свободные лошади, а не здешние немые клячи. Если бежишь в Нарнию, помни: Уинни не твоя лошадь — скорее уж ты её девочка.

Аравита раскрыла от удивления рот, но заговорила не сразу: вероятно, раньше так не думала.

— А всё-таки зачем нам ехать вместе? Ведь так нас скорее заметят.

— Нет, — возразил Игого, а Уинни его поддержала:

— Поедем вместе, поедем! Я буду меньше бояться, да и дороги толком не знаю. Такой замечательный конь, куда умнее меня.

Шаста сказал:

— Оставь ты их! Видишь, они не хотят...

— Мы хотим! — перебила его Уинни.

— Вот что, — сказала девочка. — Против вас, господин конь, я ничего не имею, но откуда вы знаете, что этот мальчишка нас не выдаст?

— Скажи уж прямо, что я тебе не компания! — воскликнул Шаста.

— Не кипятись, — сказал ему конь. — Госпожа права.

Обернувшись к Аравите, Игого вежливо продолжил:

— Нет, не предаст: я за него ручаюсь. Он добрый товарищ, к тому же, несомненно, из Нарнии или Орландии.

— Хорошо, поедем вместе, — согласилась девочка, обращаясь к коню.

'Splendid!' said Bree. 'And now that we've got the water between us and those dreadful animals, what about you two humans taking off our saddles and our all having a rest and hearing one another's stories.'

Both the children unsaddled their horses and the horses had a little grass and Aravis produced rather nice things to eat from her saddle-bag. But Shasta sulked and said, No thanks, and that he wasn't hungry. And he tried to put on what he thought very grand and stiff manners, but as a fisherman's hut is not usually a good place for learning grand manners, the result was dreadful. And he half knew that it wasn't a success and then became sulkier and more awkward than ever. Meanwhile the two horses were getting on splendidly. They remembered the very same places in Narnia — 'the grasslands up above Beaversdam' and found that they were some sort of second cousins once removed. This made things more and more uncomfortable for the humans until at last Bree said, 'And now, Tarkheena, tell us your story. And don't hurry it — I'm feeling comfortable now.'

Aravis immediately began, sitting quite still and using a rather different tone and style from her usual one. For in Calormen, story-telling (whether the stories are true or made up) is a thing you're taught, just as English boys and girls are taught essay-writing. The difference is that people want to hear the stories, whereas I never heard of anyone who wanted to read the essays.

— Я очень рад! — сказал тот. — Что ж, вода позади, звери — тоже. Не расседлать ли вам нас, не отдохнуть ли и не послушать ли друг про друга?

Дети расседлали коней, и те принялись щипать траву. Аравита вынула из сумы много всяких вкусностей, но Шаста есть отказался, стараясь говорить как можно учтивей, словно настоящий вельможа, но в рыбачьей хижине этому не научишься и получалось плохо. Он это, в сущности, понимал, поэтому становился всё угрюмей, вёл себя совсем уж неловко. Кони же прекрасно поладили. Вспоминая любимые места в Нарнии, они выяснили, что приходятся друг другу троюродными братом и сестрой. Понимая, что дети никак не могут найти общего языка, мудрый Игого предложил:

— Маленькая госпожа, поведай нам свою повесть. И не спеши: за нами никто не гонится.

Аравита немедленно села, красиво скрестив ноги, и важно начала свой рассказ. Надо заметить, что в этой стране и правду, и неправду рассказывают особым слогом — этому учат с детства, как учат у нас писать сочинения. Только рассказы эти слушать можно, а сочинений, если не ошибаюсь, не читает никто и никогда.

Chapter 3
AT THE GATES OF TASHBAAN

'My name,' said the girl at once, 'is Aravis Tarkheena and I am the only daughter of Kidrash Tarkaan, the son of Rishti Tarkaan, the son of Kidrash Tarkaan, the son of Ilsombreh Tisroc, the son of Ardeeb Tisroc who was descended in a right line from the god Tash. My father is the lord of the province of Calavar and is one who has the right of standing on his feet in his shoes before the face of Tisroc himself (may he live for ever). My mother (on whom be the peace of the gods) is dead and my father has married another wife. One of my brothers has fallen in battle against the rebels in the far west and the other is a child. Now it came to pass that my father's wife, my stepmother, hated me, and the sun appeared dark in her eyes as long as I lived in my father's house. And so she persuaded my father to promise me in marriage to Ahoshta Tarkaan. Now this Ahoshta is of base birth, though in these latter years he has won the favour of the Tisroc (may he live for ever) by flattery and evil counsels, and is now made a Tarkaan and the lord of many cities and is likely to be chosen as the Grand Vizier when the present Grand Vizier dies. Moreover he is at least sixty years old and has a hump on his back and his face resembles that of an ape. Nevertheless my father, because of the wealth and power of this Ahoshta, and being persuaded by his wife, sent messengers offering me in marriage, and the offer was favourably accepted and Ahoshta sent word that he would marry me this very year at the time of high summer.

Глава 3

У ВРАТ ТАШБААНА

— Меня зовут Аравита, — начала рассказчица. — Я прихожусь единственной дочерью могучему Кидраш-тархану, сыну Ришти-тархана, сына Кидраш-тархана, сына Ильсомбраз-тисрока, сына Ардиб-тисрока, потомка богини Таш. Отец мой, владетель Калавара, наделён правом стоять в туфлях перед Тисроком (да живёт он вечно). Мать моя ушла к богам, и отец женился снова. Один из моих братьев пал в бою с мятежниками, другой ещё мал. Случилось так, что мачеха меня невзлюбила, и солнце казалось ей чёрным, пока я жила в отчем доме. Потому она и подговорила своего супруга, а моего отца, выдать меня за Ахошту-тархана. Человек этот низок родом, но вошёл в милость к Тисроку (да живёт он вечно), ибо льстив и весьма коварен, и стал тарханом, и получил во владение города, а вскоре станет великим визирем. Годами он стар, видом гнусен, кособок и повадкою схож с обезьяной. Но мой отец, повинуясь жене и прельстившись его богатством, послал к нему гонцов, которых Ахошта принял и прислал с ними послание о том, что женится на мне нынешним летом.

'When this news was brought to me the sun appeared dark in my eyes and I laid myself on my bed and wept for a day. But on the second day I rose up and washed my face and caused my mare Hwin to be saddled and took with me a sharp dagger which my brother had carried in the western wars and rode out alone. And when my father's house was out of sight and I was come to a green open place in a certain wood where there were no dwellings of men, I dismounted from Hwin my mare and took out the dagger. Then I parted my clothes where I thought the readiest way lay to my heart and I prayed to all the gods that as soon as I was dead I might find myself with my brother. After that I shut my eyes and my teeth and prepared to drive the dagger into my heart. But before I had done so, this mare spoke with the voice of one of the daughters of men and said, 'O my mistress, do not by any means destroy yourself, for if you live you may yet have good fortune but all the dead are dead alike.'

'I didn't say it half so well as that,' muttered the mare.

'Hush, Ma'am, hush,' said Bree, who was thoroughly enjoying the story. 'She's telling it in the grand Calormene manner and no story-teller in a Tisroc's court could do it better. Pray go on, Tarkheena.'

'When I heard the language of men uttered by my mare,' continued Aravis, 'I said to myself, the fear of death has disordered my reason and subjected me to delusions. And I became full of shame for none of my lineage ought to fear death more than the biting of a gnat. Therefore I addressed myself a second time to the stabbing, but Hwin came near to me and put her head in between me and the dagger and discoursed to me most excellent reasons and rebuked me as a mother rebukes her daughter. And now my wonder was so great that I forgot about

Когда я это узнала, солнце померкло для меня, я легла на ложе и проплакала целые сутки, а наутро встала, умылась, велела оседлать кобылу по имени Уинни, взяла кинжал моего брата, погибшего в западных битвах, и поскакала в зелёный дол. Там я спешилась, разорвала одежды, чтобы сразу найти сердце, и взмолилась к богам, чтобы поскорее оказаться там же, где брат. Потом я закрыла глаза, сжала зубы, но тут кобыла моя промолвила, как дочь человеческая: «О госпожа, не губи себя! Если останешься жить, то ещё будешь счастлива, а мёртвые — мертвы».

— Я выразилась не так красиво, — заметила Уинни.

— Ничего, госпожа, так надо! — сказал ей Игого, наслаждавшийся рассказом. — Это высокий тархистанский стиль. Хозяйка твоя прекрасно им владеет. Продолжай, тархина!

— Услышав такие слова, — опять заговорила Аравита, — я подумала, что разум мой помутился с горя, и устыдилась, ибо предки мои боялись смерти не больше, чем комариного жала. Снова занесла я нож, но Уинни просунула морду между ним и мною и обратилась ко мне с разумнейшей речью, ласково укоряя меня, как мать укоряла бы дочь. Удивление мое было так сильно, что я забыла и о себе, и об Ахоште. «Как ты научилась говорить, о кобыла?» — обратилась я к ней, и она поведала то, что вы уже

killing myself and about Ahoshta and said, "O my mare, how have you learned to speak like one of the daughters of men?" And Hwin told me what is known to all this company, that in Narnia there are beasts that talk, and how she herself was stolen from thence when she was a little foal. She told me also of the woods and waters of Narnia and the castles and the great ships, till I said, "In the name of Tash and Azaroth and Zardeenah Lady of the Night, I have a great wish to be in that country of Narnia." "O my mistress," answered the mare, "if you were in Narnia you would be happy, for in that land no maiden is forced to marry against her will."

'And when we had talked together for a great time hope returned to me and I rejoiced that I had not killed myself. Moreover it was agreed between Hwin and me that we should steal ourselves away together and we planned it in this fashion. We returned to my father's house and I put on my gayest clothes and sang and danced before my father and pretended to be delighted with the marriage which he had prepared for me. Also I said to him, "O my father and O the delight of my eyes, give me your licence and permission to go with one of my maidens alone for three days into the woods to do secret sacrifices to Zardeenah, Lady of the Night and of Maidens, as is proper and customary for damsels when

знаете: там, в Нарнии, живут говорящие звери, и её украли оттуда, когда она была жеребёнком. Рассказы её о тёмных лесах, и светлых реках, и кораблях, и замках были столь прекрасны, что я воскликнула: «Молю тебя богиней Таш, и Азаротом, и Зардинах, владычицей мрака, отвези меня в эту дивную землю!» — «О госпожа! — отвечала мне кобыла моя Уинни. — В Нарнии ты обрела бы счастье, ибо там ни одну девицу не выдают замуж насильно». Надежда вернулась ко мне, и я благодарила богов, что не успела себя убить. Мы решили вернуться домой и украсть друг друга. Выполняя задуманное, я облачилась в доме отца в лучшие свои одежды и принялась петь и плясать, притворяясь весёлой, а через несколько дней обратилась к Кидраш-тархану с такими словами: «О услада моих очей, могучий Кидраш, разреши мне удалиться в лес на три дня с одной из моих прислужниц, дабы принести тайные жертвы Зардинах, владычице мрака и девства, как и подобает девице, выходящей замуж, ибо я вскоре уйду от неё к другим богам». И он отвечал мне: «Услада моих очей, да будет так».

they must bid farewell to the service of Zardeenah and prepare themselves for marriage." And he answered, "O my daughter and O the delight of my eyes, so shall it be."

'But when I came out from the presence of my father I went immediately to the oldest of his slaves, his secretary, who had dandled me on his knees when I was a baby and loved me more than the air and the light. And I swore him to be secret and begged him to write a certain letter for me. And he wept and implored me to change my resolution but in the end he said, "To hear is to obey," and did all my will. And I sealed the letter and hid it in my bosom."

'But what was in the letter?' asked Shasta.

'Be quiet, youngster,' said Bree. 'You're spoiling the story. She'll tell us all about the letter in the right place. Go on, Tarkheena.'

'Then I called the maid who was to go with me to the woods and perform the rites of Zardeenah and told her to wake me very early in the morning. And I became merry with her and gave her wine to drink; but I had mixed such things in her cup that I knew she must sleep for a night and a day. As soon as the household of my father had committed themselves to sleep I arose and put on an armour of my brother's which I always kept in my chamber in his memory. I put into my girdle all the money I had and certain choice jewels and provided myself also with food, and saddled the mare with my own hands and rode away in the second watch of the night. I directed my course not to the woods where my father supposed that I would go but north and east to Tashbaan.

'Now for three days and more I knew that my father would not seek me, being deceived by the words I had said to him. And on the fourth day we arrived at the city of Azim Balda. Now Azim Balda stands at

Покинув отца, я немедленно отправилась к старейшему из его рабов, мудрому советнику, который был мне нянькой в раннем детстве и любил меня больше, чем воздух или ясный солнечный свет. Я велела ему написать за меня письмо. Он рыдал и молил меня остаться дома, но потом смирился и сказал: «Слушаю, о госпожа, и повинуюсь!» И я запечатала это письмо и спрятала на груди.

— А что там было написано? — спросил Шаста.

— Подожди, мой маленький друг, — сказал Иго-го. — Ты портишь рассказ. Мы всё узнаем во благовременье. Продолжай, тархина.

— Потом я кликнула рабыню и велела ей разбудить меня до зари, и угостила её вином, и подмешала к нему сонного зелья. Когда весь дом уснул, я надела кольчугу погибшего брата, которая хранилась в моих покоях, взяла все деньги, какие у меня были, и драгоценные камни, и еду. Я сама оседлала Уинни, и ещё до второй стражи мы с нею ушли — не в лес, как думал отец, а на север и на восток, к Ташбаану.

Я знала, что трое суток, не меньше, отец не будет искать меня, обманутый моими словами. На четвёртый же день мы были в городе Азым-Балдах, откуда идут дороги во все стороны нашего царства и осо-

the meeting of many roads and from it the posts of the Tisroc (may he live for ever) ride on swift horses to every part of the empire: and it is one of the rights and privileges of the greater Tarkaans to send messages by them. I therefore went to the Chief of the Messengers in the House of Imperial Posts in Azim Balda and said, "O dispatcher of messages, here is a letter from my uncle Ahoshta Tarkaan to Kidrash Tarkaan, lord of Calavar. Take now these five crescents and cause it to be sent to him." And the Chief of the Messengers said, "To hear is to obey."

'This letter was feigned to be written by Ahoshta and this was the signification of the writing: "Ahoshta Tarkaan to Kidrash Tarkaan, salutation and peace. In the name of Tash the irresistible, the inexorable. Be it known to you that as I made my journey towards your house to perform the contract of marriage between me and your daughter Aravis Tarkheena, it pleased fortune and the gods that I fell in with her in the forest when she had ended the rites and sacrifices of Zardeenah according to the custom of maidens. And when I learned who she was, being delighted with her beauty and discretion, I became inflamed with love and it appeared to me that the sun would be dark to me if I did not marry her at once. Accordingly I prepared the necessary sacrifices and married your daughter the same hour that I met her and have returned with her to my own house. And we both pray and charge you to come hither as speedily as you may that we may be delighted with your face and speech; and also that you may bring with you the dowry of my wife, which, by reason of my great charges and expenses, I require without delay. And because thou and I are brothers I assure myself that you will not be angered by the haste of my marriage which is wholly occasioned by the great love

бо знатные тарханы могут послать письмо с гонцами Тисрока (да живёт он вечно). Потому я пошла к начальнику этих гонцов и сказала: «О несущий весть, вот письмо от Ахошты-тархана к Кидрашу, владетелю Калавара! Возьми эти пять полумесяцев и пошли гонца». А начальник сказал мне: «Слушаю и повинуюсь».

В этом письме было написано:

«От Ахошты к Кидраш-тархану привет и мир. Во имя великой Таш, непобедимой, непостижимой, знай, что на пути к тебе я милостью судеб встретил твою дочь, тархину Аравиту, которая приносила жертвы великой Зардинах, как и подобает девице. Узнав, кто передо мною, я был поражён её красой и добродетелью. Сердце мое воспылало, и солнце показалось бы мне чёрным, если бы я не заключил с ней немедля брачный союз. Я принёс должные жертвы, в тот же час женился и увёз прекрасную тархину в мой дом. Оба мы молим и просим тебя поспешить к нам, дабы порадовать нас ликом своим и речью и захватить с собой приданое моей жены, которое нужно мне незамедлительно, ибо я потратил немало на свадебный пир. Надеюсь и уповаю, что тебя, моего истинного брата, не разгневает поспешность, вызванная лишь тем, что я полюбил твою дочь великой любовью. Да хранят тебя боги».

I bear your daughter. And I commit you to the care of all the gods."

'As soon as I had done this I rode on in all haste from Azim Balda, fearing no pursuit and expecting that my father, having received such a letter, would send messages to Ahoshta or go to him himself, and that before the matter was discovered I should be beyond Tashbaan. And that is the pith of my story until this very night when I was chased by lions and met you at the swimming of the salt water.'

'And what happened to the girl — the one you drugged?' asked Shasta.

'Doubtless she was beaten for sleeping late,' said Aravis coolly. 'But she was a tool and spy of my stepmother's. I am very glad they should beat her.'

'I say, that was hardly fair,' said Shasta.

'I did not do any of these things for the sake of pleasing *you*,' said Aravis.

'And there's another thing I don't understand about that story,' said Shasta. 'You're not grown up, I don't believe you're any older than I am. I don't believe you're as old. How could you be getting married at your age?'

Aravis said nothing, but Bree at once said, 'Shasta, don't display your ignorance. They're always married at that age in the great Tarkaan families.'

Shasta turned very red (though it was hardly light enough for the others to see this) and felt snubbed. Aravis asked Bree for his story. Bree told it, and Shasta thought that he put in a great deal more than he needed about the falls and the bad riding. Bree obviously thought it very funny, but Aravis did not laugh. When Bree had finished they all went to sleep.

Next day all four of them, two horses and two humans, continued their journey together. Shasta thought

Отдав это письмо, я поспешила покинуть Азым-Балдах, дабы миновать Ташбаан к тому дню, когда отец мой прибудет туда или пришлёт гонцов. На этом пути за нами погнались львы и мы повстречались с вами.

— А что было дальше с той девочкой? — спросил Шаста.

— Её высекли, конечно, за то, что проспала. И поделом: она наушничала мачехе.

— А по-моему, это нехорошо, — возразил Шаста.

— Прости, — съязвила Аравита, — тебя не спросила!

— И ещё вот чего я не понял, — не обратил внимания на колкость мальчик. — Ты не взрослая, не старше меня, а то и моложе. Разве тебя можно выдать замуж?

Аравита не ответила, но Игого сказал:

— Шаста, не срамись! У тархистанских вельмож так заведено.

Мальчик покраснел (хотя в темноте никто этого не заметил), смутился и надолго замолчал. Игого тем временем поведал Аравите их историю, и Шасте показалось, что он слишком часто упоминает всякие падения и неудачи. Видимо, конь считал, что это забавно, хотя девочка вовсе и не смеялась. Потом все легли спать.

Наутро продолжили путь вчетвером, и Шаста подумал, что вдвоём было лучше. Теперь Игого бе-

it had been much pleasanter when he and Bree were on their own. For now it was Bree and Aravis who did nearly all the talking. Bree had lived a long time in Calormen and had always been among Tarkaans and Tarkaans' horses, and so of course he knew a great many of the same people and places that Aravis knew. She would always be saying things like, 'But if you were at the fight of Zulindreh you would have seen my cousin Alimash,' and Bree would answer, 'Oh, yes, Alimash, he was only captain of the chariots, you know. I don't quite hold with chariots or the kind of horses who draw chariots. That's not real cavalry. But he is a worthy nobleman. He filled my nosebag with sugar after the taking of Teebeth.' Or else Bree would say, 'I was down at the lake of Mezreel that summer,' and Aravis would say, 'Oh, Mezreel! I had a friend there, Lasaraleen Tarkheena. What a delightful place it is. Those gardens, and the Valley of the Thousand Perfumes!' Bree was not in the least trying to leave Shasta out of things, though Shasta sometimes nearly thought he was. People who know a lot of the same things can hardly help talking about them, and if you're there you can hardly help feeling that you're out of it.

Hwin the mare was rather shy before a great war-horse like Bree and said very little. And Aravis never spoke to Shasta at all if she could help it.

Soon, however, they had more important things to think of. They were getting near Tashbaan. There were more, and larger, villages, and more people on the roads. They now did nearly all their travelling by night and hid as best they could during the day. And at every halt they argued and argued about what they were to do when they reached Tashbaan. Everyone had been putting off this difficulty, but now it could be put off no longer. During these discussions Aravis became a little, a very little,

седовал не с ним, а с Аравитой. Благородный конь долго жил в Тархистане, среди тарханов и тархин, и знал почти всех знакомых своей неожиданной попутчицы. «Если ты был под Зулиндрехом, то должен был видеть Алимаша, моего родича», — говорила Аравита, а он отвечал: «Ну как же! Колесница не то что мы, кони, но всё же он храбрый воин и добрый человек. После битвы, когда мы взяли Тебёф, он дал мне много сахару». А то начинал Игого: «Помню, у озера Мезраэль...», — и Аравита вставляла: «Ах, там жила моя подруга Лазорилина. Дол Тысячи Запахов... Какие сады, какие цветы, ах и ах!» Конь никак не думал оттеснить своего маленького приятеля, но когда встречаются существа одного круга, это выходит само собой.

Уинни сильно робела перед таким конем и говорила не много, а хозяйка её — или подруга — и вовсе ни разу не обратилась к Шасте.

Вскоре, однако, им пришлось подумать о другом. Они подходили к Ташбаану. Селения стали больше, дороги не так пустынны. Теперь они ехали ночью, днём где-нибудь прятались и часто спорили о том, что делать в столице. Каждый предлагал своё, и Аравита, быть может, обращалась чуть-чуть приветливее к Шасте: человек становится лучше, когда обсуждает важные вещи, а не просто болтает.

less unfriendly to Shasta; one usually gets on better with people when one is making plans than when one is talking about nothing in particular.

Bree said the first thing now to do was to fix a place where they would all promise to meet on the far side of Tashbaan even if, by any ill luck, they got separated in passing the city. He said the best place would be the Tombs of the Ancient Kings on the very edge of the desert. 'Things like great stone bee-hives,' he said, 'you can't possibly miss them. And the best of it is that none of the Calormenes will go near them because they think the place is haunted by ghouls and are afraid of it.' Aravis asked if it wasn't really haunted by ghouls. But Bree said he was a free Narnian horse and didn't believe in these Calormene tales. And then Shasta said he wasn't a Calormene either and didn't care a straw about these old stories of ghouls. This wasn't quite true. But it rather impressed Aravis (though at the moment it annoyed her too) and of course she said she didn't mind any number of ghouls either. So it was settled that the Tombs should be their assembly place on the other side of Tashbaan, and everyone felt they were getting on very well till Hwin humbly pointed out that the real problem was not where they should go when they had got through Tashbaan but how they were to get through it.

'We'll settle that tomorrow, Ma'am,' said Bree. 'Time for a little sleep now.'

But it wasn't easy to settle. Aravis's first suggestion was that they should swim across the river below the city during the night and not go into Tashbaan at all. But Bree had two reasons against this. One was that the river-mouth was very wide and it would be far too long a swim for Hwin to do, especially with a rider on her back. (He thought it would be too long for himself too, but he said

Игого считал, что самое главное — условиться поточнее, где они встретятся по ту сторону столицы, если их почему-либо разлучат. Он предлагал старое кладбище — там стояли усыпальницы древних царей, а за ними начиналась пустыня. «Эти усыпальницы нельзя не заметить, они как огромные ульи, — говорил конь. — И никто к ним не подойдёт, здесь очень боятся привидений». Аравиту немного испугали его слова, но Игого заверил, что это пустые тархистанские толки. Шаста поспешил сказать, что он не тархистанец и никаких привидений не боится. Так это было или не так, но Аравита сразу же откликнулась (хотя и немного обиделась) и, конечно, сообщила, что не боится и она. Итак, решили встретиться среди усыпальниц, когда минуют город, и успокоились, но тут Уинни тихо заметила, что надо ещё его миновать.

— Об этом, госпожа, мы потолкуем завтра, — сказал Игого. — Спать пора.

Однако назавтра, уже перед самой столицей, они столковаться не смогли. Аравита предлагала переплыть ночью огибавшую город реку и вообще в Ташбаан не заходить. Игого возразил ей, что для Уинни эта река широка, особенно — с всадником (умолчав, что она широка и для него), да и вообще там и днём и ночью много разных судов. Как не заметить, что

much less about that). The other was that it would be full of shipping and of course anyone on the deck of a ship who saw two horses swimming past would be almost certain to be inquisitive.

Shasta thought they should go up the river above Tashbaan and cross it where it was narrower. But Bree explained that there were gardens and pleasure houses on both banks of the river for miles and that there would be Tarkaans and Tarkheenas living in them and riding about the roads and having water parties on the river. In fact it would be the most likely place in the world for meeting someone who would recognize Aravis or even himself.

'We'll have to have a disguise,' said Shasta.

Hwin said it looked to her as if the safest thing was to go right through the city itself from gate to gate because one was less likely to be noticed in the crowd. But she approved of the idea of disguise as well. She said, 'Both the human will have to dress in rags and look like peasants or slaves. And all Aravis's armour and our saddles and things must be made into bundles and put on our backs, and the children must pretend to drive us and people will think we're only pack-horses.'

'My dear Hwin!' said Aravis rather scornfully. 'As anyone could mistake Bree for anything but a war-horse however you disguised him!'

'I should think not, indeed,' said Bree, snorting and letting his ears go ever so little back.

'I know it's not a *very* good plan,' said Hwin. 'But I think it's our only chance. And we haven't been groomed for ages and we're not looking quite ourselves (at least, I'm sure I'm not). I do think if we get well plastered with mud and go along with our heads down as if we're tired and lazy — and don't lift our hooves hardly at

плывут две лошади, и не проявить излишнего любопытства?

Шаста предложил переплыть реку в другом, более узком месте, но Игого объяснил, что там по обоим берегам дворцы и сады, а в садах ночи напролёт веселятся тарханы и тархины. Именно в этих местах кто-нибудь непременно узнает Аравиту.

— Может, нам как-нибудь переодеться? — сказал Шаста.

Уинни предложила идти прямо через город, от ворот до ворот, стараясь держаться в густой толпе, а всадникам и впрямь хорошо бы переодеться, чтобы походить на крестьян или рабов, а седла и красивую кольчугу увязать в тюки и приладить к лошадиным спинам. Тогда народ подумает, что дети ведут вьючных лошадей.

— Ну, знаешь ли! — фыркнула Аравита. — Кого-кого, а *такого* коня за крестьянскую лошадь вряд ли примут.

— Надеюсь, что так, — вставил Игого, чуть-чуть прижимая уши.

— Конечно, мой план не очень хорош, — согласилась Уинни, — но иначе нам не пройти. Нас с Игого давно не чистили, мы хуже выглядим — во всяком случае я, — так что если мы хорошенько выкатаемся в глине и будем еле волочить ноги и глядеть в землю, может, и обойдётся. Да, под-

all — we might not be noticed. And our tails ought to be cut shorter: not neatly, you know, but all ragged.'

'My dear Madam,' said Bree. 'Have you pictured to yourself how very disagreeable it would be to arrive in Narnia in *that* condition?'

'Well,' said Hwin humbly (she was a very sensible mare), 'the main thing is to get there.'

Though nobody much liked it, it was Hwin's plan which had to be adopted in the end. It was a troublesome one and involved a certain amount of what Shasta called stealing, and Bree called 'raiding'. One farm lost a few sacks that evening and another lost a coil of rope the next: but some tattered old boy's clothes for Aravis to wear had to be fairly bought and paid for in a village. Shasta returned with them in triumph just as evening was closing in. The others were waiting for him among the trees at the foot of a low range of wooded hills which lay right across their path. Everyone was feeling excited because this was the last hill; when they reached the ridge at the top they would be looking down on Tashbaan. 'I do wish we were safely past it,' muttered Shasta to Hwin. 'Oh I do, I do,' said Hwin fervently.

That night they wound their way through the woods up to the ridge by a wood-cutter's track. And when they came out of the woods at the top they could see thousands of lights in the valley down below them. Shasta had had no notion of what a great city would be like and it frightened him. They had their supper and the children got some sleep. But the horses woke them very early in the morning.

The stars were still out and the grass was terribly cold and wet, but daybreak was just beginning, far to their right across the sea. Aravis went a few steps away into

стригите нам хвосты покороче и, если можно, неровно, клочками.

— Дорогая моя госпожа, — возразил Игого, — подумала ли ты, каково предстать в *таком* виде? Это же столица!

— Что поделаешь!.. — смиренно проговорила лошадь, проявив благоразумие. — Главное — через столицу пройти.

Пришлось на всё это согласиться. Шаста украл в деревне пару мешков и верёвку (Игого назвал это «позаимствовал») и честно купил старую мальчишечью рубаху для Аравиты.

Вернулся он, торжествуя, когда уже смеркалось. Все ждали его в роще, у подножия холма, радуясь, что холм этот — последний. С его вершины они уже могли видеть Ташбаан.

— Только бы город пройти... — тихо сказал Шаста, а Уинни ответила:

— Ах, правда, правда!

Ночью они взобрались по тропке на холм, и перед ними открылся огромный город, сияющий тысячью огней. Шаста, видевший это в первый раз, немного испугался, но всё же поужинал и поспал. Лошади разбудили его затемно.

Звёзды ещё сверкали, трава была влажной и очень холодной; далеко внизу, справа, над морем, едва занималась заря. Аравита отошла за дерево и вско-

the wood and came back looking odd in her new, ragged clothes and carrying her real ones in a bundle. These, and her armour and shield and scimitar and the two saddles and the rest of the horses' fine furnishings were put into the sacks. Bree and Hwin had already got themselves as dirty and bedraggled as they could and it remained to shorten their tails. As the only tool for doing this was Aravis's scimitar, one of the packs had to be undone again in order to get it out. It was a longish job and rather hurt the horses.

'My word!' said Bree, 'if I wasn't a Talking Horse what a lovely kick in the face I could give you! I thought you were going to cut it, not pull it out. That's what it feels like.'

But in spite of semi-darkness and cold fingers all was done in the end, the big packs bound on the horses, the rope halters (which they were now wearing instead of bridles and reins) in the children's hands, and the journey began.

'Remember,' said Bree. 'Keep together if we possibly can. If not, meet at the Tombs of the Ancient Kings, and whoever gets there first must wait for the others.'

'And remember,' said Shasta. 'Don't you two horses forget yourselves and start *talking*, whatever happens.'

ре вышла в мешковатой одежде, с узелком в руках. Узелок этот, и кольчугу, и ятаган, и седло сложили в мешки. Лошади уже перепачкались, как только могли, а чтобы подрезать им хвосты, пришлось снова вынуть ятаган. Хвосты подрезали долго и не очень умело.

— Ну что это! — возмутился Игого. — Ах так бы и лягнулся, не будь я говорящим конём! Мне казалось, вы подстрижёте хвосты, а не повыдёргиваете...

Было почти темно, пальцы коченели от холода, но в конце концов с делом справились. Потом нагрузили поклажу, взяли верёвки (ими заменили уздечки и поводья) и двинулись вниз. Занимался день.

— Будем держаться вместе сколько сможем, — напомнил Игого. — Если же нас разлучат, встретимся на старом кладбище. Тот, кто придёт туда первым, будет ждать остальных.

— Что бы ни случилось, — сказал лошадям Шаста, — не говорите ни слова.

Chapter 4

SHASTA FALLS IN WITH THE NARNIANS

At first Shasta could see nothing in the valley below him but a sea of mist with a few domes and pinnacles rising from it; but as the light increased and the mist cleared away he saw more and more. A broad river divided itself into two streams and on the island between them stood the city of Tashbaan, one of the wonders of the world. Round the very edge of the island, so that the water lapped against the stone, ran high walls strengthened with so many towers that he soon gave up trying to count them. Inside the walls the island rose in a hill and every bit of that hill, up to the Tisroc's palace and the great temple of Tash at the top, was completely covered with buildings — terrace above terrace, street above street, zigzag roads or huge flights of steps bordered with orange trees and lemon trees, roofgardens, balconies, deep archways, pillared colonnades, spires, battlements, minarets, pinnacles. And when at last the sun rose out of the sea and the great silver-plated dome of the temple flashed back its light, he was almost dazzled.

'Get on, Shasta,' Bree kept saying.

The river banks on each side of the valley were such a mass of gardens that they looked at first like forest, until you got closer and saw the white walls of innumerable houses peeping out from beneath the trees. Soon after that, Shasta noticed a delicious smell of flowers and fruit. About fifteen minutes later they were down among them,

Глава 4

КОРОЛЬ И КОРОЛЕВА

Сперва Шаста видел внизу только море мглы, над которым вставали купола и шпили, но когда рассвело и туман рассеялся, ему открылось больше. Широкая река обнимала двумя рукавами великую столицу, одно из чудес света. По краю острова стояла стена, укреплённая башенками, — их было так много, что Шаста скоро перестал считать. Остров был, как круглый пирог — посередине выше, и склоны его густо покрывали дома; наверху же гордо высился дворец Тисрока и храм богини Таш. Между домами причудливо вились улочки, обсаженные лимонными и апельсиновыми деревьями, на крышах зеленели сады, повсюду пестрели и переливались арки, колоннады, шпили, минареты, балконы, плоские крыши. Когда серебряный купол засверкал на солнце, у Шасты сердце забилось от восторга.

— Идём же! — в который раз сказал ему конь.

Оба берега были покрыли густыми, как лес, садами, а когда спустились ниже и Шаста ощутил сладостный запах фруктов и цветов, стало видно, что из-за деревьев выглядывают белые домики. Ещё через четверть часа путники шли меж белёных стен, из-за которых свешивались густые ветви.

plodding on a level road with white walls on each side and trees bending over the walls.

'I say,' said Shasta in an awed voice. 'This is a wonderful place!'

'I daresay,' said Bree. 'But I wish we were safely through it and out at the other side. Narnia and the North!'

At that moment a low, throbbing noise began which gradually swelled louder and louder till the whole valley seemed to be swaying with it. It was a musical noise, but so strong and solemn as to be a little frightening.

'That's the horns blowing for the city gates to be open,' said Bree. 'We shall be there in a minute. Now, Aravis, do droop your shoulders a bit and step heavier and try to look less like a princess. Try to imagine you've been kicked and cuffed and called names all your life.'

'If it comes to that,' said Aravis, 'what about you drooping your head a bit more and arching your neck a bit less and trying to look less like a war-horse?'

'Hush,' said Bree. 'Here we are.'

And they were. They had come to the river's edge and the road ahead of them ran along a many-arched bridge. The water danced brightly in the early sunlight; away to the right nearer the river's mouth, they caught a glimpse of ships' masts. Several other travellers were before them on the bridge, mostly peasants driving laden donkeys and mules or carrying baskets on their heads. The children and horses joined the crowd.

'Is anything wrong?' whispered Shasta to Aravis, who had an odd look on her face.

'Oh it's all very well for you,' whispered Aravis rather savagely. 'What would you care about Tashbaan? But I ought to be riding in on a litter with soldiers before me and slaves behind, and perhaps going to a feast in the

— Ах какая красота! — восхищённо воскликнул Шаста.

— Скорей бы она осталась позади, — заметил Игого. — К северу, в Нарнию!

В этот миг торжественно и громко затрубили трубы, и хоть звук был красив, путники немножко испугались.

— Это сигнал, — объяснил конь. — Сейчас откроют ворота. Ну, госпожа моя Аравита, опусти плечи, ступай тяжелее. Забудь, что ты тархина. Постарайся вообразить, что тобой всю жизнь помыкали.

— Если на то пошло, — заметила Аравита, — почему бы и тебе не согнуть немного шею? Забудь, что ты боевой конь.

— Тише, — попросил Игого. — Мы пришли.

Так оно и было. Река перед ними разделялась на два рукава, и вода на утреннем солнце ярко сверкала. Справа, немного подальше, белели паруса; прямо впереди возвышался многоарочный мост, по которому неспешно брели крестьяне. Одни несли корзины на голове, другие вели осликов и мулов. Как можно незаметнее путники наши присоединились к ним.

— В чём дело? — шепнул Шаста Аравите, заметив, что девочка надулась.

— Тебе-то что! — почти прошипела та. — Что тебе Ташбаан! А меня должны нести в паланкине: впереди — солдаты, позади — слуги... И прямо во дворец, к Тисроку (да живёт он вечно). Да, тебе что...

Tisroc's palace (may he live for ever) — not sneaking in like this. It's different for you.'

Shasta thought all this very silly.

At the far end of the bridge the walls of the city towered high above them and the brazen gates stood open in the gateway which was really wide but looked narrow because it was so very high. Half a dozen soldiers, leaning on their spears, stood on each side. Aravis couldn't help thinking, 'They'd all jump to attention and salute me if they knew whose daughter I am.' But the others were only thinking of how they'd get through and hoping the soldiers would not ask any questions. Fortunately they did not. But one of them picked a carrot out of a peasant's basket and threw it at Shasta with a rough laugh, saying:

'Hey! Horse-boy! You'll catch it if your master finds you've been using his saddle-horse for pack work.'

This frightened him badly for of course it showed that no one who knew anything about horses would mistake Bree for anything but a charger.

'It's my master's orders, so there!' said Shasta. But it would have been better if he had held his tongue for the soldier gave him a box on the side of his face that nearly knocked him down and said, 'Take that, you young filth, to teach you how to talk to freemen.' But they all slunk into the city without being stopped. Shasta cried only a very little; he was used to hard knocks.

Inside the gates Tashbaan did not at first seem so splendid as it had looked from a distance. The first street was narrow and there were hardly any windows in the walls on each side. It was much more crowded than Shasta had expected: crowded partly by the peasants (on their way to market) who had come in with them, but also with watersellers, sweetmeat sellers, porters, soldiers, beggars, ragged children, hens, stray dogs, and bare-footed slaves.

Шаста подумал, что всё это очень глупо.

За мостом гордо высилась городская стена. Медные ворота были открыты, и по обе стороны, опираясь на копья, стояли солдаты, пятеро. Аравита невольно подумала: «Они бы мигом встали по стойке «смирно!», если бы узнали, кто мой отец!..» — а друзья её — о том, чтобы солдаты не обратили на них внимания. К счастью, так и вышло, только один из них схватил морковку из чьей-то корзины, запустил ею в Шасту и крикнул, грубо захохотав:

— Эй, парень! Худо тебе придётся, если хозяин узнает, что ты возишь поклажу на его коне!

Шаста испугался, что ни один воин или вельможа не примет Игого за вьючную лошадь, но всё же нашёл в себе силы ответить:

— Он сам так велел!

Лучше бы ему промолчать — солдат тут же ударил его по уху и сказал:

— Поговори мне ещё!

А Шаста даже не заплакал — привык к битью.

За стеной столица показалась ему не такой красивой. Улицы были узкие и грязные, стены — сплошные, без окон, народу гораздо больше, чем он думал.

Крестьяне шли на рынок, но были тут и водоносы, и торговцы сладостями, и носильщики, и нищие, и босоногие рабы, и бродячие собаки, и куры. Если бы вы оказались там, то прежде всего ощутили бы

What you would chiefly have noticed if you had been there was the smells, which came from unwashed people, unwashed dogs, scent, garlic, onions, and the piles of refuse which lay everywhere.

Shasta was pretending to lead but it was really Bree, who knew the way and kept guiding him by little nudges with his nose. They soon turned to the left and began going up a steep hill. It was much fresher and pleasanter, for the road was bordered by trees and there were houses only on the right side; on the other they looked out over the roofs of houses in the lower town and could see some way up the river. Then they went round a hairpin bend to their right and continued rising. They were zigzagging up to the centre of Tashbaan. Soon they came to finer streets. Great statues of the gods and heroes of Calormen — who are mostly impressive rather than agreeable to look at — rose on shining pedestals. Palm trees and pillared arcades cast shadows over the burning pavements. And through the arched gateways of many a palace Shasta caught sight of green branches, cool fountains, and smooth lawns. It must be nice inside, he thought.

запах немытых людей, бродячих собак, лука, чеснока, мусора и помоев.

Шаста делал вид, что всех ведёт он, хотя вёл Иго-го, указывая, куда свернуть. Они долго шли вверх, сильно петляя, пока не оказались наконец на обсаженной деревьями улице. Воздух тут был получше. С одной стороны стояли дома, а с другой, за зеленью, виднелись крыши на уступе пониже и даже река далеко внизу. Чем выше подымались наши путники, тем становилось чище и красивее. То и дело попадались статуи богов и героев (скорее величественные, чем красивые), пальмы и аркады бросали тень на раскалённые плиты мостовой. За арками ворот зеленели деревья, пестрели цветы, сверкали фонтаны, и Шаста подумал, что там очень неплохо.

At every turn Shasta hoped they were getting out of the crowd, but they never did. This made their progress very slow, and every now and then they had to stop altogether. This usually happened because a loud voice shouted out 'Way, way, way, for the Tarkaan', or 'for the Tarkheena', or 'for the fifteenth Vizier', 'or for the Ambassador', and everyone in the crowd would crush back against the walls; and above their heads Shasta would sometimes see the great lord or lady for whom all the fuss was being made, lolling upon a litter which four or even six gigantic slaves carried on their bare shoulders. For in Tashbaan there is only one traffic regulation, which is that everyone who is less important has to get out of the way for everyone who is more important; unless you want a cut from a whip or punch from the butt end of a spear.

It was in a splendid street very near the top of the city (the Tisroc's palace was the only thing above it) that the most disastrous of these stoppages occurred.

'Way! Way! Way!' came the voice. 'Way for the White Barbarian King, the guest of the Tisroc (may he live for ever)! Way for the Narnian lords.'

Shasta tried to get out of the way and to make Bree go back. But no horse, not even a Talking Horse from Narnia, backs easily. And a woman with a very edgy basket in her hands, who was just behind Shasta, pushed the basket hard against his shoulders, and said, 'Now then! Who are you shoving!' And then someone else jostled him from the side and in the confusion of the moment he lost hold of Bree. And then the whole crowd behind him became so stiffened and packed tight that he couldn't move at all. So he found himself, unintentionally, in the first row and had a fine sight of the party that was coming down the street.

Толпа, однако, была по-прежнему густой. Идти приходилось медленно, нередко — останавливаться; то и дело раздавались крики: «Дорогу, дорогу, дорогу тархану», — или: «...тархине», — или: «...пятнадцатому визирю», — или: «...посланнику». И все, кто шёл по улице, прижимались к стене, а над головами Шаста видел носилки, которые несли на обнажённых плечах шесть рабов-великанов. В Тархистане только один закон уличного движения: уступи дорогу тому, кто важнее, если не хочешь, чтобы тебя хлестнули бичом или укололи копьём.

На очень красивой улице, почти у вершины (где стоял дворец Тисрока), случилась самая неприятная из всех этих встреч.

— Дорогу светлоликому королю, гостю Тискора (да живёт он вечно)! — провозгласил кто-то зычным голосом.

Шаста посторонился и потянул за собой Игого, но ни один конь, даже говорящий, не любит пятиться задом, а тут ещё их толкнула женщина с корзинкой, так что бедный мальчик неведомо как выпустил поводья. Толпа тем временем стала такой плотной, что отодвинуться дальше к стене он не мог и волей-неволей оказался в первом ряду.

It was quite unlike any other party they had seen that day. The crier who went before it shouting 'Way, way!' was the only Calormene in it. And there was no litter; everyone was on foot. There were about half a dozen men and Shasta had never seen anyone like them before. For one thing, they were all as fair-skinned as himself, and most of them had fair hair. And they were not dressed like men of Calormen. Most of them had legs bare to the kneee. Their tunics were of fine, bright, hardy colours — woodland green, or gay yellow, or fresh blue. Instead of turbans they wore steel or silver caps, some of them set with jewels, and one with little wings on each side of it. A few were bareheaded. The swords at their sides were long and straight, not curved like Calormene scimitars. And instead of being grave and mysterious like most Calormenes, they walked with a swing and let their arms and shoulders free, and chatted and laughed. One was whistling. You could see that they were ready to be friends with anyone who was friendly and didn't give a fig for anyone who wasn't. Shasta thought he had never seen anything so lovely in his life.

But there was no time to enjoy it for at once a really dreadful thing happened. The leader of the fair-headed men suddenly pointed at Shasta, cried out, 'There he is! There's our runaway!' and seized him by the shoulder. Next moment he gave Shasta a smack — not a cruel one to make you cry but a sharp one to let you know you are in disgrace and added, shaking:

'Shame on you, my lord! Fie for shame! Queen Susan's eyes are red with weeping because of you. What! Truant for a whole night! Where have you been?'

Shasta would have darted under Bree's body and tried to make himself scarce in the crowd if he had had the least chance; but the fair-haired men were all round him by now and he was held firm.

Он не увидел никаких носилок. Посередине улицы шли пешком чрезвычайно странные люди, человек шесть. Тархистанец был один — тот, что кричал: «Дорогу!..», — остальные были светлые, белокожие, как он, а двое ещё и белокурые. Одеты они были тоже не так, как одеваются в Тархистане, — без шаровар и халатов, в чём-то вроде рубах до колена (одна зелёная, как лес, две ярко-жёлтые, две голубые). Вместо тюрбанов у некоторых были стальные или серебряные шапочки, усыпанные драгоценными камнями, а у одного даже с крылышками. Мечи у них были длинные, прямые, а не изогнутые, как ятаган. А главное — в них самих он не заметил и следа присущей здешним вельможам важности. Они улыбались, смеялись, один — насвистывал, и сразу было видно, что они рады подружиться с любым, кто с ними хорош, и просто не замечают тех, кто с ними неприветлив. Глядя на них, Шаста подумал, что в жизни не видел таких приятных людей.

Однако насладиться зрелищем он не успел, ибо тот, кто шёл впереди, схватил его за плечо и воскликнул:

— Вот он, смотрите! Как вам не стыдно, ваше высочество! Королева глаза выплакала. Где же это видано — пропасть на всю ночь?!

Шаста спрятался бы под брюхом у коня или в толпе, но не мог — светлые люди окружили его.

Of course his first impulse was to say that he was only poor Arsheesh the fisherman's son and that the foreign lord must have mistaken him for someone else. But then, the very last thing he wanted to do in that crowded place was to start explaining who he was and what he was doing. If he started on that, he would soon be asked where he had got his horse from, and who Aravis was — and then, goodbye to any chance of getting through Tashbaan. His next impulse was to look at Bree for help. But Bree had no intention of letting all the crowd know that he could talk, and stood looking just as stupid as a horse can. As for Aravis, Shasta did not even dare to look at her for fear of drawing attention. And there was no time to think, for the leader of the Narnians said at once:

'Take one of his little lordship's hands, Peridan, of your courtesy, and I'll take the other. And now, on. Our royal sister's mind will be greatly eased when she sees our young scapegrace safe in our lodging.'

And so, before they were half-way through Tashbaan, all their plans were ruined, and without even a chance to say goodbye to the others Shasta found himself being marched off among strangers and quite unable to guess what might be going to happen next. The Narnian King — for Shasta began to see by the way the rest spoke to him that he must be a king — kept on asking him questions; where he had been, how he had got out, what he had done with his clothes, and didn't he know that he had been very naughty. Only the king called it 'naught' instead of naughty.

And Shasta said nothing in answer, because he couldn't think of anything to say that would not be dangerous.

'What! All mum?' asked the king. 'I must plainly tell you, prince, that this hangdog silence becomes one of

Конечно, можно было сказать, что он бедный сын рыбака и вельможа обознался, но тогда пришлось бы объяснить, откуда взялся конь и кто такая Аравита. Мальчик оглянулся, надеясь на помощь Игого, но тот не собирался оповещать толпу о своём особом даре. Что до Аравиты, на неё Шаста и взглянуть не смел, опасаясь выдать. Да и времени не было — глава белокожих сказал:

— Будь любезен, Перидан, возьми его высочество за руку, а я — за другую. Ну, идём. Обрадуем поскорей сестру нашу, королеву.

Потом человек этот (наверное, король, потому что все говорили ему «ваше величество») принялся расспрашивать Шасту, где он был, как выбрался из дому, куда дел одежду, не стыдно ли ему и так далее. Правда, он сказал не «стыдно», а «совестно».

Шаста молчал, ибо не мог придумать, что бы такое ответить и не попасть в беду.

— Молчишь? — сказал король. — Знаешь, принц, тебе это не пристало! Сбежать может всякий маль-

your blood even less than the scape itself. To run away might pass for a boy's frolic with some spirit in it. But the king's son of Archenland should avouch his deed; not hang his head like a Calormene slave.'

This was very unpleasant, for Shasta felt all the time that this young king was the very nicest kind of grown-up and would have liked to make a good impression on him.

The strangers led him — held tightly by both hands — along a narrow street and down a flight of shallow stairs and then up another to a wide doorway in a white wall with two tall, dark cypress trees, one on each side of it. Once through the arch, Shasta found himself in a courtyard which was also a garden. A marble basin of clear water in the centre was kept continually rippling by the fountain that fell into it. Orange trees grew round it out of smooth grass, and the four white walls which surrounded the lawn were covered with climbing roses. The noise and dust and crowding of the streets seemed suddenly far away. He was led rapidly across the garden and then into a dark doorway. The crier remained outside. After that they took him along a corridor, where the stone floor felt beautifully cool to his hot feet, and up some stairs. A moment later he found himself blinking in the light of a big, airy room with wide open windows, all looking North so that no sun came in. There was a carpet on the floor more wonderfully coloured than anything he had ever seen and his feet sank down into it as if he were treading in thick moss. All round the walls there were low sofas with rich cushions on them, and the room seemed to be full of people; very queer people some of them, thought Shasta. But he had no time to think of that before the most beautiful lady he

чик. Но наследник Орландии не станет трусить, как тархистанский раб.

Тут Шаста совсем расстроился, ибо молодой король понравился ему больше всех взрослых, которых он видел, и хотелось ему понравиться.

Удерживая за руки, незнакомцы провели его узкой улочкой, спустились по ветхим ступенькам и поднялись по красивой лестнице к широким воротам в белой стене, по обе стороны которых росли кипарисы. За воротами и дальше, за аркой, оказался двор, или, скорее, сад, в центре которого журчал прозрачный фонтан. Вокруг него, над мягкой травой, росли апельсиновые деревья; белые стены были увиты розами.

Пыль и грохот исчезли. Белокожие люди вошли в какую-то дверь, тархистанец остался. Миновав коридор, где мраморный пол приятно холодил ноги, они прошли несколько ступенек — и Шасту ослепила светлая большая комната окнами на север, так что солнце здесь не пекло. По стенам стояли низкие диваны, на которых лежали расшитые подушки, и народу было много, причём очень странного. Но Шаста не успел толком об этом подумать, потому что самая красивая девушка из всех, что ему довелось видеть, кинулась к ним и со слезами стала его целовать.

had ever seen rose from her place and threw her arms round him and kissed him, saying:

'Oh Corin, Corin, how could you? And thou and I such close friends ever since thy mother died. And what should I have said to thy royal father if I came home without thee? Would have been a cause almost of war between Archenland and Narnia which are friends time out of mind. It was naught, playmate, very naught of thee to use us so.'

'Apparently,' thought Shasta to himself, 'I'm being mistaken for a prince of Archenland, wherever that is. And these must be the Narnians. I wonder where the real Corin is?' But these thoughts did not help him say anything out loud.

'Where hast been, Corin?' said the lady, her hands still on Shasta's shoulders.

'I — I don't know,' stammered Shasta.

'There it is, Susan,' said the King. 'I could get no tale out of him, true or false.'

'Your Majesties! Queen Susan! King Edmund!' said a voice: and when Shasta turned to look at the speaker he nearly jumped out of his skin with surprise. For this was one of these queer people whom he had noticed out of the corner of his eye when he first came into the room. He was about the same height as Shasta himself. From the waist upwards he was like a man, but his legs were hairy like a goat's, and shaped like a goat's and he had goat's hooves and a tail. His skin was rather red and he had curly hair and a short pointed beard and two little horns. He was in fact a Faun, which is a creature Shasta had never seen a picture of or even heard of. And if you've read a book called *The Lion, the Witch and the Wardrobe* you may like to know that this was the very same Faun, Tumnus by name, whom Queen

— О Корин, Корин! Как ты мог?! Что я сказала бы королю Луму? Мы же с тобой такие друзья! Орландия с Нарнией всегда в мире, а тут могли бы поссориться... Как тебе не совестно?

«Меня принимают за принца какой-то Орландии, — подумал Шаста. — А они, должно быть, из Нарнии. Где же этот Корин, хотел бы я знать?»

Но мысли эти не подсказали ему, как ответить.

— Где ты был? — спросила красавица, обнимая его, и он наконец ответил:

— Я... я н-не знаю...

— Вот видишь, Сьюзен! — воскликнул король. — Ничего не говорит, даже солгать не хочет.

— Ваши величества! Королева Сьюзен! Король Эдмунд! — послышался голос, и, обернувшись, Шаста чуть не подпрыгнул от удивления.

Говоривший (из тех странных людей, которых он заметил, войдя в комнату) был не выше его и от пояса вверх вполне походил на человека, а ноги у него были лохматые и с копытцами, сзади же торчал хвост. Кожа у него была красноватая, волосы вились, а из них торчали маленькие рожки. То был фавн — Шаста в жизни их не видел, но мы-то с вами знаем, кто они такие. Надеюсь, вам приятно узнать, что фавн тот самый, мистер Тумнус, которого Люси, сестра королевы Сьюзен, встретила в Нарнии, как только туда попала, только очень постаревший, ибо Питер, Сьюзен, Эдмунд и Люси правили здесь уже несколько лет.

Susan's sister Lucy had met on the very first day when she found her way into Narnia. But he was a good deal older now for by this time Peter and Susan and Edmund and Lucy had been Kings and Queens of Narnia for several years.

'Your Majesties,' he was saying, 'His little Highness has had a touch of the sun. Look at him! He is dazed. He does not know where he is.'

Then of course everyone stopped scolding Shasta and asking him questions and he was made much of and laid on a sofa and cushions were put under his head and he was given iced sherbet in a golden cup to drink and told to keep very quiet.

Nothing like this had ever happened to Shasta in his life before. He had never even imagined lying on anything so comfortable as that sofa or drinking anything so delicious as that sherbet. He was still wondering what had happened to the others and how on earth he was going to escape and meet them at the Tombs, and what would happen when the real Corin turned up again. But none of these worries seemed so pressing now that he was comfortable. And perhaps, later on, there would be nice things to eat!

Meanwhile the people in that cool airy room were very interesting. Besides the Faun there were two Dwarfs (a kind of creature he had never seen before) and a very large Raven.

The rest were all humans; grown-ups, but young, and all of them, both men and women, had nicer faces and voices than most Calormenes. And soon Shasta found himself taking an interest in the conversation. 'Now, Madam,' the King was saying to Queen Susan (the lady who had kissed Shasta). 'What think you? We have been in this city fully three weeks. Have you yet settled in your

— У его высочества, — продолжил фавн, — похоже, лёгкий солнечный удар. Взгляните на него! Он ничего не помнит, даже не понимает, где находится!

Тогда все перестали наконец расспрашивать и ругать Шасту, положили на мягкий диван, дали ему ледяного шербета в золотой чаше и сказали, чтобы не волновался. Такого с ним в жизни не бывало, он даже не думал, что есть такие мягкие ложа и такие вкусные напитки. Конечно, он беспокоился о друзьях, и прикидывал, как бы сбежать, и гадал, что с этим Корином, но все эти заботы как-то меркли. Думая о том, что вскоре его и покормят, он рассматривал занятнейших существ, которых тут было немало.

За фавном стояли два гнома (их он тоже никогда не видел) и очень большой ворон. Прочие были люди, взрослые, но молодые, с приветливыми лицами и весёлыми добрыми голосами. Шаста стал прислушиваться к их разговору.

— Ну, Сьюзен, — обратился король к той девушке, которая целовала Шасту, — мы торчим тут скоро месяц. Что же ты решила? Хочешь выйти за этого темнолицего типа?

mind whether you will marry this dark-faced lover of yours, this Prince Rabadash, or no?'

The lady shook her head. 'No, brother,' she said, 'not for all the jewels in Tashbaan.' ('Hullo!' thought Shasta. 'Although they're king and queen, they're brother and sister, not married to one another.')

'Truly, sister,' said the King, 'I should have loved you the less if you had taken him. And I tell you that at the first coming of the Tisroc's ambassadors into Narnia to treat of this marriage, and later when the Prince was our guest at Cair Paravel, it was a wonder to me that ever you could find it in your heart to show him so much favour.'

'That was my folly, Edmund,' said Queen Susan, 'of which I cry you mercy. Yet when he was with us in Narnia, truly this Prince bore himself in another fashion than he does now in Tashbaan. For I take you all to witness what marvellous feats he did in that great tournament and hastilude which our brother the High King made for him, and how meekly and courteously he consorted with us the space of seven days. But here, in his own city, he has shown another face.'

'Ah!' croaked the Raven. 'It is an old saying: see the bear in his own den before you judge of his conditions.'

'That's very true, Sallowpad,' said one of the Dwarfs. 'And another is, Come, live with me and you'll know me.'

'Yes,' said the King. 'We have now seen him for what he is: that is, a most proud, bloody, luxurious, cruel, and selfpleasing tyrant.'

'Then in the name of Aslan,' said Susan, 'let us leave Tashbaan this very day.'

Королева покачала головой.

— Нет, дорогой брат. Ни за какие сокровища Ташбаана.

А Шаста подумал: «Ах вот оно что! Они король и королева, но не муж и жена, а брат и сестра».

— Я очень рад, — сказал король. — Когда он гостил в Кэр-Паравале, мы все удивлялись, что ты в нём нашла.

— Прости меня, Эдмунд: я такая глупая! Но вспомни: там, у нас, он был иной. Какие давал пиры, как дрался на турнирах, как любезно и милостиво говорил! А здесь, у себя, это совершенно другой человек.

— Стар-ро как мир! — прокаркал ворон. — Недаром говорится: «В берлоге не побываешь — медведя не узнаешь».

— Вот именно, — сказал один из гномов. — И ещё: «Вместе не поживёшь — друг друга не поймёшь».

— Да, — сказал король, — теперь мы увидели его дома, а не в гостях. Здесь, у себя, он гордый, жестокий, распутный бездельник.

— Асланом тебя прошу, — сказала королева, — уедем сегодня!

'There's the rub, sister,' said Edmund. 'For now I must open to you all that has been growing in my mind these last two days and more. Peridan, of your courtesy look to the door and see that there is no spy upon us. All well? So. For now we must be secret.'

Everyone had begun to look very serious. Queen Susan jumped up and ran to her brother. 'Oh, Edmund,' she cried. 'What is it? There is something dreadful in your face.'

— Не так всё просто, сестра, — ответил король. — Сейчас я открою, о чём думал последние дни. Перидан, будь добр, затвори дверь да погляди, нет ли кого в коридоре. Так. Теперь можно поговорить о важных и тайных делах.

Все стали серьёзны, а королева Сьюзен подбежала к брату.

— Эдмунд! Что случилось? У тебя такие страшные глаза!..

Chapter 5

PRINCE CORIN

'My dear sister and very good Lady,' said King Edmund, 'you must now show your courage. For I tell you plainly we are in no small danger.'

'What is it, Edmund?' asked the Queen.

'It is this,' said Edmund. 'I do not think we shall find it easy to leave Tashbaan. While the Prince had hope that you would take him, we were honoured guests. But by the Lion's Mane, I think that as soon as he has your flat denial we shall be no better than prisoners.'

One of the Dwarfs gave a low whistle.

'I warned your Majesties, I warned you,' said Sallowpad the Raven. 'Easily in but not easily out, as the lobster said in the lobster pot!'

'I have been with the Prince this morning,' continued Edmund. 'He is little used (more's the pity) to having his will crossed. And he is very chafed at your long delays and doubtful answers. This morning he pressed very hard to know your mind. I put it aside — meaning at the same time to diminish his hopes — with some light common jests about women's fancies, and hinted that his suit was likely to be cold. He grew angry and dangerous. There was a sort of threatening, though still veiled under a show of courtesy, in every word he spoke.'

'Yes,' said Tumnus. 'And when I supped with the Grand Vizier last night, it was the same. He asked me how I like Tashbaan. And I (for I could not tell him I hated every stone of it and I would not lie) told him

Глава 5

ПРИНЦ КОРИН

— Дорогая сестра и королева, — сказал король Эдмунд, — пришло тебе время доказать свою отвагу. Не стану скрывать: нам грозит большая опасность.

— Какая? — спросила королева.

— Боюсь, что мы не уедем отсюда. Пока царевич ещё надеялся, мы были почётными гостями, но с той минуты, как ты ему откажешь, клянусь гривой Аслана, станем пленниками.

Один из гномов тихо свистнул, а ворон заметил:

— Я пр-р-редупреждал ваши величества. Войти легко — выйти трудно, как сказал омар, когда его варили.

— Я видел царевича утром, — продолжил король. — Как ни жаль, он не привык, чтобы ему перечили. Он требовал от меня — то есть от тебя — окончательного ответа. Я шутил как мог над женскими капризами, но всё же дал понять, что надежды у него мало. Он страшно рассердился: даже угрожал мне, — конечно, в их слащавой манере.

— Да, — сказал фавн, — когда я ужинал с великим визирем, было то же самое. Он спросил, нравится ли мне Ташбаан. Конечно, я не мог сказать, что мне тут каждый камень противен, а лгать не умею, вот и ответил, что летом, в жару, сердце моё томится

that now, when high summer was coming on, my heart turned to the cool woods and dewy slopes of Narnia. He gave a smile that meant no good and said, "There is nothing to hinder you from dancing there again, little goat-foot; *always provided you leave us in exchange a bride for our prince.*"'

'Do you mean he would make me his wife by force?' exclaimed Susan.

'That's my fear, Susan,' said Edmund: 'Wife: or slave which is worse.'

'But how can he? Does the Tisroc think our brother the High King would suffer such an outrage?'

'Sire,' said Peridan to the King. 'They would not be so mad. Do they think there are no swords and spears in Narnia?'

'Alas,' said Edmund. 'My guess is that the Tisroc has very small fear of Narnia. We are a little land. And little lands on the borders of a great empire were always hateful to the lords of the great empire. He longs to blot them out, gobble them up. When first he suffered the Prince to come to Cair Paravel as your lover, sister, it may be that he was only seeking an occasion against us. Most likely he hopes to make one mouthful of Narnia and Archenland both.'

'Let him try,' said the second Dwarf. 'At sea we are as big as he is. And if he assaults us by land, he has the desert to cross.'

'True, friend,' said Edmund. 'But is the desert a sure defence? What does Sallowpad say?'

'I know that desert well,' said the Raven. 'For I have flown above it far and wide in my younger days,' (you may be sure that Shasta pricked up his ears at this point). 'And this is certain; that if the Tisroc goes by the great oasis he can never lead a great army across it into Archenland.

по прохладным лесам и мокрым травам. Он неприятно улыбнулся и сказал: «Никто тебя не держит, козлиное копытце: езжай, пляши в своих лесах, — а нам оставь жену для царевича».

— Ты думаешь, он сделает меня своей женой насильно? — воскликнула Сьюзен в испуге.

— Женой... Спасибо, если не рабыней.

— Как же он может? Разве царь Тисрок это потерпит?

— Не сошёл же он с ума! — сказал Перидан. — Он знает, что в Нарнии есть добрые копья.

— Мне кажется, — сказал Эдмунд, — что Тисрок очень мало боится нас. Страна у нас небольшая. Владетелям империй не нравятся маленькие страны у их границ, поэтому они стремятся их захватить и поглотить. Не затем ли он послал к нам царевича, чтобы затеять ссору? Он рад бы прибрать к рукам и Нарнию, и Орландию.

— Пускай попробует! — вскричал гном. — Между ним и нами лежит пустыня! Что скажешь, ворон?

— Я знаю её: облетел вдоль и поперёк, когда был молод. (Не сомневайтесь, тут Шаста навострил уши.) Если Тисрок пойдёт через большой оазис, то Орландии не достигнет: его людям и коням не хватит воды, — но есть и другая дорога. (Шаста стал слушать

For though they could reach the oasis by the end of their first day's march, yet the springs there would be too little for the thirst of all those soldiers and their beasts. But there is another way.'

Shasta listened more attentively still.

'He that would find that way,' said the Raven, 'must start from the Tombs of the Ancient Kings and ride northwest so that the double peak of Mount Pire is always straight ahead of him. And so, in a day's riding or a little more, he shall come to the head of a stony valley, which is so narrow that a man might be within a furlong of it a thousand times and never know that it was there. And looking down this valley he will see neither grass nor water nor anything else good. But if he rides on down it he will come to a river and can ride by the water all the way into Archenland.'

'And do the Calormenes know of this Western way?' asked the Queen.

'Friends, friends,' said Edmund, 'what is the use of all this discourse? We are not asking whether Narnia or Calormen would win if war arose between them. We are asking how to save the honour of the Queen and our own lives out of this devilish city. For though my brother, Peter the High King, defeated the Tisroc a dozen times over, yet long before that day our throats would be cut and the

ещё внимательнее.) Ведёт она от древних усыпальниц на северо-запад, и тому, кто по ней движется, всё время видна гора с двойной вершиной — Олвин. Довольно скоро, через сутки, начнётся каменистое ущелье, очень узкое, почти незаметное со стороны. Кажется, в нём нет ни травы, ни воды — ничего. Но если спуститься туда, увидишь, что по нему течёт речка. Если идти по её берегу, можно добраться до самой Орландии.

— Знают ли тархистанцы об этой дороге? — спросила королева.

— Друзья мои, — воскликнул король, — о чём мы говорим! Дело не в том, кто победит, если Тархистан нападёт на нас. Нам надо спасти честь королевы и собственную жизнь. Конечно, брат мой Питер, Верховный король, одолеет Тисрока, но мы уже будем давно мертвецами, а сестра моя, королева, — женой или рабыней царевича.

Queen's grace would be the wife, or more likely, the slave, of this prince.'

'We have our weapons, King,' said the first Dwarf. 'And this is a reasonably defensible house.'

'As to that,' said the King, 'I do not doubt that every one of us would sell our lives dearly in the gate and they would not come at the Queen but over our dead bodies. Yet we should be merely rats fighting in a trap when all's said.'

'Very true,' croaked the Raven. 'These last stands in a house make good stories, but nothing ever came of them. After their first few repulses the enemy always set the house on fire.'

'I am the cause of all this,' said Susan, bursting into tears. 'Oh, if only I had never left Cair Paravel. Our last happy day was before those ambassadors came from Calormen. The Moles were planting an orchard for us . . . oh . . . oh.'

And she buried her face in her hands and sobbed.

'Courage, Su, courage,' said Edmund. 'Remember — but what is the matter with *you*, Master Tumnus?' For the Faun was holding both his horns with his hands as if he were trying to keep his head on by them and writhing to and fro as if he had a pain in his inside.

'Don't speak to me, don't speak to me,' said Tumnus. 'I'm thinking. I'm thinking so that I can hardly breathe. Wait, wait, do wait.'

There was a moment's puzzled silence and then the Faun looked up, drew a long breath, mopped its forehead and said:

'The only difficulty is how to get down to our ship — with some stores, too — without being seen and stopped.'

'Yes,' said a Dwarf dryly. 'Just as the beggar's only difficulty about riding is that he has no horse.'

— У нас есть оружие, — напомнил гном. — Мы можем защитить этот замок.

— Я не сомневаюсь, — сказал король, — что каждый из нас дорого продаст свою жизнь. Королеву они получат только через наши трупы. Но мы тут как мыши в мышеловке.

— Недар-р-ом гово-р-рится: «В доме остаться — с жизнью расстаться», — прокаркал ворон. — И еще: «В доме запрут — дом подожгут».

— Ах, всё это из-за меня! — заплакала Сьюзен. — Не надо мне было покидать Кэр-Параваль! Как было хорошо! Кроты же почти кончили перекапывать сад... а я... а я... — И она закрыла лицо руками.

— Ну что ты, Сью... — начал король Эдмунд, но вдруг увидел, что фавн, сжав руками голову, раскачивается как от боли и бормочет:

— Минутку, минутку... Я думаю, я сейчас придумаю... Подождите, сейчас, сейчас!..

Наконец мистер Тумнус с облегчением вздохнул, вытер лоб и сказал:

— Трудно одно: добраться до корабля так, чтобы нас не заметили и не схватили.

— Да, — согласился гном. — «Рад бы нищий скакать, да коня не сыскать».

'Wait, wait,' said Mr Tumnus impatiently. 'All we need is some pretext for going down to our ship today and taking stuff on board.'

'Yes,' said King Edmund doubtfully.

'Well, then,' said the Faun, 'how would it be if your majesties bade the Prince to a great banquet to be held on board our own galleon, the *Splendour Hyaline*, tomorrow night? And let the message be worded as graciously as the Queen can contrive without pledging her honour: so as to give the Prince a hope that she is weakening.'

'This is very good counsel, Sire,' croaked the Raven.

'And then,' continued Tumnus excitedly, 'everyone will expect us to be going down to the ship all day, making preparations for our guests. And let some of us go to the bazaars and spend every minim we have at the fruiterers and the sweetmeat sellers and the wine merchants, just as we would if we were really giving a feast. And let us order magicians and jugglers and dancing girls and flute players, all to be on board tomorrow night.'

'I see, I see,' said King Edmund, rubbing his hands.

'And then,' said Tumnus, 'we'll all be on board tonight. And as soon as it is quite dark — '

'Up sails and out oars — !' said the King.

'And so to sea,' cried Tumnus, leaping up and beginning to dance.

'And our nose Northward,' said the first Dwarf.

'Running for home! Hurrah for Narnia and the North!' said the other.

'And the Prince waking next morning and finding his birds flown!' said Peridan, clapping his hands.

— Постой, постой, — остановил его фавн. — Нужно вот что: попасть под каким-нибудь предлогом на корабль, оставить там матросов...

— Наверное, ты прав... — согласился король Эдмунд.

— Ваше величество, — опять заговорил фавн, — не пригласите ли царевича на пир? Устроим мы его на вашем корабле завтра вечером. Ради пользы дела намекните, что её величество может дать там ответ, не нанося урона своей чести. Царевич подумает, что она готова уступить.

— Пр-рекрасный совет! — одобрительно прокаркал ворон.

— Все будут думать, — взволнованно проговорил фавн, — что мы готовимся к пиру. Кого-нибудь пошлём на базар купить сластей, вина и фруктов... Пригласим шутов, и колдунов, и плясуний, и флейтистов...

— Так-так, — сказал король, потирая руки.

— А когда стемнеет, — добавил фавн, — мы уже будем на борту...

— Поставим паруса, возьмём вёсла! — воскликнул король.

— И выйдем в море! — закончил фавн и пустился в пляс.

— На север! — вскричал гном.

— В Нарнию! — крикнули все. — Ура!

'Oh Master Tumnus, dear Master Tumnus,' said the Queen, catching his hands and swinging with him as he danced. 'You have saved us all.'

'The Prince will chase us,' said another lord, whose name Shasta had not heard.

'That's the least of my fears,' said Edmund. 'I have seen all the shipping in the river and there's no tall ship of war nor swift galley there. I wish he may chase us! For the *Splendour Hyaline* could sink anything he has to send after her — if we were overtaken at all.'

'Sire,' said the Raven. 'You shall hear no better plot than the Faun's though we sat in council for seven days. And now, as we birds say, nests before eggs. Which is as much as to say, let us all take our food and then at once be about our business.'

Everyone arose at this and the doors were opened and the lords and the creatures stood aside for the King and Queen to go out first. Shasta wondered what he ought to do, but Mr Tumnus said, 'Lie there, your Highness, and I will bring you up a little feast to yourself in a few moments. There is no need for you to move until we are all ready to embark.'

Shasta laid his head down again on the pillows and soon he was alone in the room.

'This is perfectly dreadful,' thought Shasta. It never came into his head to tell these Narnians the whole truth and ask for their help. Having been brought up by a hard, close-fisted man like Arsheesh, he had a fixed habit of never telling grown-ups anything if he could help it: he thought they would always spoil or stop whatever you were trying to do. And he thought that even if the Narnian King might be friendly to the two horses, because they were Talking Beasts of Narnia, he would hate Aravis, because she was a Calormene, and either sell her

— Дорогой мой Тумнус, ты меня спас! — растроганно проговорила королева и, схватив его за руки, закружилась по комнате. — Ты спас нас всех!

— Царевич пустится в погоню, — заметил вельможа, чьего имени Шаста не знал.

— Ничего, — сказал король. — У него нет хороших кораблей и быстрых галер. Царь Тисрок держит их для себя. Пускай гонятся! Мы потопим их, если они вообще нас догонят.

— Совещайся мы неделю, — добавил ворон, — лучше не придумаешь, однако недаром говорится: «Сперва — гнездо, потом — яйцо». Прежде чем приняться за дело, надо подкрепиться.

Все встали, открыли двери и пропустили первыми королеву и короля. Шаста замешкался, но фавн сказал ему:

— Отдохните, ваше высочество: я сейчас принесу вам поесть сюда. Лежите, пока не настанет пора перебираться на корабль.

Шаста опустил голову на мягкие подушки и, оставшись в комнате один, подумал: «Какой ужас!..» Ему и в голову не приходило сказать всю правду и попросить о помощи. Вырос он среди жестоких, чёрствых людей и привык ничего не говорить взрослым, чтобы хуже не было. Может быть, этот король не обидит говорящих коней, они из Нарнии, но Аравита — здешняя, он продаст её в рабство или вернёт отцу. «А я, — продолжил размышлять мальчик, — даже не посмею сказать им, что вовсе не принц Корин. Я слышал их тайны. Если они узнают, что я чужак, то живым меня не

for a slave or send her back to her father. As for himself, 'I simply daren't tell them I'm not Prince Corin *now*,' thought Shasta. 'I've heard all their plans. If they knew I wasn't one of themselves, they'd never let me out of this house alive. They'd be afraid I'd betray them to the Tisroc. They'd kill me. And if the real Corin turns up, it'll all come out, and they *will*!' He had, you see, no idea of how noble and free-born people behave.

'What am I to do? What am I to do?' he kept saying to himself. 'What — hullo, here comes that goaty little creature again.'

The Faun trotted in, half dancing, with a tray in its hands which was nearly as large as itself. This he set on an inlaid table beside Shasta's sofa, and sat down himself on the carpeted floor with his goaty legs crossed.

'Now, princeling,' he said. 'Make a good dinner. It will be your last meal in Tashbaan.'

It was a fine meal after the Calormene fashion. I don't know whether you would have liked it or not, but Shasta did. There were lobsters, and salad, and snipe stuffed with almonds and truffles, and a complicated dish made of chicken-livers and rice and raisins and nuts, and there were cool melons and gooseberry fools and mulberry fools, and every kind of nice thing that can be made with ice. There was also a little flagon of the sort of wine that is called 'white' though it is really yellow.

While Shasta was eating, the good little Faun, who thought he was still dazed with sunstroke, kept talking to him about the fine times he would have when they all got home; about his good old father King Lune of Archenland and the little castle where he lived on the southern slopes of the pass. 'And don't forget,' said Mr Tumnus, 'that you are promised your first suit of armour and your first war horse on your next birthday. And then your

отпустят — убьют. А если Корин придёт? Тогда уж наверняка...»

Понимаете, Шаста не знал, как ведут себя свободные, благородные люди.

«Что же мне делать, что делать? А вон и козлик этот идёт!..»

Фавн, слегка приплясывая, внёс в комнату огромный поднос, поставил на столик у дивана и, усевшись на ковёр скрестив ноги, сказал:

— Ну, милый принц, ешь — это последний твой обед в Ташбаане.

Обед был хорош. Не знаю, понравился бы он вам, но Шасте понравился. Он жадно съел омаров, и овощи, и бекаса, фаршированного трюфелями и миндалём, и сложное блюдо из риса, изюма, орехов и цыплячьих печёнок, и дыню, и ягоды, и какие-то дивные ледяные сласти вроде нашего мороженого. Выпил он и вина, которое зовётся белым, хотя оно светло-жёлтое.

Фавн тем временем развлекал его беседой. Думая, что принц нездоров, Тумнус пытался его обрадовать и говорил о том, как они вернутся домой, и о добром короле Луме, и о небольшом замке на склоне горы.

— Не забывай, — добавил фавн, — что ко дню рождения тебе обещали кольчугу и коня, а года через два сам король Питер посвятит тебя в рыцари. Пока что мы часто будем ездить к вам, вы — к нам, через

Highness will begin to learn how to tilt and joust. And in a few years, if all goes well, King Peter has promised your royal father that he himself will make you Knight at Cair Paravel. And in the meantime there will be plenty of comings and goings between Narnia and Archenland across the neck of the mountains. And of course you remember you have promised to come for a whole week to stay with me for the Summer Festival, and there'll be bonfires and all-night dances of Fauns and Dryads in the heart of the woods and, who knows? — we might see Aslan himself!'

When the meal was over the Faun told Shasta to stay quietly where he was. 'And it wouldn't do you any harm to have a little sleep,' he added. 'I'll call you in plenty of time to get on board. And then, Home. Narnia and the North!'

Shasta had so enjoyed his dinner and all the things Tumnus had been telling him that when he was left alone his thoughts took a different turn. He only hoped now that the real Prince Corin would not turn up until it was too late and that he would be taken away to Narnia by ship. I am afraid he did not think at all of what might happen to the real Corin when he was left behind in Tashbaan. He was a little worried about Aravis and Bree waiting for him at the Tombs. But then he said to himself, 'Well, how can I help it?' and, 'Anyway, that Aravis thinks she's too good to go about with me, so she can jolly well go alone,' and at the same time he couldn't help feeling that it would be much nicer going to Narnia by sea than toiling across the desert.

When he had thought all this he did what I expect you would have done if you had been up very early and had a long walk and a great deal of excitement and then a very good meal, and were lying on a sofa in a cool room

горы. Ты помнишь, конечно, что обещал приехать ко мне на летний праздник, где будут костры и ночные пляски с дриадами, а может — кто знает? — нас посетит сам Аслан.

Когда Шаста съел всё подчистую, фавн предложил:

— А теперь поспи. Не бойся, я за тобой зайду, когда будем перебираться на корабль. А потом — домой, на север!

Шасте так понравился и обед, и рассказы фавна, что он уже не мог думать о неприятном. Он надеялся, что принц Корин не придёт, опоздает, и его самого увезут на север. Боюсь, он не подумал, что станется с принцем, если тот будет один в Ташбаане. Об Аравите и о лошадях он чуть-чуть беспокоился, но сказал себе: «Что поделаешь? И вообще Аравите самой так лучше — очень я ей нужен», — ощущая при этом, что куда приятней плыть по морю, чем одолевать пустыню.

Подумав так, он заснул, как заснули бы и вы, если бы встали затемно, долго шли, а потом, лежа на мягком диване, столько съели.

with no noise in it except when a bee came buzzing in through the wide open windows. He fell asleep.

What woke him was a loud crash. He jumped up off the sofa, staring. He saw at once from the mere look of the room — the lights and shadows all looked different — that he must have slept for several hours. He saw also what had made the crash: a costly porcelain vase which had been standing on the window-sill lay on the floor broken into about thirty pieces. But he hardly noticed all these things. What he did notice was two hands gripping the window-sill from outside. They gripped harder and harder (getting white at the knuckles) and then up came a head and a pair of shoulders. A moment later there was a boy of Shasta's own age sitting astride the sill with one leg hanging down inside the room.

Shasta had never seen his own face in a looking-glass. Even if he had, he might not have realized that the other boy was (at ordinary times) almost exactly like himself. At the moment this boy was not particularly like anyone

Разбудил его громкий звон. Испуганно привстав, он увидел, что и тени, и свет сместились, а на полу лежат осколки драгоценной вазы. Но главное было не это: в подоконник вцепились чьи-то руки, причём так крепко, что побелели костяшки пальцев, потом появились голова и плечи, а через секунду какой-то мальчик перемахнул через подоконник и сел, свесив одну ногу.

Шаста никогда не гляделся в зеркало, а если бы и гляделся, не понял бы, что незнакомец очень похож на него, ибо тот был сейчас ни на кого не похож. Под глазом у него красовался огромный синяк, под носом

for he had the finest black eye you ever saw, and a tooth missing, and his clothes (which must have been splendid ones when he put them on) were torn and dirty, and there was both blood and mud on his face.

'Who are you?' said the boy in a whisper.

'Are you Prince Corin?' said Shasta.

'Yes, of course,' said the other. 'But who are you?'

'I'm nobody, nobody in particular, I mean,' said Shasta. 'King Edmund caught me in the street and mistook me for you. I suppose we must look like one another. Can I get out the way you've got in?'

'Yes, if you're any good at climbing,' said Corin. 'But why are you in such a hurry? I say: we ought to be able to get some fun out of this being mistaken for one another.'

'No, no,' said Shasta. 'We must change places at once. It'll be simply frightful if Mr Tumnus comes back and finds us both here. I've had to pretend to be you. And you're starting tonight — secretly. And where were you all this time?'

'A boy in the street made a beastly joke about Queen Susan,' said Prince Corin, 'so I knocked him down. He ran howling into a house and his big brother came out. So I knocked the big brother down. Then they all followed me until we ran into three old men with spears who are called the Watch. So I fought the Watch and they knocked me down. It was getting dark by now. Then the Watch took me along to lock me up somewhere. So I asked them if they'd like a stoup of wine and they said they didn't mind if they did. Then I took them to a wine shop and got them some and they all sat down and drank till they fell asleep. I thought it was time for me to be off so I came out quietly and then I found the first boy — the one who had started all the trouble — still hanging about.

запеклась кровь, одного зуба не было, одежда, некогда очень красивая, висела лохмотьями.

— Ты кто такой? — шёпотом спросил мальчик.

— А ты принц Корин? — в свою очередь спросил Шаста.

— Конечно. А ты-то кто?

— Никто, наверное. Король Эдмунд увидел меня на улице и решил, что это ты. Можно как-то отсюда выбраться?

— Можно, если хорошо лазаешь. Только куда спешить? Мы так похожи — давай ещё кого-нибудь разыграем!

— Нет-нет, — заторопился Шаста. — Мне нельзя оставаться. Вдруг фавн придёт и увидит нас вместе? Мне пришлось притвориться, что я — это ты. Вы сегодня отплываете. А где ты был всё время?

— Один мальчишка сказал гадость про королеву Сьюзен, — ответил принц. — Я его побил. Он заорал и побежал за братом. Тогда я побил брата. За мной погнались такие люди с копьями, называются «стража». Я подрался и с ними. Тут стало темнеть. Они меня куда-то увели. По дороге я предложил им выпить вина. Они напились и заснули, а я тихо выбрался и пошёл дальше, но встретил опять того мальчишку. Ну, мы подрались. Я его побил ещё раз, влез по водосточной трубе на крышу и стал ждал, когда рассветёт. А потом искал дорогу. Попить нету?

So I knocked him down again. After that I climbed up a pipe on to the roof of a house and lay quiet till it began to get light this morning. Ever since that I've been finding my way back. I say, is there anything to drink?'

'No, I drank it,' said Shasta. 'And now, show me how you got in. There's not a minute to lose. You'd better lie down on the sofa and pretend — but I forgot. It'll be no good with all those bruises and black eye. You'll just have to tell them the truth, once I'm safely away.'

'What else did you think I'd be telling them?' asked the Prince with a rather angry look. 'And who are you?'

'There's no time,' said Shasta in a frantic whisper. 'I'm a Narnian, I believe; something Northern anyway. But I've been brought up all my life in Calormen. And I'm escaping: across the desert; with a talking Horse called Bree. And now, quick! How do I get away?'

'Look,' said Corin. 'Drop from this window onto the roof of the verandah. But you must do it lightly, on your toes, or someone will hear you. Then along to your left and you can get up to the top of that wall if you're any good at all as a climber. Then along the wall to the corner. Drop onto the rubbish heap you will find outside, and there you are.'

'Thanks,' said Shasta, who was already sitting on the sill. The two boys were looking into each other's faces and suddenly found that they were friends.

'Good-bye,' said Corin. 'And *good* luck. I do hope you get safe away.'

'Good-bye,' said Shasta. 'I say, you have been having some adventures.'

'Nothing to yours,' said the Prince. 'Now drop; lightly — I say,' he added as Shasta dropped. 'I hope we meet in Archenland. Go to my father King Lune and tell him you're a friend of mine. Look out! I hear someone coming.'

— Нет, я всё выпил, — сказал Шаста. — Покажешь, как вылезти? Надо поскорей уходить. А ты ложись на диван. Ах, они же не поверят, что это я... то есть ты... у тебя такой синяк... Придётся тебе сказать им правду.

— Как же иначе? — сердито буркнул принц. — А всё-таки, кто ты такой?

— Некогда объяснять, — быстро прошептал Шаста. — Я не здешний, с севера, но вырос здесь, а теперь бегу домой, через пустыню, с говорящим конём. Ну, как мне лезть?

— Вот смотри: тут плоская крыша. Иди очень тихо, на цыпочках, а то кто-нибудь услышит! Сверни налево, потом залезь, если умеешь лазать, на стену, пройди по ней до угла и спрыгни на кучу мусора.

— Спасибо, — сказал Шаста уже с подоконника.

Мальчики посмотрели друг на друга, и обоим показалось, что теперь они друзья.

— До свидания, — сказал Корин. — Доброго тебе пути.

— До свидания, — попрощался и Шаста. — Ну и храбрый же ты!

— Куда мне до тебя! Ну, прыгай! Да, доберёшься до Орландии, скажи моему отцу, королю Луму, что ты мой друг! Скорее, кто-то идёт!

Chapter 6

SHASTA AMONG THE TOMBS

Shasta ran lightly along the roof on tiptoes. It felt hot to his bare feet. He was only a few seconds scrambling up the wall at the far end and when he got to the corner he found himself looking down into a narrow, smelly street, and there was a rubbish heap against the outside of the wall just as Corin had told him. Before jumping down he took a rapid glance round him to get his bearings. Apparently he had now come over the crown of the island-hill on which Tashbaan is built. Everything sloped away before him, flat roofs below flat roofs, down to the towers and battlements of the city's Northern wall. Beyond that was the river and beyond the river a short slope covered with gardens. But beyond that again there was something he had never seen the like of — a great yellowish-grey thing, flat as a calm sea, and stretching for miles. On the far side of it were huge blue things, lumpy but with jagged edges, and some of them with white tops. 'The desert! the mountains!' thought Shasta.

He jumped down onto the rubbish and began trotting along downhill as fast as he could in the narrow lane, which soon brought him into a wider street where there were more people. No one bothered to look at a little ragged boy running along on bare feet. Still, he was anxious and uneasy till he turned a corner and there saw the city gate in front of him. Here he was pressed and jostled a bit, for a good many other people were also going out;

Глава 6

ШАСТА
СРЕДИ УСЫПАЛЬНИЦ

Шаста неслышно пробежал по крыше, такой горячей, что чуть не обжёг босые ноги, взлетел вверх по стене, добрался до угла и мягко спрыгнул на кучу мусора в узкой грязной улочке. Прежде чем спрыгнуть, мальчик огляделся — по-видимому, он оказался на самой вершине горы, на которой стоит Ташбаан. Вокруг всё уходило вниз, плоские крыши спускались уступами до городской стены и сторожевых башен. За ними, с севера, текла река, за которой цвели сады, а уж за ними лежало странное, голое и желтоватое, пространство, уходившее за горизонт словно неподвижное море. Где-то в небе, очень далеко, синели какие-то глыбы с белым верхом. «Пустыня и горы», — догадался Шаста.

Спрыгнув со стены, он поспешил вниз по узкой улочке и вышел на широкую. Там был народ, но никто не обращал внимания на босоногого оборвыша, однако он всё-таки боялся, пока перед ним из-за какого-то угла не возникли городские ворота. Вышел он в густой толпе, которая по мосту двигалась медленно, как очередь. Здесь, над водой, было приятно вздохнуть после жары и запахов Ташбаана.

and on the bridge beyond the gate the crowd became quite a slow procession, more like a queue than a crowd. Out there, with clear running water on each side, it was deliciously fresh after the smell and heat and noise of Tashbaan.

When once Shasta had reached the far end of the bridge he found the crowd melting away; everyone seemed to be going either to the left or right along the river bank. He went straight ahead up a road that did not appear to be much used, between gardens. In a few paces he was alone, and a few more brought him to the top of the slope. There he stood and stared. It was like coming to the end of the world for all the grass stopped quite suddenly a few feet before him and the sand began: endless level sand like on a sea shore but a bit rougher because it was never wet. The mountains, which now looked further off than before, loomed ahead. Greatly to his relief he saw, about five minutes' walk away on his left, what must certainly be the Tombs, just as Bree had described them; great masses of mouldering stone shaped like gigantic beehives, but a little narrower. They looked very black and grim, for the sun was now setting right behind them.

He turned his face West and trotted towards the Tombs. He could not help looking out very hard for any sign of his friends, though the setting sun shone in his face so that he could see hardly anything. 'And anyway,' he thought, 'of course they'll be round on the far side of the farthest Tomb, not this side where anyone might see them from the city.'

There were about twelve Tombs, each with a low arched doorway that opened into absolute blackness. They were dotted about in no kind of order, so that it took a long time, going round this one and going round

За мостом толпа стала таять: народ расходился — кто налево, кто направо, — Шаста же пошёл прямо вперёд, между какими-то садами. Дойдя до того места, где трава сменялась песком, он очутился совсем один и в удивлении остановился, словно увидел не край пустыни, а край света. Трава кончалась сразу; дальше, прямо в бесконечность, уходило что-то вроде морского берега, только пожёстче, ибо здесь песок не смачивала вода. Впереди, как будто ещё дальше, маячили горы. Минут через пять он увидел слева высокие камни вроде ульев, но поуже. Шаста знал от коня, что это и есть усыпальницы древних царей. За ними садилось солнце, и они мрачно темнели на сверкающем фоне.

Свернув на запад, Шаста направился к ним. Солнце слепило его, но всё же он ясно видел, что ни лошадей, ни девочки на кладбище нет. «Наверное, они за последней усыпальницей, — подумал мальчик. — Чтобы отсюда не заметили».

Усыпальниц было штук двенадцать, стояли они как попало. В каждой чернел низенький вход. Шаста обошёл кругом каждую из них и никого не нашёл. Когда он опустился на песок, солнце уже село.

that one, before you could be sure that you had looked round every side of every tomb. This was what Shasta had to do. There was nobody there.

It was very quiet here out on the edge of the desert; and now the sun had really set.

Suddenly from somewhere behind him there came a terrible sound. Shasta's heart gave a great jump and he had to bite his tongue to keep himself from screaming. Next moment he realized what it was: the horns of Tashbaan blowing for the closing of the gates. 'Don't be a silly little coward,' said Shasta to himself. 'Why, it's only the same noise you heard this morning.' But there is a great difference between a noise heard letting you in with your friends in the morning, and a noise heard alone at nightfall, shutting you out. And now that the gates were shut he knew there was no chance of the others joining him that evening. 'Either they're shut up in Tashbaan for the night,' thought Shasta, 'or else they've gone on without me. It's just the sort of thing that Aravis would do. But Bree wouldn't. Oh, he wouldn't. — now, would he?'

In this idea about Aravis Shasta was once more quite wrong. She was proud and could be hard enough but she was as true as steel and would never have deserted a companion, whether she liked him or not.

Now that Shasta knew he would have to spend the night alone (it was getting darker every minute) he began to like the look of the place less and less. There was something very uncomfortable about those great, silent shapes of stone. He had been trying his hardest for a long time not to think of ghouls: but he couldn't keep it up any longer.

'Ow! Ow! Help!' he shouted suddenly, for at that very moment he felt something touch his leg. I don't think anyone can be blamed for shouting if something comes up from behind and touches him; not in such a place and

В ту же минуту раздался очень страшный звук. Шаста чуть не закричал, но вспомнил: это трубы оповещают Ташбаан, что ворота закрылись, — и сказал себе: «Не трусь. Ты слышал этот звук утром». Мальчик прекрасно понимал, что одно дело — слышать такие звуки при свете, среди друзей, и совсем другое — одному и в темноте. «Теперь не придут до утра. Они там заперты. Нет, Аравита увела их раньше, без меня. С неё станется! Что это я? Игого никогда на это не согласится!»

К Аравите он был несправедлив. Она могла проявить и чёрствость, и гордость, но верности не изменяла и ни за что не бросила бы спутника, нравится он ей или нет.

Как бы то ни было, ночевать ему предстояло тут, а место это с каждой минутой привлекало его всё меньше. Большие молчаливые глыбы всё-таки пугали его. Шаста изо всех сил старался не думать о привидениях, и уже немного успокоился, когда что-то коснулось его ноги.

— Помоги-и-те! — вырвался из его горла крик, адресованный неведомо кому.

Бежать он не смел: всё-таки совсем уж плохо, когда бежишь среди могил, не смея взглянуть, кто за то-

at such a time, when he is frightened already. Shasta at any rate was too frightened to run. Anything would be better than being chased round and round the burial places of the Ancient Kings with something he dared not look at behind him. Instead, he did what was really the most sensible thing he could do. He looked round; and his heart almost burst with relief. What had touched him was only a cat.

The light was too bad now for Shasta to see much of the cat except that it was big and very solemn. It looked as if it might have lived for long, long years among the Tombs, alone. Its eyes made you think it knew secrets it would not tell.

'Puss, puss,' said Shasta. 'I suppose you're not a *talking* cat.'

The cat stared at him harder than ever. Then it started walking away, and of course Shasta followed it. It led him right through the tombs and out on the desert side of them. There it sat down bolt upright with its tail curled round its feet and its face set towards the desert and towards Narnia and the North, as still as if it were watching for some enemy. Shasta lay down beside it with his back against the cat and his face towards the Tombs, because if one is nervous there's nothing like having your face towards the danger and having something warm and solid at your back. The sand wouldn't have seemed very comfortable to you, but Shasta had been sleeping on the ground for weeks and hardly noticed it. Very soon he fell asleep, though even in his dreams he went on wondering what had happened to Bree and Aravis and Hwin.

He was wakened suddenly by a noise he had never heard before. 'Perhaps it was only a nightmare,' said Shasta to himself. At the same moment he noticed that the cat had gone from his back, and he wished it hadn't. But

бой гонится, — поэтому, собрав всё своё мужество, сделал самое разумное, что мог, — обернулся и увидел... кота.

Кот, очень тёмный в темноте, был велик и важен — гораздо важнее и больше тех его собратьев, которых Шасте доводилось встречать. Глаза его таинственно сверкали, и казалось, что он много знает — но не скажет.

— Кис-кис-кис, — неуверенно позвал Шаста. — Ты говорить не умеешь?

Кот сурово поглядел на него и медленно пошёл куда-то, и Шаста, конечно, пошёл за ним. Через некоторое время они миновали усыпальницы. Тогда кот уселся на песок, обернув хвост вокруг передних лап. Смотрел он на север — туда, где лежала Нарния, — и был так неподвижен, что Шаста спокойно лёг спиной к нему, лицом к могилам, словно чувствовал, что кот охраняет его от врагов. Когда тебе страшно, самое лучшее — повернуться лицом к опасности и почувствовать что-то тёплое и надёжное за спиной. Песок показался бы вам не очень удобным, но Шаста и прежде спал на земле, так что скоро заснул, даже во сне гадая, где сейчас Игого, Уинни и Аравита.

Разбудил мальчика странный и страшный звук, и он подумал: «Наверное, мне всё приснилось». И тут же ощутил, что кота за спиной нет, и очень огорчился, но лежал тихо, не решаясь даже открыть глаза,

he lay quite still without even opening his eyes because he felt sure he would be more frightened if he sat up and looked round at the Tombs and the loneliness: just as you or I might lie still with the clothes over our heads. But then the noise came again — a harsh, piercing cry from behind him out of the desert. Then of course he had to open his eyes and sit up.

The moon was shining brightly. The Tombs — far bigger and nearer than he had thought they would be — looked grey in the moonlight. In fact, they looked horribly like huge people, draped in grey robes that covered their heads and faces. They were not at all nice things to have near you when spending a night alone in a strange place. But the noise had come from the opposite side, from the desert. Shasta had to turn his back on the Tombs (he didn't like that much) and stare out across the level sand. The wild cry rang out again.

'I hope it's not more lions,' thought Shasta. It was in fact not very like the lion's roars he had heard on the night when they met Hwin and Aravis, and was really the cry of a jackal. But of course Shasta did not know this. Even if he had known, he would not have wanted very much to meet a jackal.

The cries rang out again and again. 'There's more than one of them, whatever they are,' thought Shasta. 'And they're coming nearer.'

I suppose that if he had been an entirely sensible boy he would have gone back through the Tombs nearer to the river where there were houses, and wild beasts would be less likely to come. But then there were (or he thought there were) the ghouls. To go back through the Tombs would mean going past those dark openings in the Tombs; and what might come out of them? It may have been silly, but Shasta felt he would rather risk the

как лежим иногда мы с вами, закрыв простынёй голову. Звук раздался снова — пронзительный вой или вопль, — и тут глаза у Шасты открылись сами, он даже сел на песке.

Ярко светила луна; усыпальницы стали как будто больше, но казались не чёрными, а серыми, и очень уж походили на чёрных людей, закрывших голову и лицо серым покрывалом. Что и говорить, это не радует. Однако звук шёл не от них, а сзади, из пустыни. Сам того не желая, Шаста обернулся и, посмотрев в ту сторону, подумал: «Хоть бы не львы!..»

Звук и впрямь не походил на рычание льва, но Шаста этого не знал. Выли шакалы (это тоже не слишком приятно). «Их много, — подумал Шаста, сам не зная о ком. — Они всё ближе...» Мне кажется, будь он поумнее, вернулся бы к реке, где стояли дома, но его пугали усыпальницы, мимо которых предстояло пройти. Кто его знает, что вылезет из чёрных отверстий? Глупо это или не глупо, Шаста предпочёл диких зверей, но крики приближались, и он изменил мнение...

wild beasts. Then, as the cries came nearer and nearer, he began to change his mind.

He was just going to run for it when suddenly, between him and the desert, a huge animal bounded into view. As the moon was behind it, it looked quite black, and Shasta did not know what it was, except that it had a very big, shaggy head and went on four legs. It did not seem to have noticed Shasta, for it suddenly stopped, turned its head towards the desert and let out a roar which re-echoed through the Tombs and seemed to shake the sand under Shasta's feet. The cries of the other creatures suddenly stopped and he thought he could hear feet scampering away. Then the great beast turned to examine Shasta.

'It's a lion, I know it's a lion,' thought Shasta. 'I'm done. I wonder will it hurt much. I wish it was over. I wonder does anything happen to people after they're dead? O-o-oh! Here it comes!' And he shut his eyes and his teeth tight.

But instead of teeth and claws he only felt something warm lying down at his feet. And when he opened his eyes he said, 'Why, it's not nearly as big as I thought! It's only half the size. No, it isn't even quarter the size. I do declare it's only the cat!! I must have dreamed all that about its being as big as a horse.'

And whether he really had been dreaming or not, what was now lying at his feet, and staring him out of countenance with its big, green, unwinking eyes, was the cat; though certainly one of the largest cats he had ever seen.

'Oh, Puss,' gasped Shasta. 'I am so glad to see you again. I've been having such horrible dreams.' And he at once lay down again, back to back with the cat as they had been at the beginning of the night. The warmth from it spread all over him.

Мальчик уже собирался бежать, когда увидел на фоне луны огромного зверя. Тот шёл медленно и степенно, как бы не замечая его, потом остановился, издал низкий, оглушительный рёв, эхом отдавшийся в камне усыпальниц, и прежние вопли стихли. Зашуршал песок, словно какие-то существа бросились врассыпную. Тогда огромный зверь обернулся к Шасте, и тот подумал: «Это лев. Вот и всё. Очень будет больно или нет?.. Ох, поскорей бы!.. А что бывает потом, когда умрёшь? Ой-ой-ой-ой!!!»

Мальчик закрыл глаза, сжал зубы, но ничего не случилось, а когда решился открыть, что-то тёплое лежало у его ног. «Да он не такой уж большой! — удивлённо подумал Шаста. — Вполовину меньше, чем мне показалось. Нет, вчетверо... Ой, это кот! Значит, лев просто приснился!»

Действительно, у его ног лежал большой кот и смотрел на него зелёными немигающими глазами. Таких огромных котов Шасте видеть ещё не приходилось.

— Как хорошо, что это ты! — воскликнул мальчик и, прижавшись к коту, почувствовал, как и прежде, его животворящее тепло. — Мне снился страшный сон.

'I'll never do anything nasty to a cat again as long as I live,' said Shasta, half to the cat and half to himself. 'I did once, you know. I threw stones at a half-starved mangy old stray. Hey! Stop that.' For the cat had turned round and given him a scratch. 'None of that,' said Shasta. 'It isn't as if you could understand what I'm saying.' Then he dozed off.

Next morning when he woke, the cat was gone, the sun was already up, and the sand hot. Shasta, very thirsty, sat up and rubbed his eyes. The desert was blindingly white and, though there was a murmur of noises from the city behind him, where he sat everything was perfectly still. When he looked a little left and west, so that the sun was not in his eyes, he could see the mountains on the far side of the desert, so sharp and clear that they looked only a stone's throw away. He particularly noticed one blue height that divided into two peaks at the top and decided that it must be Mount Pire. 'That's our direction, judging by what the Raven said,' he thought, 'so I'll just make sure of it, so as not to waste any time when the others turn up.' So he made a good, deep straight furrow with his foot pointing exactly to Mount Pire.

The next job, clearly, was to get something to eat and drink. Shasta trotted back through the Tombs — they looked quite ordinary now and he wondered how he could ever have been afraid of them — and down into the cultivated land by the river's side. There were a few people about but not very many, for the city gates had been open several hours and the early morning crowds had already gone in. So he had no diffculty in doing a little 'raiding' (as Bree called it). It involved a climb over a garden wall and the results were three oranges, a melon, a fig or two, and a pomegranate. After that, he went down to the river bank, but not too near the bridge, and had

«Больше никогда не буду обижать кошек», — сказал он себе и добавил, уже коту:

— Знаешь, я однажды бросил камнем в старую голодную кошку... Эй, ты что!

Как раз в этот миг кот его царапнул. «Ну-ну! Будто понимает...»

Наутро, когда Шаста проснулся, кота не было, ярко светило солнце, песок уже нагрелся. Очень хотелось пить. Пустыня сверкала белизной. Из города доносился смутный шум, но здесь было очень тихо. Повернувшись так, чтобы солнце не слепило, он увидел вдали — чуть левее, к западу — горы, такие чёткие, что казалось, будто они совсем близко (одна из них имела две вершины), и, подумав: «Вот туда и надо идти», — провёл ногой по песку ровную полосу, чтобы не терять времени, когда все придут, а потом решил чего-нибудь поесть и направился к реке.

Усыпальницы оказались совсем не страшными, и теперь Шаста удивился, отчего они его так пугали. Народ здесь был, ворота открылись давно, толпа уже вошла в город, и оказалось не трудно, как сказал бы Игого, что-нибудь «позаимствовать». Он перелез через стену и сорвал в саду три апельсина, пару смокв и гранат. После того как перекусил, мальчик подошёл к реке у самого моста и напился. Вода так понравилась, что он ещё и выкупался — ведь при жизни на берегу плавать и ходить он научился одновременно. Потом он лёг на траву и стал смотреть на Ташбаан, гордый, большой и прекрасный. Вспомнил он

a drink. The water was so nice that he took off his hot, dirty clothes and had a dip; for of course Shasta, having lived on the shore all his life, had learned to swim almost as soon as he had learned to walk. When he came out he lay on the grass looking across the water at Tashbaan — all the splendour and strength and glory of it. But that made him remember the dangers of it too. He suddenly realized that the others might have reached the Tombs while he was bathing ('and gone on without me, as likely as not'), so he dressed in a fright and tore back at such a speed that he was all hot and thirsty when he arrived and so the good of his bathe was gone.

Like most days when you are alone and waiting for something this day seemed about a hundred hours long. He had plenty to think of, of course, but sitting alone, just thinking, is pretty slow. He thought a good deal about the Narnians and especially about Corin. He wondered what had happened when they discovered that the boy who had been lying on the sofa and hearing all their secret plans wasn't really Corin at all. It was very unpleasant to think of all those nice people imagining him a traitor.

But as the sun slowly, slowly climbed up to the top of the sky and then slowly, slowly began going downwards to the West, and no one came and nothing at all happened, he began to get more and more anxious. And of course he now realized that when they arranged to wait for one another at the Tombs no one had said anything about How Long. He couldn't wait here for the rest of his life! And soon it would be dark again, and he would have another night just like last night. A dozen different plans went through his head, all wretched ones, and at last he fixed on the worst plan of all. He decided to wait till it was dark and then go back to the river and steal as many melons as he could carry and set out for Mount

и о том, как опасно там было, и вдруг заподозрил, что, пока купался, Аравита и лошади, наверное, добрались до кладбища, не нашли его и ушли. Быстро одевшись, Шаста побежал обратно и так запыхался и вспотел, словно и не купался, но среди усыпальниц никого не было.

Солнце медленно ползло вверх по небу, потом медленно опускалось, но никто не пришёл и ничего не случилось, и мальчику стало совсем не по себе. Теперь он понял, что они решили здесь встретиться и ждать друг друга, но не договорились, как долго. Не до старости же! Скоро стемнеет, опять начнётся ночь... Десятки планов сменялись в его мозгу, пока он не выбрал самый худший: подождать до темноты, вернуться к реке, украсть столько дынь, сколько сможет, и пойти к той горе одному.

Если бы Шаста, как ты, читал книги о путешествиях через пустыню, то понял бы, что это очень глупо, но он не читал.

Pire alone, trusting for his direction to the line he had drawn that morning in the sand. It was a crazy idea and if he had read as many books as you have about journeys over deserts he would never have dreamed of it. But Shasta had read no books at all.

Before the sun set something did happen. Shasta was sitting in the shadow of one of the Tombs when he looked up and saw two horses coming towards him. Then his heart gave a great leap, for he recognized them as Bree and Hwin. But the next moment his heart went down into his toes again. There was no sign of Aravis. The Horses were being led by a strange man, an armed man pretty handsomely dressed like an upper slave in a great family. Bree and Hwin were no longer got up like pack-horses, but saddled and bridled. And what could it all mean? 'It's a trap,' thought Shasta. 'Somebody has caught Aravis and perhaps they've tortured her and she's given the whole thing away. They want me to jump out and run up and speak to Bree and then I'll be caught too! And yet if I don't, I may be losing my only chance to meet the others. Oh I do wish I knew what had happened.' And he skulked behind the Tomb, looking out every few minutes, and wondering which was the least dangerous thing to do.

Прежде чем солнце село, кое-что всё-таки произошло. Когда тени усыпальниц стали совсем длинными, а Шаста давно съел все свои припасы, сердце у него подпрыгнуло: вдали показались две лошади. Вне всякого сомнения, это были Уинни и Игого, прекрасные и гордые, как прежде, но теперь под дорогими сёдлами, и вёл их человек в кольчуге, похожий на слугу из знатного дома. «Аравиту поймали, — в ужасе решил Шаста. — Она всё рассказала, и этого человека послали за мной. Они хотят, чтобы я кинулся к Игого и заговорил! А если не кинусь — тогда я точно остался один... Что же теперь делать?» И он юркнул за усыпальницу, чтобы подумать, как поступить.

Chapter 7

ARAVIS IN TASHBAAN

What had really happened was this. When Aravis saw Shasta hurried away by the Narnians and found herself alone with two horses who (very wisely) wouldn't say a word, she never lost her head even for a moment. She grabbed Bree's halter and stood still, holding both the horses; and though her heart was beating as hard as a hammer, she did nothing to show it. As soon as the Narnian lords had passed she tried to move on again. But before she could take a step, another crier ('Bother all these people,' thought Aravis) was heard shouting out, 'Way, way, way! Way for the Tarkheena Lasaraleen!' and immediately, following the crier, came four armed slaves and then four bearers carrying a litter which was all a-flutter with silken curtains and all a-jingle with silver bells and which scented the whole street with perfumes and flowers. After the litter, female slaves in beautiful clothes, and then a few grooms, runners, pages, and the like. And now Aravis made her first mistake.

She knew Lasaraleen quite well — almost as if they had been at school together — because they had often stayed in the same houses and been to the same parties. And Aravis couldn't help looking up to see what Lasaraleen looked like now that she was married and a very great person indeed.

It was fatal. The eyes of the two girls met. And immediately Lasaraleen sat up in the litter and burst out at the top of her voice.

Глава 7
ВСТРЕЧА СТАРЫХ ПОДРУГ

А на самом деле случилось вот что. Когда Аравита увидела, что Шасту куда-то тащат, и осталась одна с лошадьми, которые весьма разумно молчали, то ни на миг не растерялась. Сердце у неё сильно билось, но она ничем это не выказала. Как только белокожие господа прошли мимо, она попыталась двинуться дальше, однако снова раздался крик: «Дорогу! Дорогу тархине!» — и появились четыре вооружённых раба, а за ними четыре носильщика, на плечах у которых едва покачивался роскошный паланкин. За ним, в облаке ароматов, следовали рабыни, гонцы, пажи и ещё какие-то слуги. И тут Аравита совершила первую свою ошибку.

Она прекрасно знала ту, что лениво покоилась на носилках. Это была Лазорилина, недавно вышедшая замуж за одного из самых богатых и могущественных тарханов. Девочки часто встречались в гостях, а это почти то же самое, что учиться в одной школе. Ну как тут было не посмотреть, какой стала старая подруга, после того как вышла замуж и обрела большую власть? Вот Аравита и посмотрела, а подруга — на неё...

'Aravis! What on earth are you doing here? Your father — '

There was not a moment to lose. Without a second's delay Aravis let go the Horses, caught the edge of the litter, swung herself up beside Lasaraleen and whispered furiously in her ear.

'Shut up! Do you hear? Shut up. You must hide me. Tell your people — '

'But darling — ' began Lasaraleen in the same loud voice. (She didn't in the least mind making people stare; in fact she rather liked it.)

'Do what I tell you or I'll never speak to you again,' hissed Aravis. 'Please, please be quick, Las. It's frightfully important. Tell your people to bring those two horses along. Pull all the curtains of the litter and get away somewhere where I can't be found. And do *hurry*.'

'All right, darling,' said Lasaraleen in her lazy voice. 'Here. Two of you take the Tarkheena's horses.' (This was to the slaves.) 'And now home. I say, darling, do you think we really want the curtains drawn on a day like this? I mean to say — '

But Aravis had already drawn the curtains, enclosing Lasaraleen and herself in a rich and scented, but rather stuffy, kind of tent.

'I mustn't be seen,' 'she said. 'My father doesn't know I'm here. I'm running away.'

'My dear, how perfectly thrilling,' said Lasaraleen. 'I'm dying to hear all about it. Darling, you're sitting on my dress. Do you mind? That's better. It is a new one. Do you like it? I got it at — '

'Oh, Las, do be serious,' said Aravis. 'Where is my father?'

'Didn't you know?' said Lasaraleen. 'He's here, of course. He came to town yesterday and is asking about

— Аравита! Что ты здесь делаешь? А твой отец...

Отпустив лошадей, беглянка ловко вскочила в паланкин и быстро прошептала:

— Тише! Спрячь меня. Скажи своим людям...

— Нет, это ты мне скажи... — громко перебила её Лазорилина, как всегда, привлекая к себе внимание.

— Скорее! — прошипела Аравита. — Это очень важно!.. Прикажи своим людям, чтобы вели за нами вон тех лошадей, и задёрни полог. Ах, поскорее!

— Хорошо, хорошо, — томно ответила тархина. — Эй, вы, возьмите лошадей! А зачем задёргивать занавески в такую жару, не понимаю?..

Но Аравита уже задёрнула их сама, и обе тархины оказались в некоем подобии палатки, душной, сладко благоухающей.

— Отец не знает, что я здесь: сбежала из дому, — призналась Аравита.

— Какой ужас... — протянула Лазорилина. — Расскажи же всё поскорей... Ах, ты сидишь на моём покрывале! Слезь, пожалуйста. Вот так. Оно тебе нравится? Представляешь, я его...

you everywhere. And to think of you and me being here together and his not knowing anything about it! It's the funniest thing I ever heard.' And she went off into giggles. She always had been a terrible giggler, as Aravis now remembered.

'It isn't funny at all,' she said. 'It's dreadfully serious. Where can you hide me?'

'No difficulty at all, my dear girl,' said Lasaraleen. 'I'll take you home. My husband's away and no one will see you. Phew! It's not much fun with the curtains drawn. I want to see people. There's no point in having a new dress on if one's to go about shut up like this.'

'I hope no one heard you when you shouted out to me like that,' said Aravis.

'No, no, of course, darling,' said Lasaraleen absent-mindedly. 'But you haven't even told me yet what you think of the dress.'

'Another thing,' said Aravis. 'You must tell your people to treat those two horses very respectfully. That's part of the secret. They're really Talking Horses from Narnia.'

'Fancy!' said Lasaraleen. 'How exciting! And oh, darling, have you seen the barbarian queen from Narnia? She's staying in Tashbaan at present. They say Prince Rabadash is madly in love with her. There have been the most wonderful parties and hunts and things all this last fortnight. I can't see that she's so very pretty myself. But some of the Narnian *men* are lovely. I was taken out on a river party the day before yesterday, and I was wearing my — '

'How shall we prevent your people telling everyone that you've got a visitor — dressed like a beggar's brat — in your house? It might so easily get round to my father.'

'Now don't keep on fussing, there's a dear,' said Lasaraleen. 'We'll get you some proper clothes in a moment. And here we are!'

— Потом, потом, — перебила её Аравита. — Где ты можешь меня спрятать?

— У себя во дворце, конечно. Муж уехал, никто тебя не увидит. Ах как жаль, кстати, что никто не видит сейчас моего нового покрывала! Так нравится оно тебе?

— И вот ещё что, — продолжала о своём Аравита. — С этими лошадьми надо обращаться особенно. Они говорящие, из Нарнии, понимаешь?

— Не может быть... — протянула Лазорилина. — Как интересно... Кстати, ты видела эту дикарку, королеву? Не понимаю, что в ней находят!.. Говорят, Рабадаш от неё без ума. Вот мужчины у них — красавцы. Какие теперь балы, какие пиры, охота!.. Позавчера пировали у реки, и на мне было...

— А твои люди не пустят слух, что у тебя гостит какая-то нищая в отрепьях? Дойдёт до отца...

— Ах, не беспокойся ты по пустякам! Мы тебя переоденем. Ну вот мы и на месте.

The bearers had stopped and the litter was being lowered. When the curtains had been drawn Aravis found that she was in a courtyard-garden very like the one that Shasta had been taken into a few minutes earlier in another part of the city. Lasaraleen would have gone indoors at once but Aravis reminded her in a frantic whisper to say something to the slaves about not telling anyone of their mistress's strange visitor.

'Sorry, darling, it had gone right out of my head,' said Lasareleen. 'Here. All of you. And you, doorkeeper. No one is to be let out of the house today. And anyone I catch talking about this young lady will be first beaten to death and then burned alive and after that be kept on bread and water for six weeks. There.'

Although Lasaraleen had said she was dying to hear Aravis's story, she showed no sign of really wanting to hear it at all. She was, in fact, much better at talking than at listening. She insisted on Aravis having a long and

Носильщики остановились и опустили паланкин на землю. Раздвинув занавески, Аравита увидела, что они в красивом саду, примерно таком же, как тот, куда привели и Шасту некоторое время назад. Лазорилина пошла было в дом, но беглянка шёпотом напомнила ей, что надо предупредить слуг.

— Ах, прости, совсем забыла! — сказала хозяйка. — Эй, вы! Сегодня никто никуда не выйдет. Узнаю, что пошли слухи, сожгу живьём, засеку до смерти, а потом посажу на хлеб и воду.

Хоть Лазорилина и сказала, что желала бы услышать историю Аравиты, но всё время говорила сама. Она настояла, чтобы подруга искупалась (в Тархистане купаются долго и очень роскошно), потом

luxurious bath (Calormene baths are famous) and then dressing her up in the finest clothes before she would let her explain anything. The fuss she made about choosing the dresses nearly drove Aravis mad. She remembered now that Lasaraleen had always been like that, interested in clothes and parties and gossip. Aravis had always been more interested in bows and arrows and horses and dogs and swimming. You will guess that each thought the other silly. But when at last they were both seated after a meal (it was chiefly of the whipped cream and jelly and fruit and ice sort) in a beautiful pillared room (which Aravis would have liked better if Lasaraleen's spoiled pet monkey hadn't been climbing about it all the time) Lasaraleen at last asked her why she was running away from home.

When Aravis had finished telling her story, Lasaraleen said, 'But, darling, why *don't* you marry Ahoshta Tarkaan? Everyone's crazy about him. My husband says he is beginning to be one of the greatest men in Calormen. He has just been made Grand Vizier now old Axartha has died. Didn't you know?'

'I don't care. I can't stand the sight of him,' said Aravis.

'But, darling, only think! Three palaces, and one of them that beautiful one down on the lake at Ilkeen. Positively ropes of pearls, I'm told. Baths of asses' milk. And you'd see such a lot of me.'

'He can keep his pearls and palaces as far as I'm concerned,' said Aravis.

'You always *were* a queer girl, Aravis,' said Lasaraleen. 'What more *do* you want?'

In the end, however, Aravis managed to make her friend believe that she was in earnest and even to discuss plans. There would be no difficulty now about getting the two horses out of the North gate and then on to the Tombs. No one would stop or question a groom in

предложила ей лучшие одежды, которые выбирала так долго, что Аравита чуть с ума не сошла. Теперь она вспомнила, что Лазорилина всегда любила наряды и сплетни, в то время как сама предпочитала собак, лошадей и охоту. Не трудно догадаться, что каждой из них другая казалась глупой. Наконец они поели (главным образом сладостей: взбитых сливок, и желе, и фруктов, и мороженого), расположились в красивой комнате (которая понравилась бы гостье ещё больше, если бы ручная обезьянка не лазила всё время по колоннам), и Лазорилина спросила, почему же подруга убежала из дому, а когда Аравита закончила свой рассказ, вскричала:

— Ах, непременно выходи за Ахошту-тархана! У нас тут все от него без ума. Мой муж говорит, что он будет великим человеком. Теперь, когда старый Ашарта умер, он стал великим визирем, ты знаешь?

— Не знаю и знать не хочу! — отрезала Аравита.

— Нет, ты подумай! Три дворца, один — тот, красивый, у озера Илкина, горы жемчуга... Купается в ослином молоке... А кроме того, мы сможем часто видеться!

— Не нужны мне его дворцы и жемчуга.

— Ты всегда была чудачкой, — сухо сказала Лазорилина. — Не пойму, что тебе нужно.

Помочь она всё же согласилась, решив, что это само по себе занятно. Молодые тархины подумали, что слуга из богатого дома с двумя породистыми лошадьми не вызовет никаких подозрений. Выйти же из города Аравите было много труднее: никто

fine clothes leading a war horse and a lady's saddle horse down to the river, and Lasaraleen had plenty of grooms to send. It wasn't so easy to decide what to do about Aravis herself. She suggested that she could be carried out in the litter with the curtains drawn. But Lasaraleen told her that litters were only used in the city and the sight of one going out through the gate would be certain to lead to questions.

When they had talked for a long time — and it was all the longer because Aravis found it hard to keep her friend to the point — at last Lasaraleen clapped her hands and said, 'Oh, I have an idea. There is one way of getting out of the city without using the gates. The Tisroc's garden (may he live for ever!) runs right down to the water and there is a little water-door. Only for the palace people of course — but then you know, dear (here she tittered a little) we almost *are* palace people. I say, it is lucky for you that you came to *me*. The dear Tisroc (may he live for ever!) is so kind. We're asked to the palace almost every day and it is like a second home. I love all the dear princes and princesses and I positively adore Prince Rabadash. I might run in and see any of the palace ladies at any hour of the day or night. Why shouldn't I slip in with you, after dark, and let you out by the water-door? There are always a few punts and things tied up outside it. And even if we were caught — '

'All would be lost,' said Aravis.

'Oh darling, don't get so excited,' said Lasaraleen. 'I was going to say, even if we were caught everyone would only say it was one of my mad jokes. I'm getting quite well known for them. Only the other day — do listen, dear, this is frightfully funny — '

'I meant, all would be lost *for me*,' said Aravis a little sharply.

и никогда не выносил закрытые паланкины за ворота.

Наконец Лазорилина захлопала в ладоши и воскликнула:

— Ах, я придумала! Мы пройдём к реке садом Тисрока (да живёт он вечно). Там есть дверца. Только вот придворные... Знаешь, тебе повезло, что ты пришла ко мне! Мы ведь и сами почти придворные. Тисрок такой добрый (да живёт он вечно). Нас приглашают во дворец каждый день, мы буквально живём там. Я просто *обожаю* царевича Рабадаша. Значит, я проведу тебя в темноте. Если нас поймают...

— Тогда всё погибло, — закончила Аравита.

— Милочка, не перебивай! Говорю тебе: меня все знают, при дворе привыкли к моим выходкам. Вот послушай, вчера...

— Я хочу сказать, всё погибло *для меня*, — пояснила Аравита.

'Oh — ah — yes — I *do* see what you mean, darling. Well, can you think of any better plan?'

Aravis couldn't, and answered, 'No. We'll have to risk it. When can we start?'

'Oh, not tonight,' said Lasaraleen. 'Of course not tonight. There's a great feast on tonight (I must start getting my hair done for it in a few minutes) and the whole place will be a blaze of lights. And such a crowd too! It would have to be tomorrow night.'

This was bad news for Aravis, but she had to make the best of it. The afternoon passed very slowly and it was a relief when Lasaraleen went out to the banquet, for Aravis was very tired of her giggling and her talk about dresses and parties, weddings and engagements and scandals. She went to bed early and that part she did enjoy: it was so nice to have pillows and sheets again.

But the next day passed very slowly. Lasaraleen wanted to go back on the whole arrangement and kept on telling Aravis that Narnia was a country of perpetual snow and ice inhabited by demons and sorcerers, and she was mad to think of going there. 'And with a peasant boy, too!' said Lasaraleen. 'Darling, think of it! It's not Nice.' Aravis had thought of it a good deal, but she was so tired of Lasaraleen's silliness by now that, for the first time, she began to think that travelling with Shasta was really rather more fun than fashionable life in Tashbaan. So she only replied, 'You forget that I'll be nobody, just like him, when we get to Narnia. And anyway, I promised.'

'And to think,' said Lasaraleen, almost crying, 'that if only you had sense you could be the wife of a Grand Vizier!' Aravis went away to have a private word with the horses.

'You must go with a groom a little before sunset down to the Tombs,' she said. 'No more of those packs. You'll be

— А, ну да, конечно... Но что тут ещё можно придумать?

— Ничего, так что придётся рискнуть. Когда же мы пойдём?

— Только не сегодня! — воскликнула Лазорилина. — Сегодня пир... Когда же я сделаю причёску? Столько народу будет! Давай завтра вечером.

Аравита огорчилась, но решила потерпеть. Когда Лазорилина ушла, девочка вздохнула с облегчением: очень уж ей надоели рассказы о нарядах, свадьбах, пирах и нескромных происшествиях.

Следующий день тянулся бесконечно. Лазорилина не раз принималась отговаривать гостью, непрестанно повторяя, что в Нарнии снег, и лед, и демоны, и колдуны, да ещё какой-то деревенский мальчишка в попутчиках! Это же неприлично...

Аравита и сама порой так думала, но теперь, когда смертельно устала от глупости, ей пришло в голову, что путешествовать с Шастой куда веселее, чем вести светскую жизнь в столице, поэтому сказала:

— Там, в Нарнии, я буду просто девочкой. И потом, я обещала.

Лазорилина чуть не заплакала.

— Что же это такое? Будь ты поумней, стала бы женой *визиря*!

Аравита предпочла поговорить с лошадьми.

— Как только на землю спустятся сумерки, ступайте к могилам, но без поклажи. Вас снова оседла-

saddled and bridled again. But there'll have to be food in Hwin's saddle-bags and a full water-skin behind yours, Bree. The man has orders to let you both have a good long drink at the far side of the bridge.'

'And then, Narnia and the North!' whispered Bree. 'But what if Shasta is not at the Tombs?'

'Wait for him of course,' said Aravis. 'I hope you've been quite comfortable.'

'Never better stabled in my life,' said Bree. 'But if the husband of that tittering Tarkheena friend of yours is paying his head groom to get the best oats, then I think the head groom is cheating him.'

Aravis and Lasaraleen had supper in the pillared room.

About two hours later they were ready to start. Aravis was dressed to look like a superior slave-girl in a great house and wore a veil over her face. They had agreed that if any questions were asked Lasaraleen would pretend that Aravis was a slave she was taking as a present to one of the princesses.

The two girls went out on foot. A very few minutes brought them to the palace gates. Here there were of course soldiers on guard but the officer knew Lasaraleen quite well and called his men to attention and saluted. They passed at once into the Hall of Black Marble. A fair number of courtiers, slaves and others were still moving about here but this only made the two girls less conspicuous. They passed on into the Hall of Pillars and then into the Hall of Statues and down the colonnade, passing the great beaten-copper doors of the throne room. It was all magnificent beyond description; what they could see of it in the dim light of the lamps.

ют, только у тебя, Уинни, будут сумы с провизией, а у тебя, Игого, — бурдюки с водой. Слуге приказано напоить вас как следует за мостом, у реки.

— А потом — на север, в Нарнию! — возликовал Игого. — Послушай, вдруг Шаста не добрался до кладбища?

— Тогда подождите его — как же иначе. Надеюсь, вам тут было хорошо?

— Куда уж лучше! Но если муж твоей болтуньи думает, что конюх покупает самый лучший овёс, то ошибается.

Через два часа, поужинав в красивой комнате, Аравита и Лазорилина вышли из дому. Аравита закрыла лицо чадрой и оделась так, чтобы её приняли за рабыню из богатого дома. Они решили: если кто-нибудь спросит, Лазорилина скажет, что собралась подарить её одной из царевен.

Шли они пешком, и вскоре оказались у ворот дворца. Конечно, тут была стража, но начальник узнал госпожу и отдал ей честь. Девочки прошли чёрный мраморный зал, где было много народу (но это и к лучшему: никто не обратил на них внимания), потом был колонный зал, за ним — два ряда статуй и колоннада, из которой можно попасть в тронный зал, медные двери которого были сейчас закрыты.

Presently they came out into the garden-court which sloped downhill in a number of terraces. On the far side of that they came to the Old Palace. It had already grown almost quite dark and they now found themselves in a maze of corridors lit only by occasional torches fixed in brackets to the walls. Lasaraleen halted at a place where you had to go either left or right.

'Go on, do go on,' whispered Aravis, whose heart was beating terribly and who still felt that her father might run into them at any corner.

'I'm just wondering...' said Lasaraleen. 'I'm not absolutely sure which way we go from here. I *think* it's the left. Yes, I'm almost sure it's the left. What fun this is!'

They took the left hand way and found themselves in a passage that was hardly lighted at all and which soon began going down steps.

'It's all right,' said Lasaraleen. 'I'm sure we're right now. I remember these steps.' But at that moment a moving light appeared ahead. A second later there appeared from round a distant corner, the dark shapes of two men walking backwards and carrying tall candles. And of course it is only before royalties that people walk backwards. Aravis felt Lasaraleen grip her arm — that sort of sudden grip which is almost a pinch and which means that the person who is gripping you is very frightened indeed. Aravis thought it odd that Lasaraleen should be so afraid of the Tisroc if he were really such a friend of hers, but there was no time to go on thinking. Lasaraleen was hurrying her back to the top of the steps, on tiptoes, and groping wildly along the wall.

'Here's a door,' she whispered. 'Quick.'

They went in, drew the door very softly behind them, and found themselves in pitch darkness. Aravis

Наконец девочки вышли в сад, уступами спускавшийся к реке. Подальше в саду стоял Старый дворец. Когда они до него добрались, уже стемнело и в лабиринте коридоров на стенах зажгли редкие факелы.

— Иди, не трусь! — шепнула Аравита, хотя сердце у неё билось так, словно из-за угла вот-вот появится отец.

— Куда же свернуть? — услышала она размышления подруги. — Всё-таки налево... Как смешно!

И тут оказалось, что Лазорилина толком не помнит, куда свернуть: направо или налево.

Они свернули налево и очутились в длинном коридоре. Не успела Лазорилина сказать: «Ну вот! Я помню эти ступеньки», — как в дальнем конце показались две тени, пятившиеся задом, — так ходят только перед царем. Лазорилина вцепилась в руку подруги, и та удивилась, чего она боится, если Тисрок друг её мужа. Тем временем Лазорилина втащила её в какую-то комнату, бесшумно закрыла дверь, и они очутились в полной темноте.

— Охрани нас Таш! — услышала Аравита её шёпот. — Только бы они не вошли!.. Ползи под диван.

could hear by Lasaraleen's breathing that she was terrified.

'Tash preserve us!' whispered Lasaraleen. 'What *shall* we do if he comes in here. Can we hide?'

There was a soft carpet under their feet. They groped forward into the room and blundered on to a sofa.

'Let's lie down behind it,' whimpered Lasaraleen. 'Oh, I do wish we hadn't come.'

There was just room between the sofa and the curtained wall and the two girls got down. Lasaraleen managed to get the better position and was completely covered. The upper part of Aravis's face stuck out beyond the sofa, so that if anyone came into that room with a light and happened to look in exactly the right place they would see her. But of course, because she was wearing a veil, what they saw would not at once look like a forehead and a pair of eyes. Aravis shoved desperately to try to make Lasaraleen give her a little more room. But Lasaraleen, now quite selfish in her panic, fought back and pinched her feet. They gave it up and lay still, panting a little. Their own breath semed dreadfully noisy, but there was no other noise.

'Is it safe?' said Aravis at last in the tiniest possible whisper.

'I — I — *think* so,' began Lasaraleen. 'But my poor nerves — ' and then came the most terrible noise they could have heard at that moment: the noise of the door opening. And then came light. And because Aravis couldn't get her head any further in behind the sofa, she saw everything.

First came the two slaves (deaf and dumb, as Aravis rightly guessed, and therefore used at the most secret councils) walking backwards and carrying the candles. They took up their stand one at each end of the sofa.

Они спрятались под диваном, но всё место заняла Лазорилина. Если бы в комнату внесли свечи, то все увидели бы голову Аравиты. Правда, девочка была в чадре, так что ничего, кроме глаз да лба не увидишь, но всё-таки... Словом, она старалась отвоевать побольше места, но Лазорилина ущипнула её за ногу.

На том борьба и кончилась. Обе тяжело дышали, и это были единственные звуки.

— Тут нас не схватят? — спросила Аравита как можно тише.

— На-надеюсь, — пролепетала Лазорилина. — Ах как я измучилась!..

И тут раздался страшный звук — открылась дверь. Аравита втянула голову сколько могла, но видела всё.

Первыми вошли рабы со свечами в руках (девочка догадалась, что они глухонемые) и встали слева и справа от дивана. Это было хорошо: они прикрыли беглянку, а она всё видела. Потом появился не-

This was a good thing, for of course it was now harder for anyone to see Aravis once a slave was in front of her and she was looking between his heels. Then came an old man, very fat, wearing a curious pointed cap by which she immediately knew that he was the Tisroc. The least of the jewels with which he was covered was worth more than all the clothes and weapons of the Narnian lords put together: but he was so fat and such a mass of frills and pleats and bobbles and buttons and tassels and talismans that Aravis couldn't help thinking the Narnian fashions (at any rate for men) looked nicer. After him came a tall young man with a feathered and jewelled turban on his head and an ivory-sheathed scimitar at his side. He seemed very excited and his eyes and teeth flashed fiercely in the candlelight. Last of all came a little humpbacked, wizened old man in whom she recognized with a shudder the new Grand Vizier and her own betrothed husband, Ahoshta Tarkaan himself.

As soon as all three had entered the room and the door was shut, the Tisroc seated himself on the divan with a sigh of contentment, the young man took his place, standing before him, and the Grand Vizier got down on his knees and elbows and laid his face flat on the carpet.

вероятно толстый человек в странной островерхой шапочке. Самый маленький из драгоценных камней, украшавших его одежды, стоил больше, чем всё, что было у людей из Нарнии. Аравита подумала, что нарнийская мода — во всяком случае мужская — как-то приятнее. За ним вошёл высокий юноша в тюрбане с длинным пером и ятаганом в ножнах слоновой кости. Он очень волновался, зубы у него злобно сверкали. Последним появился горбун, в котором она с ужасом узнала своего жениха.

Дверь закрылась. Тисрок сел на диван, вздохнув с облегчением. Царевич встал перед ним, а великий визирь опустился на четвереньки и припал лицом к ковру.

Chapter 8
IN THE HOUSE OF THE TISROC

'Oh-my-father-and-oh-the-delight-of-my-eyes,' began the young man, muttering the words very quickly and sulkily and not at all as if the Tisroc *were* the delight of his eyes. 'May you live for ever, but you have utterly destroyed me. If you had given me the swiftest of the galleys at sunrise when I first saw that the ship of the accursed barbarians was gone from her place I would perhaps have overtaken them. But you persuaded me to send first and see if they had not merely moved round the point into better anchorage. And now the whole day has been wasted. And they are gone — gone — out of my reach! The false jade, the — ' and here he added a great many descriptions of Queen Susan which would not look at all nice in print. For of course this young man was Prince Rabadash and of course the false jade was Susan of Narnia.

'Compose yourself, O my son,' said the Tisroc. 'For the departure of guests makes a wound that is easily healed in the heart of a judicious host.'

'But I *want* her,' cried the Prince. 'I must have her. I shall die if I do not get her — false, proud, black-hearted daughter of a dog that she is! I cannot sleep and my food has no savour and my eyes are darkened because of her beauty. I must have the barbarian queen.'

Глава 8

ЗАГОВОР ТИСРОКА, ЦАРЕВИЧА РАБАДАША И ВИЗИРЯ АХОШТЫ

— Отец мой и услада моих очей! — начал молодой человек очень быстро и очень злобно. — Живите вечно, но меня вы погубили. Если б вы дали мне ещё на рассвете самый лучший корабль, я бы нагнал этих варваров. Теперь мы потеряли целый день, а эта ведьма, эта лгунья, эта... эта...

И он прибавил несколько слов, которые я не рискну повторять. Молодой человек был царевич Рабадаш, а ведьма и лгунья — королева Сьюзен.

— Успокойся, о сын мой! — сказал Тисрок. — Расставание с гостем ранит сердце, но разум исцеляет.

— Она мне *нужна*! — воскликнул царевич. — Я умру без этой гнусной, гордой, неверной собаки! Я не сплю, и не ем, и ничего не вижу из-за её красоты.

'How well it was said by a gifted poet,' observed the Vizier, raising his face (in a somewhat dusty condition) from the carpet, 'that deep draughts from the fountain of reason are desirable in order to extinguish the fire of youthful love.'

This seemed to exasperate the Prince. 'Dog,' he shouted, directing a series of well-aimed kicks at the hindquarters of the Vizier, 'do not dare to quote the poets to me. I have had maxims and verses flung at me all day and I can endure them no more.' I am afraid Aravis did not feel at all sorry for the Vizier.

The Tisroc was apparently sunk in thought, but when, after a long pause, he noticed what was happening, he said tranquilly:

'My son, by all means desist from kicking the venerable and enlightened Vizier: for as a costly jewel retains its value even if hidden in a dung-hill, so old age and discretion are to be respected even in the vile persons of our subjects. Desist therefore, and tell us what you desire and propose.'

'I desire and propose, O my father,' said Rabadash, 'that you immediately call out your invincible armies and invade the thrice-accursed land of Narnia and waste it with fire and sword and add it to your illimitable empire, killing their High King and all of his blood except the queen Susan. For I must have her as my wife, though she shall learn a sharp lesson first.'

'Understand, O my son,' said the Tisroc, 'that no words you can speak will move me to open war against Narnia.'

'If you were not my father, O ever-living Tisroc,' said the Prince, grinding his teeth, 'I should say that was the word of a coward.'

— Прекрасно сказал поэт: «Водой здравомыслия гасится пламень любви», — вставил визирь, приподняв несколько запылённое лицо.

Царевич дико взревел и ловко пнул визиря в приподнятый зад.

— Пёс! Ещё стихи читает!

Боюсь, что Аравита не испытала при этом жалости.

— Сын мой, — спокойно и отрешённо промолвил Тисрок, — учись сдерживать себя, когда хочется пнуть достопочтенного и просвещённого визиря. Изумруд ценен и в мусорной куче, а старость и скромность — в подлейшем из наших подданных. Поведай лучше, что собираешься делать.

— Я собираюсь, отец мой, — сказал Рабадаш, — призвать твоё непобедимое войско, захватить трижды проклятую Нарнию, присоединить к твоей великой державе и перебить всех поголовно, кроме королевы Сьюзен. Она будет моей женой, хотя её надо проучить.

— Пойми, о сын мой: никакие твои речи не побудят меня воевать с Нарнией, — возразил Тисрок.

— Если бы ты не был мне отцом, о услада моих очей, — сказал царевич, скрипнув зубами, — я бы назвал тебя трусом.

'And if you were not my son, O most inflammable Rabadash,' replied his father, 'your life would be short and your death slow when you had said it.' (The cool, placid voice in which he spoke these words made Aravis's blood run cold.)

'But why, O my father,' said the Prince — this time in a much more respectful voice, 'why should we think twice about punishing Narnia any more than about hanging an idle slave or sending a worn-out horse to be made into dog's-meat? It is not the fourth size of one of your least provinces. A thousand spears could conquer it in five weeks. It is an unseemly blot on the skirts of your empire.'

'Most undoubtedly,' said the Tisroc. 'These little barbarian countries that call themselves *free* (which is as much as to say, idle, disordered, and unprofitable) are hateful to the gods and to all persons of discernment.'

'Then why have we suffered such a land as Narnia to remain thus long unsubdued?'

'Know, O enlightened Prince,' said the Grand Vizier, 'that until the year in which your exalted father began his salutary and unending reign, the land of Narnia was

— Если бы ты не был мне сыном, о пылкий Рабадаш, — парировал Тисрок, — жизнь твоя была бы короткой, а смерть — долгой.

(Приятный спокойный его голос совсем перепугал Аравиту.)

— Почему же, отец мой, ты не накажешь Нарнию? Мы вешаем нерадивого раба, бросаем псам старую лошадь. Нарния меньше самой малой из наших округ. Тысяча копий справятся с ней за месяц.

— Несомненно, — согласился Тисрок, — эти варварские страны, которые называют себя свободными, а на самом деле просто не знают порядка, гнусны и богам, и достойным людям.

— Чего ж мы их терпим? — вскричал Рабадаш.

— Знай, о достойный царевич, — подхватил визирь, повинуясь знаку царя, — что в тот самый год, когда твой великий отец (да живёт он вечно) начал

covered with ice and snow and was moreover ruled by a most powerful enchantress.'

'This I know very well, O loquacious Vizier,' answered the Prince. 'But I know also that the enchantress is dead. And the ice and snow have vanished, so that Narnia is now wholesome, fruitful, and delicious.'

'And this change, O most learned Prince, has doubtless been brought to pass by the powerful incantations of those wicked persons who now call themselves kings and queens of Narnia.'

'I am rather of the opinion,' said Rabadash, 'that it has come about by the alteration of the stars and the operation of natural causes.'

'All this,' said the Tisroc, 'is a question for the disputations of learned men. I will never believe that so great an alteration, and the killing of the old enchantress, were effected without the aid of strong magic. And such things are to be expected in that land, which is chiefly inhabited by demons in the shape of beasts that talk like men, and monsters that are half man and half beast. It is commonly reported that the High King of Narnia (whom may the gods utterly reject) is supported by a demon of hideous aspect and irresistible maleficence who appears in the shape of a Lion. Therefore the attacking of Narnia is a dark and doubtful enterprise, and I am determined not to put my hand out farther than I can draw it back.'

'How blessed is Calormen,' said the Vizier, popping up his face again, 'on whose ruler the gods have been pleased to bestow prudence and circumspection! Yet as the irrefutable and sapient Tisroc has said it is very grievous to be constrained to keep our hands off such a dainty dish as Narnia. Gifted was that poet who said — ' but at this point Ahoshta noticed an impatient

своё благословенное царствование, гнусной Нарнией правила могущественная колдунья.

— Я слышал это сотни раз, о многоречивый визирь, — ответил царевич, — как слышал и то, что она повержена. Снега и льды растаяли, и Нарния прекрасна, как сад.

— О многознающий царевич! — воскликнул визирь. — Случилось всё потому, что те, кто правит Нарнией сейчас, — злые колдуны.

— А я думаю, — сказал Рабадаш, — что тут виной звёзды и прочие естественные причины.

— Учёным людям стоит об этом поспорить, — заметил Тисрок. — Никогда не поверю, что старую чародейку можно было убить без могучих чар. Чего и ждать от страны, где обитают демоны в обличье зверей, говорящих, как люди, и страшные чудища с копытами, но с человеческой головой. Мне доносят, что тамошнему королю (да уничтожат его боги) помогает мерзейший и сильнейший демон, принимающий обличье льва. Поэтому я на эту страну нападать не стану.

— Сколь благословенны жители нашей страны, — вставил визирь, — ибо всемогущие боги одарили её правителя великой мудростью! Премудрый Тисрок (да живёт он вечно) изрёк: «Как нельзя есть из грязного блюда, так нельзя трогать Нарнию». Недаром поэт сказал...

Царевич приподнял ногу, и он умолк.

movement of the Prince's toe and became suddenly silent.

'It is very grievous,' said the Tisroc in his deep, quiet voice. 'Every morning the sun is darkened in my eyes, and every night my sleep is the less refreshing, because I remember that Narnia is still free.'

'O my father,' said Rabadash. 'How if I show you a way by which you can stretch out your arm to take Narnia and yet draw it back unharmed if the attempt prove unfortunate?'

'If you can show me that, O Rabadash,' said the Tisroc, 'you will be the best of sons.'

'Hear then, O father. This very night and in this hour I will take but two hundred horse and ride across the desert. And it shall seem to all men that you know nothing of my going. On the second morning I shall be at the gates of King Lune's castle of Anvard in Archenland. They are at peace with us and unprepared and I shall take Anvard before they have bestirred themselves. Then I will ride through the pass above Anvard and down through Narnia to Cair Paravel. The High King will not be there; when I left them he was already preparing a raid against the giants on his northern border. I shall find Cair Paravel, most likely with open gates, and ride in. I shall exercise prudence and courtesy and spill as little Narnian blood as I can. And what then remains but to sit there till the *Splendour Hyaline* puts in, with Queen Susan on board, catch my strayed bird as she sets foot ashore, swing her into the saddle, and then, ride, ride, ride back to Anvard?'

'But is it not probable, O my son,' said the Tisroc, 'that at the taking of the woman either King Edmund or you will lose his life?'

'They will be a small company,' said Rabadash, 'and I will order ten of my men to disarm and bind him: re-

— Всё это весьма печально, — сказал Тисрок. — Солнце меня не радует, сон не освежает при одной только мысли, что Нарния свободна.

— Отец, — воскликнул Рабадаш, — сию же минуту я соберу двести воинов! Никто и не услышит, что ты об этом знал. Назавтра мы будем у королевского замка в Орландии. Они с нами в мире, так что опомниться не успеют, как я возьму замок. Оттуда мы поскачем в Кэр-Параваль. Верховный король сейчас на севере. Когда я у них был, он собирался попугать великанов. Ворота его замка, наверное, открыты. Я дождусь их корабля, схвачу королеву Сьюзен, а люди мои расправятся со всеми остальными.

— Не боишься ли ты, сын мой, что король Эдмунд убьёт тебя?

— Их мало, так что десятка моих людей хватит, чтобы связать его и обезоружить. Я не стану его

straining my vehement desire for his blood so that there shall be no deadly cause of war between you and the High King.'

'And how if the *Splendour Hyaline* is at Cair Paravel before you?'

'I do not look for that with these winds, O my father.'

'And lastly, O my resourceful son,' said the Tisroc, 'you have made clear how all this might give you the barbarian woman, but not how it helps me to the overthrowing of Narnia.'

'O my father, can it have escaped you that though I and my horsemen will come and go through Narnia like an arrow from a bow, yet we shall have Anvard for ever? And when you hold Anvard you sit in the very gate of Narnia, and your garrison in Anvard can be increased by little and little till it is a great host.'

'It is spoken with understanding and foresight. But how do I draw back my arm if all this miscarries?'

'You shall say that I did it without your knowledge and against your will, and without your blessing, being constrained by the violence of my love and the impetuosity of youth.'

'And how if the High King then demands that we send back the barbarian woman, his sister?'

'O my father, be assured that he will not. For though the fancy of a woman has rejected this marriage, the High King Peter is a man of prudence and understanding who will in no way wish to lose the high honour and advantage of being allied to our House and seeing his nephew and grand nephew on the throne of Calormen.'

'He will not see that if I live for ever as is no doubt your wish,' said the Tisroc in an even drier voice than usual.

убивать, и тебе не придётся воевать с Верховным королём.

— А что, если корабль тебя опередит?

— Отец мой, навряд ли, при таком ветре...

— И, мой хитроумный сын, — сказал Тисрок, — объясни мне наконец, как поможет всё это уничтожить Нарнию.

— Разве ты не понял, отец мой? Мои люди захватят по пути Орландию, а значит, мы останемся у самой нарнийской границы и будем понемногу пополнять гарнизон.

— Что ж, это разумно и мудро, — одобрил Тисрок. — А что, если ты не преуспеешь и Верховный король потребует от меня ответа?

— Ты скажешь, что ничего не знал: я действовал сам, гонимый любовью и молодостью.

— А если он потребует, чтобы я вернул эту дикарку?

— Поверь, этого не будет. Король человек разумный и на многое закроет глаза ради того, чтобы увидеть своих племянников на тархистанском престоле.

— Как он их увидит, если я буду жить вечно? — суховато спросил Тисрок.

'And also, O my father and O the delight of my eyes,' said the Prince, after a moment of awkward silence, 'we shall write letters as if from the Queen to say that she loves me and has no desire to return to Narnia. For it is well known that women are as changeable as weather-cocks. And even if they do not wholly believe the letters, they will not dare to come to Tashbaan in arms to fetch her.'

'O enlightened Vizier,' said the Tisroc, 'bestow your wisdom upon us concerning this strange proposal.'

'O eternal Tisroc,' answered Ahoshta, 'the strength of paternal affection is not unknown to me and I have often heard that sons are in the eyes of their fathers more precious than carbuncles. How then shall I dare freely to unfold to you my mind in a matter which may imperil the life of this exalted Prince?'

'Undoubtedly you will dare,' replied the Tisroc. 'Because you will find that the dangers of not doing so are at least equally great.'

'To hear is to obey,' moaned the wretched man. 'Know then, O most reasonable Tisroc, in the first place, that the danger of the Prince is not altogether so great as might appear. For the gods have withheld from the barbarians the light of discretion, as that their poetry is not, like ours, full of choice apophthegms and useful maxims, but is all of love and war. Therefore nothing will appear to them more noble and admirable than such a mad enterprise as this of — ow!' For the Prince, at the word 'mad', had kicked him again.

'Desist, O my son,' said the Tisroc. 'And you, estimable Vizier, whether he desists or not, by no means allow the flow of your eloquence to be interrupted. For nothing is more suitable to persons of gravity and de-

— А кроме того, отец мой и услада моих очей, — проговорил царевич после неловкого молчания, — мы напишем письмо от имени королевы, в котором будет сказано, что она меня обожает и возвращаться не хочет. Всем известно, что женское сердце изменчиво.

— О многомудрый визирь, — сказал Тисрок, — просвети нас. Что ты думаешь об этих удивительных замыслах?

— О вечный Тисрок! Я слышал, что сын для отца дороже алмаза. Посмею ли я открыть мои мысли, когда речь идёт о замысле, который опасен для царевича?

— Посмеешь, — разрешил Тисрок. — Ибо тебе известно, что молчать для тебя ещё опасней.

— Слушаюсь и повинуюсь! — сказал злой Ахошта. — Знай же, о кладезь мудрости, что опасность не так уж велика. Боги скрыли от варваров свет разумения, стихи их — о любви и битвах — ничему не учат, поэтому им кажется, что этот поход прекрасен и благороден, а не безумен...

При этом слове царевич опять его пнул, и визирь охнул.

— Держи себя в руках, сын мой! — чуть повысил голос Тисрок. — А ты, достойный визирь, говори, смирится король или нет. Людям достойным и разумным пристало терпеть малые невзгоды.

corum than to endure minor inconveniences with constancy.'

'To hear is to obey,' said the Vizier, wriggling himself round a little so as to get his hinder parts further away from Rabadash's toe. 'Nothing, I say, will seem as pardonable, if not estimable, in their eyes as this — er — hazardous attempt, especially because it is undertaken for the love of a woman. Therefore, if the Prince by misfortune fell into their hands, they would assuredly not kill him. Nay, it may even be, that though he failed to carry off the queen, yet the sight of his great valour and of the extremity of his passion might incline her heart to him.'

'That is a good point, old babbler,' said Rabadash. 'Very good, however it came into your ugly head.'

'The praise of my masters is the light of my eyes,' said Ahoshta. 'And secondly, O Tisroc, whose reign must and shall be interminable, I think that with the aid of the gods it is very likely that Anvard will fall into the Prince's hands. And if so, we have Narnia by the throat.'

There was a long pause and the room became so silent that the two girls hardly dared to breathe. At last the Tisroc spoke.

'Go, my son,' he said. 'And do as you have said. But expect no help nor countenance from me. I will not avenge you if you are killed and I will not deliver you if the barbarians cast you into prison. And if, either in success or failure, you shed a drop more than you need of Narnian noble blood and open war arises from it, my favour shall never fall upon you again and your next brother shall have your place in Calormen. Now go. Be swift, secret, and fortunate. May the strength of Tash the inexorable, the irresistible be in your sword and lance.'

— Слушаю и повинуюсь, — проговорил визирь, чуть отодвинувшись. — Итак, им понравится этот... э-э... диковинный замысел, особенно потому, что причиной тому — любовь к женщине. Если царевича схватят, то не убьют... Более того: отвага и сила страсти могут тронуть сердце королевы.

— Неглупо, старый болтун, — сказал Рабадаш, явно довольный. — Даже умно. Как ты только додумался...

— Похвала владык — услада моих ушей, — раболепно вымолвил Ахошта. — А ещё, о Тисрок, живущий вечно, если силой богов мы возьмём Анвард, то сможем схватить Нарнию за горло.

Надолго воцарилась тишина, и девочки затаили дыхание. Наконец Тисрок молвил:

— Иди, мой сын, делай как задумал, но помощи от меня не жди. Я не стану мстить, если ты погибнешь, и не пришлю выкуп, если попадёшь в плен. Если же втянешь меня в ссору с Нарнией, наследником будешь не ты, а твой младший брат. Итак, иди. Действуй быстро, тайно, успешно. Да хранит тебя великая Таш.

'To hear is to obey,' cried Rabadash, and after kneeling for a moment to kiss his father's hands he rushed from the room. Greatly to the disappointment of Aravis, who was now horribly cramped, the Tisroc and Vizier remained.

'O Vizier,' said the Tisroc, 'is it certain that no living soul knows of this council we three have held here tonight?'

'O my master,' said Ahoshta, 'it is not possible that any should know. For that very reason I proposed, and you in your wisdom agreed, that we should meet here in the Old Palace where no council is ever held and none of the household has any occasion to come.'

'It is well,' said the Tisroc. 'If any man knew, I would see to it that he died before an hour had passed. And do you also, O prudent Vizier, forget it. I sponge away from my own heart and from yours all knowledge of the Prince's plans. He is gone without my knowledge or my consent, I know not whither, because of his violence and the rash and disobedient disposition of youth. No man will be more astonished than you and I to hear that Anvard is in his hands.'

'To hear is to obey,' said Ahoshta.

'That is why you will never think even in your secret heart that I am the hardest hearted of fathers who thus send my first-born son on an errand so likely to be his death; pleasing as it must be to you who do not love the Prince. For I see into the bottom of your mind.'

'O impeccable Tisroc,' said the Vizier. 'In comparison with you I love neither the Prince nor my own life nor bread nor water nor the light of the sun.'

'Your sentiments,' said the Tisroc, 'are elevated and correct. I also love none of these things in comparison with the glory and strength of my throne. If the Prince

Рабадаш преклонил колени и поспешно вышел из комнаты. К неудовольствию Аравиты, Тисрок и визирь остались.

— Уверен ли ты, что ни одна душа не слышала нашей беседы?

— О владыка! — сказал Ахошта. — Кто же мог услышать? Потому я и предложил, а ты согласился, чтобы мы беседовали здесь, в Старом дворце, куда не заходят слуги.

— Прекрасно, — сказал Тисрок. — Если кто что узнает, то умрёт через час, не позже. И ты, благоразумный визирь, забудь всё! Сотрём из наших сердец память о замыслах царевича. Он ничего мне не говорил — молодость пылка, опрометчива и строптива. Когда он возьмёт Анвард, мы очень удивимся.

— Слушаю... — начал было Ахошта, но Тисрок продолжил:

— Вот почему тебе и в голову не придёт, что я, жестокий отец, посылаю сына на верную смерть, как ни желанна тебе эта мысль, ибо ты не любишь царевича.

— О просветлённый Тисрок! — воскликнул визирь. — Перед любовью к тебе ничтожны мои чувства и к царевичу, и к себе самому.

— Похвально. Для меня тоже всё ничтожно перед любовью к могуществу. Если царевич преуспеет, мы обретём Орландию, а там — и Нарнию, ну а если

succeeds, we have Archenland, and perhaps hereafter Narnia. If he fails — I have eighteen other sons and Rabadash, after the manner of the eldest sons of kings, was beginning to be dangerous. More than five Tisrocs in Tashbaan have died before their time because their eldest sons, enlightened princes, grew tired of waiting for their throne. He had better cool his blood abroad than boil it in inaction here. And now, O excellent Vizier, the excess of my paternal anxiety inclines me to sleep. Command the musicians to my chamber. But before you lie down, call back the pardon we wrote for the third cook. I feel within me the manifest prognostics of indigestion.'

'To hear is to obey,' said the Grand Vizier. He crawled backwards on all fours to the door, rose, bowed, and went out. Even then the Tisroc remained seated in silence on the divan till Aravis almost began to be afraid that he had dropped asleep. But at last with a great creaking and sighing he heaved up his enormous body, signed to the slaves to precede him with the lights, and went out. The door closed behind him, the room was once more totally dark, and the two girls could breathe freely again.

погибнет... Старшие сыновья опасны, а у меня ещё восемнадцать детей. Пять моих предшественников погибли по той причине, что старшие их сыновья устали ждать. Пускай охладит свою кровь на севере. Теперь же, о многоумный визирь, меня клонит ко сну. Как-никак я отец, беспокоюсь. Вели послать музыкантов в мою опочивальню. Да, и прикажи наказать третьего повара — что-то живот побаливает...

— Слушаю и повинуюсь!

Визирь дополз задом до порога, приподнялся, коснулся головой пола и исчез за дверью. Охая и вздыхая, Тисрок медленно встал, дал знак рабам, и все покинули помещение.

Наконец-то девочки смогли перевести дух.

Chapter 9

ACROSS THE DESERT

'Hove dreadful! How perfectly dreadful!' whimpered Lasaraleen. 'Oh darling, I *am* so frightened. I'm shaking all over. Feel me.'

'Come on,' said Aravis, who was trembling herself. 'They've gone back to the new palace. Once we're out of this room we're safe enough. But it's wasted a terrible time. Get me down to that water-gate as quick as you can.'

'Darling, how *can* you?' squeaked Lasaraleen. 'I can't do anything — not now. My poor nerves! No: we must just lie still a bit and then go back.'

'Why back?' asked Aravis.

'Oh, you don't understand. You're so unsympathetic,' said Lasaraleen, beginning to cry. Aravis decided it was no occasion for mercy.

'Look here!' she said, catching Lasaraleen and giving her a good shake. 'If you say another word about going back, and if you don't start taking me to that water-gate at once — do you know what I'll do? I'll rush out into that passage and scream. Then we'll both be caught.'

'But we shall both be k-k-killed!' said Lasaraleen. 'Didn't you hear what the Tisroc (may he live for ever) said?'

'Yes, and I'd sooner be killed than married to Ahoshta. So come *on*.'

'Oh you *are* unkind,' said Lasaraleen. 'And I in such a state!'

Глава 9

ПУСТЫНЯ

— Какой ужас! Какой жуткий ужас! — захныкала Лазорилина. — Я с ума сойду... умру... Видишь — вся дрожу, потрогай мою руку!

— Они ушли, — сказала Аравита, хотя и саму её била дрожь. — Когда мы выберемся из этой комнаты, нам ничто не будет угрожать. Сколько времени потеряли! Веди меня поскорее к этой твоей калитке.

— Как ты можешь? — возопила Лазорилина. — Я без сил, совершенно разбита! Полежим и пойдём обратно.

— Да ты что! — воскликнула Аравита.

— Какая ты злая! — разрыдалась подруга. — Совсем меня не жалеешь!

Аравита в тот миг не была склонна к жалости, поэтому крикнула, хорошенько её встряхнув:

— Вот что! Если ты меня не поведёшь, я закричу, и нас найдут.

— И у-у-бьют! — прорыдала Лазорилина. — Ты слышала, что сказал Тисрок (да живёт он вечно)?

— Лучше умереть, чем выйти замуж за Ахошту, — ответила Аравита. — Идём.

— Какая ты жестокая! — продолжила причитать Лазорилина, но всё же повела Аравиту по длинным

But in the end she had to give in to Aravis. She led the way down the steps they had already descended, and along another corridor and so finally out into the open air. They were now in the palace garden which sloped down in terraces to the city wall. The moon shone brightly. One of the drawbacks about adventures is that when you come to the most beautiful places you are often too anxious and hurried to appreciate them; so that Aravis (though she remembered them years later) had only a vague impression of grey lawns, quietly bubbling fountains, and the long black shadows of cypress trees.

When they reached the very bottom and the wall rose frowning above them, Lasaraleen was shaking so that she could not unbolt the gate. Aravis did it. There, at last, was the river, full of reflected moonlight, and a little landing stage and a few pleasure boats.

'Good-bye,' said Aravis, 'and thank you. I'm sorry if I've been a pig. But think what I'm flying from!'

'Oh Aravis darling,' said Lasaraleen. 'Won't you change your mind? Now that you've seen what a very great man Ahoshta is!'

'Great man!' said Aravis. 'A hideous grovelling slave who flatters when he's kicked but treasures it all up and hopes to get his own back by egging on that horrible Tisroc to plot his son's death. Faugh! I'd sooner marry my father's scullion than a creature like that.'

'Oh Aravis, Aravis! How can you say such dreadful things; and about the Tisroc (may he live for ever) too. It must be right if *he's* going to do it!'

'Good-bye,' said Aravis, 'and I thought your dresses lovely. And I think your house is lovely too. I'm sure you'll have a lovely life — though it wouldn't suit me. Close the door softly behind me.'

коридорам в дворцовый сад, спускавшийся уступами к городской стене.

Ярко светила луна. Как это ни прискорбно, в самые красивые места мы попадаем, когда нам не до них, и Аравита смутно вспоминала потом серую траву, какие-то фонтаны и чёрные тени кипарисов.

Открывать калитку пришлось ей самой — Лазорилину просто трясло. Они увидели реку, отражавшую лунный свет, и маленькую пристань, и несколько лодок.

— Прощай, — сказала беглянка. — Спасибо, и прости, что я вела себя как свинья.

— Может, передумаешь? — с надеждой спросила подруга. — Ты же видела, какой он большой человек!

— Он гнусный холуй, — возразила Аравита. — Я скорее выйду за конюха, чем за него. Ну, бывай. Да, наряды у тебя очень хорошие. И дворец лучше некуда. И жить ты будешь счастливо — но я так не хочу. Закрой калитку потише.

She tore herself away from her friend's affectionate embraces, stepped into a punt, cast off, and a moment later was out in midstream with a huge real moon overhead and a huge reflected moon down, deep down, in the river. The air was fresh and cool and as she drew near the farther bank she heard the hooting of an owl. 'Ah! That's better!' thought Aravis. She had always lived in the country and had hated every minute of her time in Tashbaan.

When she stepped ashore she found herself in darkness, for the rise of the ground, and the trees, cut off the moonlight. But she managed to find the same road that Shasta had found, and came just as he had done to the end of the grass and the beginning of the sand, and looked (like him) to her left and saw the big, black Tombs. And now at last, brave girl though she was, her heart quailed. Supposing the others weren't there! Supposing the ghouls were! But she stuck out her chin (and a little bit of her tongue too) and went straight towards them.

But before she had reached them she saw Bree and Hwin and the groom.

'You can go back to your mistress now,' said Aravis (quite forgetting that he couldn't, until the city gates opened next morning). 'Here is money for your pains.'

'To hear is to obey,' said the groom, and at once set off at a remarkable speed in the direction of the city. There was no need to tell him to make haste: he also had been thinking a good deal about ghouls.

For the next few seconds Aravis was busy kissing the noses and patting the necks of Hwin and Bree just as if they were quite ordinary horses.

'And here comes Shasta! Thanks be to the Lion!' said Bree.

Уклонившись от пылких объятий, она прыгнула в лодку. Где-то ухала сова. «Как хорошо!» Аравита никогда не жила в городе, и он ей не понравился.

На другом берегу было совсем темно. Чутьём или чудом она нашла тропинку — ту самую, на которую набрёл Шаста, — и тоже пошла налево, и разглядела во мраке глыбы усыпальниц. Тут, хоть она и была очень смелой, ей стало жутко. И всё же девочка упрямо вскинула подбородок, прикусила кончик языка и направилась вперёд, а в следующий миг увидела лошадей и слугу.

— Иди к своей хозяйке, — сказала она ему, забыв, что ворота заперты. — Вот тебе за труды.

— Слушаю и повинуюсь, — с готовностью отозвался слуга и помчался к берегу. Кто-кто, а он привидений боялся.

— Слава льву, вон и Шаста! — воскликнул Игого.

Aravis looked round, and there, right enough, was Shasta who had come out of hiding the moment he saw the groom going away.

'And now,' said Aravis. 'There's not a moment to lose.' And in hasty words she told them about Rabadash's expedition.

'Treacherous hounds!' said Bree, shaking his mane and stamping with his hoof. 'An attack in time of peace, without defiance sent! But we'll grease his oats for him. We'll be there before he is.'

'Can we?' said Aravis, swinging herself into Hwin's saddle. Shasta wished he could mount like that.

'Brooh-hoo!' snorted Bree. 'Up you get, Shasta. Can we! And with a good start too!'

'He said he was going to start at once,' said Aravis.

'That's how humans talk,' said Bree. 'But you don't get a company of two hundred horse and horsemen watered and victualled and armed and saddled and started all in a minute. Now: what's our direction? Due North?

'No,' said Shasta. 'I know about that. I've drawn a line. I'll explain later. Bear a bit to our left, both you horses. Ah — here it is!'

'Now,' said Bree. 'All that about galloping for a day and a night, like in stories, can't really be done. It must be walk and trot: but brisk trots and short walks. And whenever we walk you two humans can slip off and walk too. Now. Are you ready, Hwin? Off we go. Narnia and the North!'

At first it was delightful. The night had now been going on for so many hours that the sand had almost finished giving back all the sun-heat it had received during the day, and the air was cool, fresh, and clear. Under the

Аравита повернулась и впрямь увидела мальчишку, который, как только слуга удалился, вышел из-за усыпальницы.

Девочка быстро поведала друзьям о том, что узнала во дворце, и конь, встряхивая гривой и цокая копытом, заржал:

— Рыцари так не поступают! Подлые псы! Но мы опередим его и предупредим северных королей!

— А мы успеем? — спросила Аравита, взлетая в седло так, что Шаста позавидовал ей.

— О-го-го!.. — ответил ей конь. — Успеем ли мы! Ещё бы! В седло, Шаста!

— Он говорил, что выступит сразу, — напомнила Аравита.

— Люди всегда так говорят, — объяснил конь. — Двести коней и воинов сразу не соберёшь. Вот мы тронемся сразу. Каков наш путь, Шаста? Прямо на север?

— Нет. Я нарисовал, смотри. Потом объясню. Значит, сперва налево.

— И вот ещё что, — добавил конь. — В книжках пишут: «Они скакали день и ночь», — но этого не бывает. Надо менять шаг на рысь. Когда мы будем идти шагом, вы можете идти рядом с нами. Ну всё. Ты готова, госпожа моя Уинни? Тогда — в Нарнию!

Сперва всё было прекрасно. За долгую ночь песок остыл, и воздух был прохладным, прозрачным и свежим. В лунном свете казалось, что перед ними вода на серебряном подносе. Тишина стояла полная, толь-

moonlight the sand, in every direction and as far as they could see, gleamed as if it were smooth water or a great silver tray. Except for the noise of Bree's and Hwin's hoofs there was not a sound to be heard. Shasta would nearly have fallen asleep if he had not had to dismount and walk every now and then.

This seemed to last for hours. Then there came a time when there was no longer any moon. They seemed to ride in the dead darkness for hours and hours. And after that there came a moment when Shasta noticed that he could see Bree's neck and head in front of him a little more clearly than before; and slowly, very slowly, he began to notice the vast grey flatness on every side. It looked absolutely dead, like something in a dead world; and Shasta felt quite terribly tired and noticed that he was getting cold and that his lips were dry. And all the time the squeak of the leather, the jingle of the bits, and the noise of the hoofs — not *propputty-propputty* as it would be on a hard road, but *thubbudy-thubbudy* on the dry sand.

At last, after hours of riding, far away on his right there came a single long streak of paler grey, low down on the horizon. Then a streak of red. It was the morning at last, but without a single bird to sing about it. He was glad of the walking bits now, for he was colder than ever.

Then suddenly the sun rose and everything changed in a moment. The grey sand turned yellow and twinkled as if it was strewn with diamonds. On their left the shadows of Shasta and Hwin and Bree and Aravis, enormously long, raced beside them. The double peak of Mount Pire, far ahead, flashed in the sunlight and Shasta saw they were a little out of the course. 'A bit left, a bit left,' he sang out. Best of all, when you looked back, Tashbaan was already small and remote. The Tombs were quite invisible: swallowed up in that single, jagged-

ко мягко ступали лошади, и Шаста, чтобы не уснуть, иногда шёл пешком.

Потом — очень не скоро — луна исчезла, и долго царила тьма. Наконец Шаста увидел холку Игого, а потом мало-помалу стал различать и серые пески. Они были мёртвыми, словно путники вступили в мёртвый мир. Похолодало. Хотелось пить. Копыта звучали глухо — не «цок-цок-цок», а вроде бы «хох-хох-хох».

Должно быть, прошло ещё немало часов, прежде чем далеко справа появилась бледная полоса, а потом порозовела.

Наступало утро, но его приход не приветствовала ни одна птица. Воздух стал не теплее, а ещё холоднее.

Вдруг появилось солнце, и всё изменилось. Песок мгновенно пожелтел и засверкал, словно усыпанный алмазами. Длинные-предлинные тени легли слева от лошадей. Далеко впереди ослепительно засияла двойная вершина, и Шаста, заметив, что они немного сбились с курса, обернулся и сказал Игого:

— Чуть-чуть левее.

Ташбаан казался ничтожным и тёмным, усыпальницы исчезли, словно их поглотил город Тисрока. От этого всем стало легче, но ненадолго: вскоре Шасту

edged hump which was the city of the Tisroc. Everyone felt better.

But not for long. Though Tashbaan looked very far away when they first saw it, it refused to look any further away as they went on. Shasta gave up looking back at it, for it only gave him the feeling that they were not moving at all. Then the light became a nuisance. The glare of the sand made his eyes ache: but he knew he mustn't shut them. He must screw them up and keep on looking ahead at Mount Pire and shouting out directions. Then came the heat. He noticed it for the first time when he had to dismount and walk: as he slipped down to the sand the heat from it struck up into his face as if from the opening of an oven door. Next time it was worse. But the third time, as his bare feet touched the sand he screamed with pain and got one foot back in the stirrup and the other half over Bree's back before you could have said knife.

'Sorry, Bree,' he gasped. 'I can't walk. It burns my feet.'

'Of course!' panted Bree. 'Should have thought of that myself. Stay on. Can't be helped.'

'It's all right for *you*,' said Shasta to Aravis who was walking beside Hwin. 'You've got shoes on.'

Aravis said nothing and looked prim. Let's hope she didn't mean to, but she did.

On again, trot and walk and trot, jingle-jingle-jingle, squeak-squeak-squeak, smell of hot horse, smell of hot self, blinding glare, headache. And nothing at all different for mile after mile. Tashbaan would never look any further away. The mountains would never look any nearer. You felt this had been going on for always — jingle-jingle-jingle, squeak-squeak-squeak, smell of hot horse, smell of hot self.

Of course one tried all sorts of games with oneself to try to make the time pass: and of course they were all no

начал мучить солнечный свет. Песок сверкал так, что глаза болели, но закрыть их мальчик не мог — глядел на двойную вершину, — а когда спешился, чтобы немного передохнуть, ощутил, как мучителен зной. Когда же спешился во второй раз, жарой дохнуло как из печи. В третий раз он вскрикнул, коснувшись песка босой ступней, и мигом взлетел в седло, сказав коню:

— Ты уж прости. Не могу, ноги обжигает.

Потом повернулся к Аравите, которая шла за своей лошадью:

— Тебе-то хорошо в туфлях.

После этого бесконечно длилось одно и то же: жара, жжение в глазах, головная боль, запах своего и конского пота. Город далеко позади не исчезал никак, даже не уменьшался, горы впереди не становились ближе. Каждый старался не думать ни о прохладной воде, ни о ледяном шербете, ни о холодном молоке, густом, нежирном, но чем больше они старались, тем хуже это удавалось.

good. And one tried very hard not to think of drinks — iced sherbet in a palace in Tashbaan, clear spring water tinkling with a dark earthy sound, cold, smooth milk just creamy enough and not too creamy — and the harder you tried not to think, the more you thought.

At last there was something different — a mass of rock sticking up out of the sand about fifty yards long and thirty feet high. It did not cast much shadow, for the sun was now very high, but it cast a little. Into that shade they crowded. There they ate some food and drank a little water. It is not easy giving a horse a drink out of a skin bottle, but Bree and Hwin were clever with their lips. No one had anything like enough. No one spoke. The Horses were flecked with foam and their breathing was noisy. The children were pale.

After a very short rest they went on again. Same noises, same smells, same glare, till at last their shadows began to fall on their right, and then got longer and longer till they seemed to stretch out to the Eastern end of the world. Very slowly the sun drew nearer to the Western horizon. And now at last he was down and, thank goodness, the merciless glare was gone, though the heat

Когда все совсем измучились, появилась скала ярдов пятьдесят шириной и тридцать — высотой. Тень была короткой (солнце стояло высоко), но всё же была. Дети поели и выпили воды. Лошадей напоили из фляжки — это очень трудно, но Игого и Уинни старались как могли. Никто не сказал ни слова. Лошади, покрытые пеной, тяжело дышали. Шаста и Аравита были очень бледны.

Потом они снова двинулись в путь, и время едва ползло, пока солнце не стало медленно спускаться по ослепительному небу. Когда оно скрылось, угас мучительный блеск песка, но жара держалась ещё долго. Ни малейших признаков ущелья, о котором говорили гном и ворон, не было и в помине. Опять тянулись часы — а может, долгие минуты, — взошла

coming up from the sand was still as bad as ever. Four pairs of eyes were looking out eagerly for any sign of the valley that Sallowpad the Raven had spoken about. But, mile after mile, there was nothing but level sand. And now the day was quite definitely done, and most of the stars were out, and still the Horses thundered on and the children rose and sank in their saddles, miserable with thirst and weariness. Not till the moon had risen did Shasta — in the strange, barking voice of someone whose mouth is perfectly dry — shout out:

'There it is!'

There was no mistaking it now. Ahead, and a little to their right, there was at last a slope: a slope downward and hummocks of rock on each side. The Horses were far too tired to speak but they swung round towards it and in a minute or two they were entering the gully. At first it was worse in there than it had been out in the open desert, for there was a breathless stuffiness between the rocky walls and less moonlight. The slope continued steeply downwards and the rocks on either hand rose to the height of cliffs. Then they began to meet vegetation — prickly cactus-like plants and coarse grass of the kind that would prick your fingers. Soon the horse-hoofs were falling on pebbles and stones instead of sand. Round every bend of the valley — and it had many bends — they looked eagerly for water. The Horses were nearly at the end of their strength now, and Hwin, stumbling and panting, was lagging behind Bree. They were almost in despair before at last they came to a little muddiness and a tiny trickle of water through softer and better grass. And the trickle became a brook, and the brook became a stream with bushes on each side, and the stream became a river and there came (after more disappointments than I could possibly describe) — a moment when Shas-

луна, и вдруг Шаста крикнул (или прохрипел — так пересохло в горле):

— Глядите!

Впереди, немного справа, начиналось ущелье. Лошади ринулись туда, ничего не ответив от усталости, но поначалу там было хуже, чем в пустыне: слишком уж душно и темно. Дальше стали попадаться растения вроде кустов и трава, которой вы порезали бы пальцы. Копыта стучали уже «цок-цок-цок», но весьма уныло, ибо воды всё не было. Много раз сворачивала тропка то вправо, то влево (ущелье оказалось чрезвычайно извилистым), пока трава не стала мягче и зеленее. Наконец Шаста — не то задремавший, не то сомлевший — вздрогнул и очнулся: Игого остановился как вкопанный. Перед ними в маленькое озерцо, скорее похожее на лужу, низвергался водопадом источник. Лошади припали к воде, а Шаста спрыгнул и полез в лужу, хотя та и оказалась ему по колено. Наверное, то была лучшая минута его жизни.

ta, who had been in a kind of doze, suddenly realized that Bree had stopped and found himself slipping off. Before them a little cataract of water poured into a broad pool: and both the Horses were already in the pool with their heads down, drinking, drinking, drinking. 'O-o-oh,' said Shasta and plunged in — it was about up to his knees — and stooped his head right into the cataract. It was perhaps the loveliest moment in his life.

It was about ten minutes later when all four of them (the two children wet nearly all over) came out and began to notice their surroundings. The moon was now high enough to peep down into the valley. There was soft grass on both sides of the river, and beyond the grass, trees and bushes sloped up to the bases of the cliffs. There must have been some wonderful flowering shrubs hidden in that shadowy undergrowth for the whole glade was full of the coolest and most delicious smells. And out of the darkest recess among the trees there came a sound Shasta had never heard before — a nightingale.

Everyone was much too tired to speak or to eat. The Horses, without waiting to be unsaddled, lay down at once. So did Aravis and Shasta.

About ten minutes later the careful Hwin said, 'But we mustn't go to sleep. We've got to keep ahead of that Rabadash.'

'No,' said Bree very slowly. 'Mustn't go sleep. Just a little rest.'

Shasta knew (for a moment) that they would all go to sleep if he didn't get up and do something about it, and felt that he ought to. In fact he decided that he would get up and persuade them to go on. But presently; not yet; not just yet...

Very soon the moon shone and the nightingale sang over two horses and two human children, all fast asleep.

Минут через десять повеселевшие лошади и мокрые дети огляделись и увидели сочную траву, кусты, деревья. Должно быть, кусты цвели: аромат разливался несказанно прекрасный, — но ещё прекраснее были звуки, которых Шаста никогда не слышал. Это пел соловей.

Лошади легли на землю, не дожидаясь, пока их расседлают. Легли и дети. Все молчали, только минут через пятнадцать Уинни проговорила:

— Спать нельзя... Надо опередить этого Рабадаша.

— Нельзя, нельзя... — сонно повторил Игого. — Отдохнём немного...

Шаста подумал, что надо что-нибудь сделать, иначе все заснут, даже *решил* встать — но не сейчас... чуточку позже...

И через минуту луна освещала детей и лошадей, крепко спавших под пение соловья.

It was Aravis who awoke first. The sun was already high in the heavens and the cool morning hours were already wasted. 'It's my fault,' she said to herself furiously as she jumped up and began rousing the others. 'One wouldn't expect Horses to keep awake after a day's work like that, even if they *can* talk. And of course that Boy wouldn't; he's had no decent training. But *I* ought to have known better.'

The others were dazed and stupid with the heaviness of their sleep.

'Neigh-ho — broo-hoo,' said Bree. 'Been sleeping in my saddle, eh? I'll never do that again. Most uncomfortable — '

'Oh, come on, come on,' said Aravis. 'We've lost half the morning already. There isn't a moment to spare.'

'A fellow's got to have a mouthful of grass,' said Bree.

I'm afraid we can't wait,' said Aravis.

'What's the terrible hurry?' said Bree. 'We've crossed the desert, haven't we?'

'But we're not in Archenland yet,' said Aravis. 'And we've got to get there before Rabadash.'

'Oh, we must be miles ahead of him,' said Bree. 'Haven't we been coming a shorter way? Didn't that Raven friend of yours say this was a short cut, Shasta?'

'He didn't say anything about *shorter*,' answered Shasta. 'He only said *better*, because you got to a river this way. If the oasis is due North of Tashbaan, then I'm afraid this may be longer.'

'Well I can't go on without a snack,' said Bree. 'Take my bridle off, Shasta.'

'P-please,' said Hwin, very shyly, 'I feel just like Bree that I *can't* go on. But when Horses have humans (with spurs and things) on their backs, aren't they often made

Первой проснулась Аравита и, увидев в небе солнце, рассердилась на себя: «Это всё я! Лошади очень устали, а он... куда ему, он ведь совсем не воспитан!.. Вот мне стыдно — ведь я тархина».

И девочка принялась будить остальных.

Совсем отупевшие со сна, они поначалу не понимали, в чём дело.

— Ай-ай-ай! — посетовал Игого. — Заснуть нерассёдланным!.. Нехорошо и неудобно.

— Да вставай ты, мы и так потеряли пол-утра! — разозлилась Аравита.

— Дай хоть позавтракать-то, — попросил конь.

— Боюсь, ждать нам нельзя, — возразила девочка, но Игого укоризненно пробормотал:

— Что за спешка? Пустыню мы прошли как-никак.

— Мы не в Орландии! А вдруг Рабадаш нас обгонит?

— Ну, он ещё далеко, — успокоил её конь. — Твой ворон говорил, что эта дорога короче, да, Шаста?

— Нет, что она *лучше*. Очень может быть, что короче — прямо на север.

— Как хочешь, но я идти не могу, пока не перекушу. Убери-ка уздечку.

— Простите, — застенчиво сказала Уинни, — мы, лошади, часто делаем то, чего не можем. Так надо людям... Неужели мы сейчас не постараемся ради Нарнии?

to go on when they're feeling like this? and then they find they can. I m-mean — oughtn't we to be able to do even more, now that we're free? It's all for Narnia.'

'I think, Ma'am,' said Bree very crushingly, 'that I know a little more about campaigns and forced marches and what a horse can stand than you do.'

To this Hwin made no answer, being, like most highly bred mares, a very nervous and gentle person who was easily put down. In reality she was quite right, and if Bree had had a Tarkaan on his back at that moment to make him go on, he would have found that he was good for several hours' hard going. But one of the worst results of being a slave and being forced to do things is that when there is no one to force you any more you find you have almost lost the power of forcing yourself.

So they had to wait while Bree had a snack and a drink, and of course Hwin and the children had a snack and a drink too. It must have been nearly eleven o'clock in the morning before they finally got going again. And even then Bree took things much more gently than yesterday. It was really Hwin, though she was the weaker and more tired of the two, who set the pace.

The valley itself, with its brown, cool river, and grass and moss and wild flowers and rhododendrons, was such a pleasant place that it made you want to ride slowly.

— Госпожа моя, — рассердился Игого, — мне кажется, я знаю больше, чем ты, что может лошадь в походе, а чего — не может.

И она замолчала, потому что, как все породистые кобылы, легко смущалась и смирялась. А права-то была она. Если бы на нём ехал тархан, Игого как-то смог бы идти дальше. Что поделаешь! Когда ты долго был рабом, трудно бороться со своими желаниями.

Словом, все ждали, пока Игого наестся и напьётся вволю, и, конечно, подкрепились сами. Тронулись в путь часам к одиннадцати. Впереди шла Уинни.

Долина была так прекрасна — и трава, и мох, и цветы, и кусты, и прохладная речка, — что все двигались медленно.

Chapter 10

THE HERMIT OF THE SOUTHERN MARCH

After they had ridden for several hours down the valley, it widened out and they could see what was ahead of them. The river which they had been following here joined a broader river, wide and turbulent, which flowed from their left to their right, towards the east. Beyond this new river a delightful country rose gently in low hills, ridge beyond ridge, to the Northern Mountains themselves. To the right there were rocky pinnacles, one or two of them with snow clinging to the ledges. To the left, pine-clad slopes, frowning cliffs, narrow gorges, and blue peaks stretched away as far as the eye could reach. He could no longer make out Mount Pire. Straight ahead the mountain range sank to a wooded saddle which of course must be the pass from Archenland into Narnia.

'Broo-hoo-hoo, the North, the green North!' neighed Bree: and certainly the lower hills looked greener and fresher than anything that Aravis and Shasta, with their southern-bred eyes, had ever imagined. Spirits rose as they clattered down to the water's-meet of the two rivers.

The eastern-flowing river, which was pouring from the higher mountains at the western end of the range, was far too swift and too broken with rapids for them to think of swimming it; but after some casting about, up and down the bank, they found a place shallow enough

Глава 10

ОТШЕЛЬНИК

После нескольких часов пути долина стала шире, ручей превратился в реку, а та влилась в другую реку, большую и бурную, которая текла слева направо. За второй рекой открывались взору зелёные холмы, восходящие уступами к северным горам. Теперь горы были так близко и вершины их так сверкали, что Шаста не мог различить, какая из них двойная. Но прямо перед нашими путниками (хотя и выше, конечно) темнел перевал — должно быть, то и был путь из Орландии в Нарнию.

— Север, север, север! — воскликнул Игого.

И впрямь, дети никогда не видели, даже вообразить не могли, таких зелёных, светлых холмов. Реку, что несла свои воды на восток, переплыть было невозможно, но, хорошенько поискав, наши путники нашли брод. Рёв воды, холодный ветер и стремительные стрекозы привели Шасту в полный восторг.

to wade. The roar and clatter of water, the great swirl against the horses' fetlocks, the cool, stirring air and the darting dragonflies, filled Shasta with a strange excitement.

'Friends, we are in Archenland!' said Bree proudly as he splashed and churned his way out on the Northern bank. 'I think that river we've just crossed is called the Winding Arrow.'

'I hope we're in time,' murmured Hwin.

Then they began going up, slowly and zigzagging a good deal, for the hills were steep. It was all open park-like country with no roads or houses in sight. Scattered trees, never thick enough to be a forest, were everywhere. Shasta, who had lived all his life in an almost tree-less grassland, had never seen so many or so many kinds. If you had been there you would probably have known (he didn't) that he was seeing oaks, beeches, silver birches, rowans, and sweet chestnuts. Rabbits scurried away in every direction as they advanced, and presently they saw a whole herd of fallow deer making off among the trees.

'Isn't it simply glorious!' said Aravis.

At the first ridge Shasta turned in the saddle and looked back. There was no sign of Tashbaan; the desert, unbroken except by the narrow green crack which they had travelled down, spread to the horizon.

'Hullo!' he said suddenly. 'What's that?'

'What's what?' said Bree, turning round. Hwin and Aravis did the same.

'That,' said Shasta, pointing. 'It looks like smoke. Is it a fire?'

'Sand-storm, I should say,' said Bree.

'Not much wind to raise it,' said Aravis.

— Друзья, мы в Орландии! — гордо сказал Игого, выходя на северный берег. — Кажется, эта река называется Орлянка.

— Надеюсь, мы не опоздали, — тихо прибавила Уинни.

Они стали медленно подниматься, петляя, ибо склоны были круты. Деревья росли редко, не образуя леса, но Шаста, выросший в пустынных краях, никогда не видел их столько сразу. Вы бы, в отличие от него, узнали дубы, буки, клёны, берёзы и каштаны. Под ними сновали кролики, вдалеке даже мелькнуло стадо оленей.

— Какая красота! — воскликнула Аравита.

На первом уступе Шаста обернулся и увидел одну лишь пустыню — Ташбаан исчез. Радость могла быть полной, если бы его взору при этом не предстало что-то вроде облака.

— Что это?

— Наверное, песчаный смерч, — сказал Игого.

— Ветер для этого слишком слаб, — возразила Аравита.

'Oh!' exclaimed Hwin. 'Look! There are things flashing in it. Look! They're helmets — and armour. And it's moving: moving this way.'

'By Tash!' said Aravis. 'It's the army. It's Rabadash.'

'Of course it is,' said Hwin. 'Just what I was afraid of. Quick! We must get to Anvard before it.' And without another word she whisked round and began galloping North. Bree tossed his head and did the same.

'Come *on*, Bree, come on,' yelled Aravis over her shoulder.

The race was very gruelling for the Horses. As they topped each ridge they found another valley and another ridge beyond it; and though they knew they were going in more or less the right direction, no one knew how far it was to Anvard. From the top of the second ridge Shasta looked back again. Instead of a dust-cloud well out in the desert he now saw a black, moving mass, rather like ants, on the far bank of the Winding Arrow. They were doubtless looking for a ford.

'They're on the river!' he yelled wildly.

'Quick! Quick!' shouted Aravis. 'We might as well not have come at all if we don't reach Anvard in time. Gallop, Bree, gallop. Remember you're a war-horse.'

It was all Shasta could do to prevent himself from shouting out similar instructions; but he thought, 'The poor chap's doing all he can already,' and held his tongue. And certainly both Horses were doing, if not all they could, all they thought they could; which is not quite the same thing. Bree had caught up with Hwin and they thundered side by side over the turf. It didn't look as if Hwin could possibly keep it up much longer.

At that moment everyone's feelings were completely altered by a sound from behind. It was not the sound they

— Смотрите! — воскликнула Уинни. — Там что-то блестит. Ой, это шлемы... и кольчуги!

— Клянусь великой Таш, — согласилась с ней Аравита, — это они, тархистанцы.

— Скорее! Опередим их! — И Уинни понеслась стрелой вверх, по крутым холмам.

Игого опустил голову и поскакал за нею.

Скакать было трудно: за каждым уступом лежала долинка. Они знали, что не сбились с дороги, но не знали, далеко ли до Анварда. Со второго уступа Шаста оглянулся опять и увидел уже не облако, а тучу или полчище муравьев у самой реки. Без сомнения, армия Рабадаша искала брод.

— Они у реки!

— Скорей, скорей! — воскликнула Аравита. — Скачи, Игого! Вспомни, ты боевой конь.

Шаста же подумал: «И так бедняга скачет изо всех сил».

На самом же деле лошади скорее *полагали,* что быстрее скакать не могут, а это не совсем одно и то же. Когда Игого поравнялся с Уинни, та хрипела. И в эту минуту сзади раздался странный звук — не звон оружия, и не цокот копыт, и не боевые крики, а рёв, который Шаста слышал той ночью, когда встретил Уинни и Аравиту. Игого узнал этот рёв, глаза его налились кровью, и он неожиданно понял,

had been expecting to hear — the noise of hoofs and jingling armour, mixed, perhaps, with Calormene battle-cries. Yet Shasta knew it at once. It was the same snarling roar he had heard that moonlit night when they first met Aravis and Hwin. Bree knew it too. His eyes gleamed red and his ears lay flat back on his skull. And Bree now discovered that he had not really been going as fast — not quite as fast — as he could. Shasta felt the change at once. Now they were really going all out. In a few seconds they were well ahead of Hwin.

'It's not fair,' thought Shasta. 'I *did* think we'd be safe from lions here!'

He looked over his shoulder. Everything was only too clear. A huge tawny creature, its body low to the ground, like a cat streaking across the lawn to a tree when a strange dog has got into the garden, was behind them. And it was nearer every second and half second.

He looked forward again and saw something which he did not take in, or even think about. Their way was barred by a smooth green wall about ten feet high. In the middle of that wall there was a gate, open. In the middle of the gateway stood a tall man dressed, down to his bare feet, in a robe coloured like autumn leaves, leaning on a straight staff. His beard fell almost to his knees.

Shasta saw all this in a glance and looked back again. The lion had almost got Hwin now. It was making snaps at her hind legs, and there was no hope now in her foam-flecked, wide-eyed face.

'Stop,' bellowed Shasta in Bree's ear. 'Must go back. Must help!'

Bree always said afterwards that he never heard, or never understood this; and as he was in general a very truthful horse we must accept his word.

Shasta slipped his feet out of the stirrups, slid both his legs over the left side, hesitated for one hideous hun-

что бежал до сих пор совсем не изо всех сил. Через несколько секунд он оставил Уинни далеко позади.

«Ну что это такое! — подумал Шаста. — И тут львы!»

Оглянувшись через плечо, он увидел огромного льва, который нёсся, стелясь по земле, как кошка, убегающая от собаки. Взглянув вперёд, Шаста тоже не увидел ничего хорошего: дорогу перегораживала зелёная стена высотой футов десять. В ней были воротца, и там стоял человек. Одежды его — цвета осенних листьев — ниспадали к босым ногам, белая борода доходила до колен.

Шаста обернулся — лев уже почти схватил Уинни — и крикнул Игого:

— Назад! Надо им помочь!

Всегда, всю свою жизнь, Игого утверждал, что не понял его или не расслышал. Всем известна его правдивость, и мы поверим ему.

Шаста спрыгнул с коня на полном скаку (а это очень трудно и, главное, страшно). Боли он не ощутил,

dredth of a second, and jumped. It hurt horribly and nearly winded him; but before he knew how it hurt him he was staggering back to help Aravis. He had never done anything like this in his life before and hardly knew why he was doing it now.

One of the most terrible noises in the world, a horse's scream, broke from Hwin's lips. Aravis was stooping low over Hwin's neck and seemed to be trying to draw her sword. And now all three — Aravis, Hwin, and the lion were almost on top of Shasta. Before they reached him the lion rose on its hind legs, larger than you would have believed a lion could be, and jabbed at Aravis with its right paw. Shasta could see all the terrible claws extended. Aravis screamed and reeled in the saddle. The lion was tearing her shoulders. Shasta, half mad with horror, managed to lurch towards the brute. He had no weapon, not even a stick or a stone. He shouted out, idiotically, at the lion as one would at a dog, 'Go home! Go home!' For a fraction of a second he was staring right into its wide-opened, raging mouth. Then, to his utter astonishment, the lion, still on its hind legs, checked itself suddenly, turned head over heels, picked itself up, and rushed away.

Shasta did not for a moment suppose it had gone for good. He turned and raced for the gate in the green wall which, now for the first time, he remembered seeing. Hwin, stumbling and nearly fainting, was just entering the gate: Aravis still kept her seat but her back was covered with blood.

'Come in, my daughter, come in,' the robed and bearded man was saying, and then, 'Come in, my son' as Shasta panted up to him. He heard the gate closed behind him; and the bearded stranger was already helping Aravis off her horse.

They were in a wide and perfectly circular enclosure, protected by a high wall of green turf. A pool of perfectly still

ибо кинулся на помощь Аравите. Никогда в жизни он так не поступал и не знал, почему делает это сейчас.

Уинни закричала: это был очень страшный и жалобный звук, — и Аравита, прижавшись к её холке, попыталась вынуть кинжал. Все трое — лошадь, Аравита и лев — нависли над Шастой, но лев тронул не его, а, поднявшись на задние лапы, ударил правой передней Аравиту. Шаста увидел его страшные когти и тут же услышал дикий крик. Аравита покачнулась в седле. У Шасты не было ни меча, ни палки, ни даже камня. Он с криком кинулся было на страшного зверя, на долю секунды заглянув в разверстую алую пасть, но, к великому его удивлению, лев перекувырнулся и не спеша удалился.

Шаста решил, что зверь вот-вот вернётся, и кинулся к зелёной стене, о которой только теперь вспомнил. Уинни, содрогаясь всем телом, вбежала тем временем в ворота. Аравита сидела прямо, но по спине у неё струилась кровь.

— Добро пожаловать, дочь моя, — сказал старик. — Добро пожаловать, сын мой. — И ворота закрылись за едва дышавшим Шастой.

Беглецы оказались в большом, совершенном круглом дворе, окружённом стеной из торфа. В самом

water, so full that the water was almost exactly level with the ground, lay before him. At one end of the pool, completely overshadowing it with its branches, there grew the hugest and most beautiful tree that Shasta had ever seen. Beyond the pool was a little low house of stone roofed with deep and ancient thatch. There was a sound of bleating and over at the far side of the enclosure there were some goats. The level ground was completely covered with the finest grass.

'Are — are — are you,' panted Shasta. 'Are you King Lune of Archenland?'

The old man shook his head. 'No,' he replied in a quiet voice, 'I am the Hermit of the Southern March. And now, my son, waste no time on questions, but obey. This damsel is wounded. Your horses are spent. Rabadash is at this moment finding a ford over the Winding Arrow. If you run now, without a moment's rest, you will still be in time to warn King Lune.'

Shasta's heart fainted at these words for he felt he had no strength left. And he writhed inside at what seemed the cruelty and unfairness of the demand. He had not yet learned that if you do one good deed your reward usually is to be set to do another and harder and better one. But all he said out loud was:

его центре поблёскивал водой небольшой пруд, возле которого, осеняя его ветвями, росло самое большое и самое красивое дерево из всех, какие Шасте доводилось видеть. В глубине двора стоял невысокий домик, крытый черепицей, и рядом с ним, на лужайке, поросшей зелёной сочной травой, паслись козы.

— Вы... вы... Лум, король Орландии? — выговорил Шаста.

Старик покачал головой.

— Нет, я отшельник. Не трать время на вопросы, а слушай меня, сын мой. Девица ранена, лошади измучены. Рабадаш только что отыскал брод. Беги, и тогда успеешь предупредить короля Лума.

Сердце у Шасты упало — он знал, что бежать не может, и подивился жестокости старика, ибо ещё не ведал, что стоит нам сделать что-нибудь хорошее, как мы должны в награду сделать то, что ещё лучше и ещё труднее.

'Where is the King?'

The Hermit turned and pointed with his staff. 'Look,' he said. 'There is another gate, right opposite to the one you entered by. Open it and go straight ahead: always straight ahead, over level or steep, over smooth or rough, over dry or wet. I know by my art that you will find King Lune straight ahead. But run, run: always run.'

Shasta nodded his head, ran to the northern gate and disappeared beyond it. Then the Hermit took Aravis, whom he had all this time been supporting with his left arm, and half led, half carried her into the house. After a long time he came out again.

'Now, cousins,' he said to the Horses. 'It is your turn.'

Without waiting for an answer — and indeed they were too exhausted to speak — he took the bridles and saddles off both of them. Then he rubbed them both down, so well that a groom in a King's stable could not have done it better.

'There, cousins,' he said, 'dismiss it all from your minds and be comforted. Here is water and there is grass. You shall have a hot mash when I have milked my other cousins, the goats.'

'Sir,' said Hwin, finding her voice at last, 'will the Tarkheena live? Has the lion killed her?'

'I who know many present things by my art,' replied the Hermit with a smile, 'have yet little knowledge of things future. Therefore I do not know whether any man or woman or beast in the whole world will be alive when the sun sets tonight. But be of good hope. The damsel is likely to live as long as any of her age.'

When Aravis came to herself she found that she was lying on her face on a low bed of extraordinary softness in a cool, bare room with walls of undressed stone. She

— Где король? — спросил он почему-то.

Отшельник обернулся и указал посохом на север.

— Гляди — вон другие ворота. Открой их и беги прямо, вверх и вниз, по воде и посуху, не сворачивая. Там найдёшь короля. Беги!

Шаста кивнул и скрылся за северными воротами. Тогда отшельник, всё это время поддерживавший Аравиту левой рукой, медленно повёл её к дому. Вышел он не скоро.

— Двоюродный брат мой, двоюродная сестра, — обратился он к лошадям, — теперь ваша очередь.

Не дожидаясь ответа, он расседлал их, почистил скребницей лучше самого королевского конюха, а потом сказал:

— Пейте воду, ешьте траву и отдыхайте. Когда подою своих двоюродных сестер, коз, принесу вам ещё поесть.

— Господин мой, — подала голос Уинни, — выживет ли тархина?

— Я знаю много о настоящем, — проговорил старец, — мало — о будущем. Никто не может сказать, доживёт ли человек или зверь до сегодняшней ночи. Но не отчаивайся. Девица здорова, и, думаю, проживёт столько, сколько любая её лет.

Очнувшись, Аравита обнаружила, что покоится на мягчайшем ложе в прохладной белёной комнате, но не могла понять, почему лежит ничком. И только

couldn't understand why she had been laid on her face; but when she tried to turn and felt the hot, burning pains all over her back, she remembered, and realized why. She couldn't understand what delightfully springy stuff the bed was made of, because it was made of heather (which is the best bedding) and heather was a thing she had never seen or heard of.

The door opened and the Hermit entered, carrying a large wooden bowl in his hand. After carefully setting this down, he came to the bedside, and asked:

'How do you find yourself, my daughter?'

'My back is very sore, father,' said Aravis, 'but there is nothing else wrong with me.'

He knelt beside her, laid his hand on her forehead, and felt her pulse.

'There is no fever,' he said. 'You will do well. Indeed there is no reason why you should not get up tomorrow. But now, drink this.'

He fetched the wooden bowl and held it to her lips. Aravis couldn't help making a face when she tasted it, for goats' milk is rather a shock when you are not used to it. But she was very thirsty and managed to drink it all and felt better when she had finished.

'Now, my daughter, you may sleep when you wish,' said the Hermit. 'For your wounds are washed and dressed and though they smart they are no more serious than if they had been the cuts of a whip. It must have been a very strange lion; for instead of catching you out of the saddle and getting his teeth into you, he has only drawn his claws across your back. Ten scratches: sore, but not deep or dangerous.'

'I say!' said Aravis. 'I *have* had luck.'

'Daughter,' said the Hermit, 'I have now lived a hundred and nine winters in this world and have never yet

когда попыталась повернуться, вскрикнула от боли и вспомнила всё. Из чего сделано ложе, она не знала и знать не могла. А то был вереск — спать на нём мягче всего.

Открылась дверь, вошёл отшельник с деревянной миской в руке и, осторожно поставив её, спросил:

— Лучше ли тебе, дочь моя?
— Спина болит, отец мой, а так ничего.

Он опустился на колени, потрогал её лоб и пощупал пульс.
— Жара нет. Завтра встанешь, а сейчас выпей это.

Пригубив молока, Аравита поморщилась — козье молоко противно с непривычки, — но выпила: очень уж мучила жажда.

— Спи сколько хочешь, дочь моя, — сказал отшельник. — Я промыл и смазал бальзамом твои раны. Они не глубже удара бича. Какой удивительный лев! Не стянул с седла, не вонзил в тебя зубы, только поцарапал. Десять полосок... Больно, но не опасно.

— Просто повезло, — пожала плечами Аравита.
— Дочь моя, я прожил сто девять зим, и ни разу не видел, чтобы кому-нибудь повезло, — возразил

met any such thing as Luck. There is something about all this that I do not understand: but if ever we need to know it, you may be sure that we shall.'

'And what about Rabadash and his two hundred horse?' asked Aravis.

'They will not pass this way, I think,' said the Hermit. 'They must have found a ford by now well to the east of us. From there they will try to ride straight to Anvard.'

'Poor Shasta!' said Aravis. 'Has he far to go? Will he get there first?'

'There is good hope of it,' said the old man.

Aravis lay down again (on her side this time) and said, 'Have I been asleep for a long time? It seems to be getting dark.'

The Hermit was looking out of the only window, which faced north. 'This is not the darkness of night,' he said presently. 'The clouds are falling down from Stormness Head. Our foul weather always comes from there in these parts. There will be thick fog tonight.'

Next day, except for her sore back, Aravis felt so well that after breakfast (which was porridge and cream) the Hermit said she could get up. And of course she at once went out to speak to the Horses. The weather had changed and the whole of that green enclosure was filled, like a great green cup, with sunlight. It was a very peaceful place, lonely and quiet.

Hwin at once trotted across to Aravis and gave her a horse-kiss.

'But where's Bree?' said Aravis when each had asked after the other's health and sleep.

'Over there,' said Hwin, pointing with her nose to the far side of the circle. 'And I wish you'd come and talk to him. There's something wrong, I can't get a word out of him.'

отшельник. — Везенья нет, есть что-то иное. Я не знаю что, но если будет надо, мне откроется и это.

— А где Рабадаш и его люди? — спросила Аравита.

— Думаю, здесь они не пойдут — возьмут правее. Они хотят попасть прямо в Анвард.

— Бедный Шаста! — воскликнула Аравита. — Далеко он убежал? Успеет?

— Надеюсь.

Аравита осторожно легла, теперь — на бок, и спросила:

— А долго я спала? Уже темнеет.

Отшельник посмотрел в окно, выходящее на север.

— Это не вечер, это тучи, и они ползут с пика Бурь — непогода в наших местах всегда идёт оттуда. Ночью будет туман.

Назавтра спина ещё болела, но Аравита совсем оправилась и после завтрака (овсянки и сливок) отшельник разрешил ей встать. Конечно, она сразу же побежала к лошадям. Погода переменилась. Зелёная чаша двора была полна до краёв сияющим светом. Здесь было очень укромно, хорошо и тихо.

— Где Игого? — спросила беглянка, когда они справились друг у друга о здоровье.

— Вон там, — ответила Уинни. — Поговори с ним, а то он молчит, когда я с ним заговариваю.

They strolled across and found Bree lying with his face towards the wall, and though he must have heard them coming, he never turned his head or spoke a word.

'Good morning, Bree,' said Aravis. 'How are you this morning?'

Bree muttered something that no one could hear.

'The Hermit says that Shasta probably got to King Lune in time,' continued Aravis, 'so it looks as if all our troubles are over. Narnia, at last, Bree!'

'I shall never see Narnia,' said Bree in a low voice.

'Aren't you well, Bree dear?' said Aravis.

Bree turned round at last, his face mournful as only a horse's can be.

'I shall go back to Calormen,' he said.

'What?' said Aravis. 'Back to slavery!'

'Yes,' said Bree. 'Slavery is all I'm fit for. How can I ever show my face among the free Horses of Narnia? — I who left a mare and a girl and a boy to be eaten by lions while I galloped all I could to save my own wretched skin!'

'We all ran as hard as we could,' said Hwin.

'Shasta didn't!' snorted Bree. 'At least he ran in the right direction: ran *back*. And that is what shames me most of all. I, who called myself a war-horse and boasted of a hundred fights, to be beaten by a little human boy — a child, a mere foal, who had never held a sword nor had any good nurture or example in his life!'

'I know,' said Aravis. 'I felt just the same. Shasta was marvellous. I'm just as bad as you, Bree. I've been snubbing him and looking down on him ever since you met us and now he turns out to be the best of us all. But I think it would be better to stay and say we're sorry than to go back to Calormen.'

Игого лежал у задней стены отвернувшись и ни на что не реагировал.

— Доброе утро, Игого, — сказала Аравита, — как ты себя чувствуешь?

Конь что-то пробурчал.

— Отшельник думает, что Шаста успел предупредить короля, — продолжила девочка. — Беды наши кончились: скоро будем в Нарнии.

— Я там не буду, — со вздохом сказал Игого.

— Тебе нехорошо? — всполошились лошадь и девочка.

Он обернулся и проговорил:

— Я вернусь в Тархистан.

— Как? — воскликнула Аравита. — Туда, в рабство?

— Я лучшего не стою. Как покажусь благородным нарнийским лошадям, я, оставивший двух дам и мальчика на съедение льву?

— Мы все убежали, — возразила Уинни.

— Мы, но не *он*! — вскричал Игого. — Он побежал спасать вас. Ах какой стыд! Я кичился перед ним, а он ребёнок, в бою не бывал, и пример ему брать не с кого...

— Да, — согласилась Аравита. — И мне стыдно. Он молодец. Я вела себя не лучше, чем ты, Игого: смотрела на него сверху вниз — тогда как он самый благородный из нас. Но я хочу просить у него прощения, а не возвращаться в Тархистан.

'It's all very well for you,' said Bree. 'You haven't disgraced yourself. But I've lost everything.'

'My good Horse,' said the Hermit, who had approached them unnoticed because his bare feet made so little noise on that sweet, dewy grass. 'My good Horse, you've lost nothing but your self-conceit. No, no, cousin. Don't put back your ears and shake your mane at me. If you are really so humbled as you sounded a minute ago, you must learn to listen to sense. You're not quite the great Horse you had come to think, from living among poor dumb horses. Of course you were braver and cleverer than *them*. You could hardly help being that. It doesn't follow that you'll be anyone very special in Narnia. But as long as you know you're nobody special, you'll be a very decent sort of Horse, on the whole, and taking one thing with another. And now, if you and my other four-footed cousin will come round to the kitchen door we'll see about the other half of that mash.'

— Как знаешь, — сказал Игого. — Ты осрамилась, не больше, а я потерял всё.

— Добрый мой конь, — заговорил отшельник, незаметно подойдя к ним, — ты не потерял ничего, кроме гордыни. Не тряси гривой. Если ты и впрямь так сильно казнишься, выслушай меня. Когда ты жил среди бедных немых коней, слишком много о себе возомнил. Конечно, ты был храбрее и умнее их — это нетрудно, — но в Нарнии немало таких, как ты. Помни, что ты один из многих, а станешь одним из лучших. А теперь, брат мой и сестра, пойдёмте, вас ждёт угощение.

Chapter 11

THE UNWELCOME FELLOW TRAVELLER

When Shasta went through the gate he found a slope of grass and a little heather running up before him to some trees. He had nothing to think about now and no plans to make: he had only to run, and that was quite enough. His limbs were shaking, a terrible stitch was beginning in his side, and the sweat that kept dropping into his eyes blinded them and made them smart. He was unsteady on his feet too, and more than once he nearly turned his ankle on a loose stone.

The trees were thicker now than they had yet been and in the more open spaces there was bracken. The sun had gone in without making it any cooler. It had become one of those hot, grey days when there seem to be twice as many flies as usual. Shasta's face was covered with them; he didn't even try to shake them off — he had too much else to do.

Suddenly he heard a horn — not a great throbbing horn like the horns of Tashbaan but a merry call, Ti-ro-to-to-ho! Next moment he came out into a wide glade and found himself in a crowd of people.

At least, it looked a crowd to him. In reality there were about fifteen or twenty of them, all gentlemen in green hunting-dress, with their horses; some in the saddle and some standing by their horses' heads. In the centre someone was holding the stirrup for a man to mount. And the man he was holding it for was the jol-

Глава 11

СТРАННЫЙ СПУТНИК

Миновав ворота, Шаста побежал дальше: сперва — по траве, потом — по вереску. Он ни о чём не думал и ничего не загадывал, только бежал. Ноги у него подкашивались, в боку сильно кололо, пот заливал лицо, мешая смотреть, а в довершение бед он чуть не вывихнул лодыжку, споткнувшись о камень.

Деревья росли всё гуще. Прохладней не стало — был один из тех душных пасмурных дней, когда мух вдвое больше, чем обычно. Мухи эти непрестанно садились ему на лоб и на нос, но он их не отгонял.

Вдруг он услышал звук охотничьего рога — не грозный, как в Ташбаане, а радостный и весёлый, — и почти сразу увидел пёструю весёлую толпу.

На самом деле то была не толпа, а всего человек двадцать в ярко-зелёных камзолах. Одни сидели в седле, другие стояли возле коней и держали их под уздцы. В самом центре высокий оруженосец придерживал стремя для своего господина — на диво приветливого круглолицего ясноглазого короля.

liest, fat, apple-cheeked, twinkling-eyed King you could imagine.

As soon as Shasta came in sight this King forgot all about mounting his horse. He spread out his arms to Shasta, his face lit up, and he cried out in a great, deep voice that seemed to come from the bottom of his chest:

'Corin! My son! And on foot, and in rags! What — '

'No,' panted Shasta, shaking his head. 'Not Prince Corin. I — I — know I'm like him... saw his Highness in Tashbaan... sent his greetings.'

The King was staring at Shasta with an extraordinary expression on his face.

'Are you K-King Lune?' gasped Shasta. And then, without waiting for an answer, 'Lord King — fly — Anvard shut the gates — enemies upon you — Rabadash and two hundred horse.'

'Have you assurance of this, boy?' asked one of the other gentlemen.

'My own eyes,' said Shasta. 'I've seen them. Raced them all the way from Tashbaan.'

'On foot?' said the gentleman, raising his eyebrows a little.

Horses — with the Hermit,' said Shasta.

'Question him no more, Darrin,' said King Lune. 'I see truth in his face. We must ride for it, gentlemen. A spare horse there, for the boy. You can ride fast, friend?'

For answer Shasta put his foot in the stirrup of the horse which had been led towards him and a moment later he was in the saddle. He had done it a hundred times with Bree in the last few weeks, and his mounting was very different now from what it had been on that first night when Bree had said that he climbed up a horse as if he were climbing a haystack.

Завидев Шасту, король не стал садиться на коня. Лицо его просветлело. Он громко и радостно закричал, протягивая к мальчику руки:

— Корин, сынок! Почему ты бежишь, почему в лохмотьях?

— Я не принц Корин, — еле выговорил Шаста. — Я... я его видел в Ташбаане... он шлёт вам привет.

Король пристальнее пригляделся к нему.

— Вы король Лум? — задыхаясь, спросил Шаста и продолжил, не дожидаясь ответа: — Бегите... в Анвард... заприте ворота... сюда идёт Рабадаш.... с ним двести воинов.

— Ты уверен в том, что говоришь? — спросил один из придворных.

— Я видел их, — ответил Шаста, — своими глазами, потому что проделал тот же путь.

— Пешком? — удивился придворный.

— Верхом. Лошади сейчас у отшельника.

— Не расспрашивай его, Дарин, — сказал король. — Он не лжёт. Подведите ему коня. Ты умеешь скакать во весь опор, сынок?

Шаста, не отвечая, взлетел в седло, и был несказанно рад, когда Дарин сказал королю:

He was pleased to hear the Lord Darrin say to the King, 'The boy has a true horseman's seat, Sire. I'll warrant there's noble blood in him.'

'His blood, aye, there's the point,' said the King. And he stared hard at Shasta again with that curious expression, almost a hungry expression, in his steady, grey eyes.

But by now — the whole party was moving off at a brisk canter. Shasta's seat was excellent but he was sadly puzzled what to do with his reins, for he had never touched the reins while he was on Bree's back. But he looked very carefully out of the corners of his eyes to see what the others were doing (as some of us have done at parties when we weren't quite sure which knife or fork we were meant to use) and tried to get his fingers right. But he didn't dare to try really directing the horse; he trusted it would follow the rest. The horse was of course an ordinary horse, not a Talking Horse; but it had quite wits enough to realize that the strange boy on its back had no whip and no spurs and was not really master of the situation. That was why Shasta soon found himself at the tail end of the procession.

— Какая выправка, ваше величество! Несомненно, этот мальчик знатного рода.

— Ах, Дарин, об этом я и думаю! — И король снова пристально посмотрел на Шасту добрыми серыми глазами.

Тот и впрямь прекрасно сидел в седле, но совершенно не знал, что делать с поводьями, поэтому внимательно, хотя и украдкой, наблюдал, что делают другие (как поступаем мы в гостях, когда не знаем, какую взять вилку), и всё же надеялся, что конь сам разберёт, куда идти. Конь был не говорящий, но умный: понимал, что мальчик без шпор ему не хозяин, — поэтому Шаста вскоре оказался в хвосте отряда.

Even so, he was going pretty fast. There were no flies now and the air in his face was delicious. He had got his breath back too. And his errand had succeeded. For the first time since the arrival at Tashbaan (how long ago it seemed!) he was beginning to enjoy himself.

He looked up to see how much nearer the mountain tops had come. To his disappointment he could not see them at all: only a vague greyness, rolling down towards them. He had never been in mountain country before and was surprised. 'It's a cloud,' he said to himself, 'a cloud coming down. I see. Up here in the hills one is really in the sky. I shall see what the inside of a cloud is like. What fun! I've often wondered.' Far away on his left and a little behind him, the sun was getting ready to set.

They had come to a rough kind of road by now and were making very good speed. But Shasta's horse was still the last of the lot. Once or twice when the road made a bend (there was now continuous forest on each side of it) he lost sight of the others for a second or two.

Then they plunged into the fog, or else the fog rolled over them. The world became grey. Shasta had not realized how cold and wet the inside of a cloud would be; nor how dark. The grey turned to black with alarming speed.

Someone at the head of the column winded the horn every now and then, and each time the sound came from a little farther off. He couldn't see any of the others now, but of course he'd be able to as soon as he got round the next bend. But when he rounded it he still couldn't see them. In fact he could see nothing at all. His horse was walking now. 'Get on, Horse, get on,' said Shasta. Then came the horn, very faint. Bree had always told him that he must keep his heels well turned out, and Shasta had got the idea that something very terrible would happen if he dug his heels into a horse's sides. This seemed to

Впервые с тех пор, как вошёл в Ташбаан, у него полегчало на сердце и он посмотрел вверх, чтобы определить, насколько приблизилась вершина, однако увидел лишь какие-то серые комья. Он никогда не бывал в горах, и ему показалось очень занятным проехать сквозь тучу. «Тут мы и впрямь в небе. Посмотрю, что в туче, внутри. Мне давно хотелось...»

Далеко слева садилось солнце.

Дорога теперь была нелёгкая, но двигались они быстро. Шаста всё ещё ехал последним. Раза два, когда тропа сворачивала, он на мгновение терял других из виду — их скрывал густой лес.

Потом они нырнули в туман, или, если хотите, туман поглотил их. Всё стало серым. Шаста не подозревал, как холодно и мокро внутри тучи и как темно. Серое слишком уж быстро становилось чёрным.

Кто-то впереди отряда иногда трубил в рог, и звук этот всё отдалялся. Шаста опять никого не видел, но думал, что увидит, за очередным поворотом. Но нет — и за поворотом никого не было. Конь шёл шагом.

— Скорей, ну скорей! — сказал ему Шаста.

Вдалеке протрубил рог. Игого вечно твердил, что его бока пяткой и коснуться нельзя, и Шаста думал, что, если коснётся, произойдёт что-то страшное, но сейчас задумался.

— Вот что, конь: если будешь так тащиться, я тебя... ну... пришпорю. Да-да!

him an occasion for trying it. 'Look here, Horse,' he said, 'if you don't buck up, do you know what I'll do? I'll dig my heels into you. I really will.' The horse, however, took no notice of this threat. So Shasta settled himself firmly in the saddle, gripped with his knees, clenched his teeth, and punched both the horse's sides with his heels as hard as he could.

The only result was that the horse broke into a kind of pretence of a trot for five or six paces and then subsided into a walk again. And now it was quite dark and they seemed to have given up blowing that horn. The only sound was a steady drip-drip from the branches of the trees.

'Well, I suppose even a walk will get us somewhere sometime,' said Shasta to himself. 'I only hope I shan't run into Rabadash and his people.'

He went on for what seemed a long time, always at a walking pace. He began to hate that horse, and he was also beginning to feel very hungry.

Presently he came to a place where the road divided into two. He was just wondering which led to Anvard when he was startled by a noise from behind him. It was the noise of trotting horses. 'Rabadash!' thought Shasta. He had no way of guessing which road Rabadash would take. 'But if I take one,' said Shasta to himself, 'he *may* take the other: and if I stay at the crossroads I'm *sure* to be caught.' He dismounted and led his horse as quickly as he could along the right-hand road.

The sound of the cavalry grew rapidly nearer and in a minute or two Shasta realized that they were at the crossroads. He held his breath, waiting to see which way they would take.

There came a low word of command — 'Halt!' — then a moment of horsey noises — nostrils blowing,

Конь не обратил на его слова внимания, и тогда Шаста сел покрепче в седло, сжал зубы и выполнил свою угрозу. Но что толку? Конь шагов пять протрусил рысью, не больше. Совсем стемнело, рог умолк, только ветки похрустывали справа и слева, и Шаста подумал: «Куда-нибудь да выйдем. Хорошо бы не к Рабадашу!..»

Коня своего он почти ненавидел, к тому же очень хотелось есть.

Наконец он доехал до развилки, и когда прикидывал, какая же дорога ведёт в Анвард, сзади послышался цокот копыт. «Рабадаш! По какой же дороге он пойдёт? Если я пойду по одной, он *может* пойти по другой, а если буду тут стоять — схватит наверняка». Шаста спешился и поспешил с конём по правой дороге.

Цокот копыт приближался, и минуты через две воины были у развилки. Шаста затаил дыхание. Тут раздался голос:

hoofs pawing, bits being champed, necks being patted. Then a voice spoke.

'Attend, all of you,' it said. 'We are now within a furlong of the castle. Remember your orders. Once we are in Narnia, as we should be by sunrise, you are to kill as little as possible. On this venture you are to regard every drop of Narnian blood as more precious than a gallon of your own. On *this* venture, I say. The gods will send us a happier hour and then you must leave nothing alive between Cair Paravel and the Western Waste. But we are not yet in Narnia. Here in Archenland it is another thing. In the assault on this castle of King Lune's, nothing matters but speed. Show your mettle. It must be mine within an hour. And if it is, I give it all to you. I reserve no booty for myself. Kill me every barbarian male within its walls, down to the child that was born yesterday, and everything else is yours to divide as you please — the women, the gold, the jewels, the weapons, and the wine. The man that I see hanging back when we come to the gates shall be burned alive. In the name of Tash the irresistible, the inexorable — forward!'

With a great cloppitty-clop the column began to move, and Shasta breathed again. They had taken the other road.

Shasta thought they took a long time going past, for though he had been talking and thinking about 'two hundred horse' all day, he had not realized how many they really were. But at last the sound died away and once more he was alone amid the drip-drip from the trees.

He now knew the way to Anvard but of course he could not now go there: that would only mean running into the arms of Rabadash's troopers. 'What on earth am I to do?' said Shasta to himself. But he remounted his horse and continued along the road he had chosen, in the

— Помните мой приказ! Завтра, в Нарнии, каждая капля их крови будет ценней, чем галлон вашей. Я сказал: «Завтра». Боги пошлют нам лучшие дни, и мы не оставим живым никого между Кэр-Паравалем и Западной степью. Но мы ещё не в Нарнии. Здесь, в Орландии, в замке Лума, важно одно: действовать побыстрей. Возьмите его за час. Вся добыча — ваша. Убивайте всех мужчин, даже новорождённых младенцев, а женщин, золото, камни, оружие, вино делите как хотите. Если кто уклонится от битвы, сожгу живьём. А теперь — во имя великой Таш — вперёд!

Звеня оружием, отряд двинулся по *другой* дороге. Шаста много раз за эти дни повторял слова «двести лошадей», но до сих пор не понимал, как долго проходит мимо такое войско. Наконец последний звук угас в тумане, и Шаста вздохнул с облегчением. Теперь он знал, какая из дорог ведёт в Анвард, но двинуться по ней не мог. Пока он думал, как быть, конь шагал по другой дороге.

faint hope of finding some cottage where he might ask for shelter and a meal. He had thought, of course, of going back to Aravis and Bree and Hwin at the hermitage, but he couldn't because by now he had not the least idea of the direction.

'After all,' said Shasta, 'this road is bound to get to somewhere.'

But that all depends on what you mean by somewhere. The road kept on getting to somewhere in the sense that it got to more and more trees, all dark and dripping, and to colder and colder air. And strange, icy winds kept blowing the mist past him though they never blew it away. If he had been used to mountain country he would have realized that this meant he was now very high up — perhaps right at the top of the pass. But Shasta knew nothing about mountains.

'I *do* think,' said Shasta, 'that I must be the most unfortunate boy that ever lived in the whole world. Everything goes right for everyone except me. Those Narnian lords and ladies got safe away from Tashbaan; I was left behind. Aravis and Bree and Hwin are all as snug as anything with that old Hermit: of course I was the one who was sent on. King Lune and his people must have got safely into the castle and shut the gates long before Rabadash arrived, but I get left out.'

And being very tired and having nothing inside him, he felt so sorry for himself that the tears rolled down his cheeks.

What put a stop to all this was a sudden fright. Shasta discovered that someone or somebody was walking beside him. It was pitch dark and he could see nothing. And the Thing (or Person) was going so quietly that he could hardly hear any footfalls. What he could hear was breathing. His invisible companion seemed to breathe

«Ну, ничего: куда-нибудь всё равно приеду», — попытался утешить себя Шаста. Дорога и впрямь куда-то вела: лес становился всё гуще, воздух — холоднее. Резкий ветер словно бы пытался и не мог развеять туман. Если бы Шаста бывал в горах, то понял бы, что это значит: они с конём уже очень высоко.

«Какой я несчастный!.. — думал Шаста. — Всем хорошо, мне одному плохо. Король и королева Нарнии вместе со свитой бежали из Ташбаана, а я остался. Аравита, Уинни и Игого сидят у отшельника и горя не знают, а меня, конечно, послали сюда. Король Лум и его люди, наверно, уже в замке и успели закрыть ворота, а я... Да что тут говорить!..»

От голода, усталости и жалости к себе он горько заплакал, но как только слёзы потекли по щекам, почувствовал, что за ним кто-то идёт. Он ничего не видел, только слышал дыхание, и ему казалось, что неведомое существо — очень большое. Он вспомнил, что в этих краях живут великаны, и теперь ему было о чём плакать — только слёзы сразу высохли.

Что-то (или *кто-то*) шло так тихо, что Шаста подумал, не померещилось ли ему, и успокоился, но

on a very large scale, and Shasta got the impression that it was a very large creature. And he had come to notice this breathing so gradually that he had really no idea how long it had been there. It was a horrible shock.

It darted into his mind that he had heard long ago that there were giants in these Northern countries. He bit his lip in terror. But now that he really had something to cry about, he stopped crying.

The Thing (unless it was a Person) went on beside him so very quietly that Shasta began to hope he had only imagined it. But just as he was becoming quite sure of it, there suddenly came a deep, rich sigh out of the darkness beside him. That couldn't be imagination! Anyway, he had felt the hot breath of that sigh on his chilly left hand.

If the horse had been any good — or if he had known how to get any good out of the horse — he would have risked everything on a breakaway and a wild gallop. But he knew he couldn't make that horse gallop. So he went on at a walking pace and the unseen companion walked and breathed beside him. At last he could bear it no longer.

'Who are you?' he said, scarcely above a whisper.

'One who has waited long for you to speak,' said the Thing. Its voice was not loud, but very large and deep.

'Are you — are you a giant?' asked Shasta.

'You might call me a giant,' said the Large Voice. 'But I am not like the creatures you call giants.'

'I can't see you at all,' said Shasta, after staring very hard. Then (for an even more terrible idea had come into his head) he said, almost in a scream, 'You're not — not something *dead*, are you? Oh please — please do go away. What harm have I ever done you? Oh, I am the unluckiest person in the whole world!'

тут услышал очень глубокий вздох и почувствовал на левой щеке горячее дыхание.

Будь бы конь получше — или если бы мальчик знал, как с ним справиться, — то пустился бы вскачь, но, увы, сейчас это невозможно.

Конь шёл неспешно, а существо шло почти рядом. Шаста терпел сколько мог, наконец спросил:

— Кто ты такой? — И услышал негромкий, но очень глубокий голос:

— Тот, кто долго тебя ждал.

— Ты... великан?

— Можешь звать меня и так, но я не из тех созданий.

— Я тебя не вижу. — Шаста вдруг страшно испугался. — А ты... ты не мёртвый? Уйди, уйди, пожалуйста! Что я тебе сделал! Нет, почему мне хуже всех?

Once more he felt the warm breath of the Thing on his hand and face. 'There,' it said, 'that is not the breath of a ghost. Tell me your sorrows.'

Shasta was a little reassured by the breath: so he told how he had never known his real father or mother and had been brought up sternly by the fisherman. And then he told the story of his escape and how they were chased by lions and forced to swim for their lives; and of all their dangers in Tashbaan and about his night among the tombs and how the beasts howled at him out of the desert. And he told about the heat and thirst of their desert journey and how they were almost at their goal when another lion chased them and wounded Aravis. And also, how very long it was since he had had anything to eat.

'I do not call you unfortunate,' said the Large Voice.

'Don't you think it was bad luck to meet so many lions?' said Shasta.

'There was only one lion,' said the Voice.

'What on earth do you mean? I've just told you there were at least two the first night, and — '

'There was only one: but he was swift of foot.'

'How do you know?'

'I was the lion.' And as Shasta gaped with open mouth and said nothing, the Voice continued. 'I was the lion who forced you to join with Aravis. I was the cat who comforted you among the houses of the dead. I was the lion who drove the jackals from you while you slept. I was the lion who gave the Horses the new strength of fear for the last mile so that you should reach King Lune in time. And I was the lion you do not remember who pushed the boat in which you lay, a child near death, so that it came

Тёплое дыхание коснулось его руки и лица, и голос спросил:

— Ну как, живой я или мёртвый? Поделись лучше со мной своими печалями.

И Шаста рассказал ему всё — что не знает своих родителей, что жил у рыбака, что сбежал, что за ним гнались львы, что настрадался от страха среди усыпальниц, а в пустыне были звери, и было жарко, и хотелось пить, а у самой цели ещё один лев погнался за ними и ранил Аравиту. Ещё сказал, что давно ничего не ел.

— Я не назвал бы тебя несчастным, — проговорил голос.

— Да как же! И львы за мной гнались, и...

— Лев был только один, — возразил голос.

— Да нет, в первую ночь их было два, а то и больше, и ещё...

— Лев был один, — повторил голос. — Просто быстро бежал.

— А ты откуда знаешь? — удивился Шаста.

— Это я и был.

Шаста онемел от удивления, а голос продолжил:

— Это я заставил тебя ехать вместе с Аравитой. Это я согревал и охранял тебя среди усыпальниц. Это я — уже львом, а не котом, — отогнал от тебя шакалов. Это я придал лошадям новые силы в самом конце пути, чтобы ты успел предупредить короля Лума. Это я, хоть ты того и не помнишь, пригнал своим дыханием к берегу лодку, в которой лежал умирающий ребёнок.

to shore where a man sat, wakeful at midnight, to receive you.'

'Then it was you who wounded Aravis?'

'It was I.'

'But what for?'

'Child,' said the Voice, 'I am telling you your story, not hers. I tell no one any story but his own.'

'Who *are* you?' asked Shasta.

'Myself,' said the Voice, very deep and low so that the earth shook: and again 'Myself', loud and clear and gay: and then the third time 'Myself', whispered so softly you could hardly hear it, and yet it seemed to come from all round you as if the leaves rustled with it.

Shasta was no longer afraid that the Voice belonged to something that would eat him, nor that it was the voice of a ghost. But a new and different sort of trembling came over him. Yet he felt glad too.

The mist was turning from black to grey and from grey to white. This must have begun to happen some time ago, but while he had been talking to the Thing he had not been noticing anything else. Now, the whiteness around him became a shining whiteness; his eyes began to blink. Somewhere ahead he could hear birds singing. He knew the night was over at last. He could see the mane and ears and head of his horse quite easily now. A golden light fell on them from the left. He thought it was the sun.

He turned and saw, pacing beside him, taller than the horse, a Lion. The horse did not seem to be afraid of it or else could not see it. It was from the Lion that the light came. No one ever saw anything more terrible or beautiful.

Luckily Shasta had lived all his life too far south in Calormen to have heard the tales that were whispered in Tashbaan about a dreadful Narnian demon that appeared in the form of a lion. And of course he knew none

— И Аравиту ранил ты?

— Да, я.

— Зачем же?

— Сын мой, мы сейчас говорим о тебе, не о ней. Я рассказываю каждому только его историю.

— Кто ты такой?

— Я — это я, — произнёс голос так, что задрожали камни, и повторил, чётко и ясно: — Я — это я, — а потом едва слышно, словно листва, обладатель голоса прошелестел: — Я — это я...

Шаста уже не боялся, что его съедят, не боялся, что кто-то — мёртвый, но всё равно *боялся* — и радовался.

Туман стал серым, потом белым, потом сияющим. Где-то впереди запели птицы. Золотой свет падал сбоку на голову лошади. «Солнце встаёт», — подумал Шаста и, поглядев в сторону, увидел огромнейшего льва. Лошадь его не боялась или не видела, хотя светился именно он — солнце ещё не встало. Лев был одновременно устрашающий и невыразимо прекрасный.

Шаста жил до сих пор так далеко, что ни разу не слышал тархистанских толков о страшном демоне, который ходит по Нарнии в обличье льва, и уж тем более не слышал правды об Аслане, Великом льве

of the true stories about Aslan, the great Lion, the son of the Emperor-over-the-sea, the King above all High Kings in Narnia. But after one glance at the Lion's face he slipped out of the saddle and fell at its feet. He couldn't say anything but then he didn't want to say anything, and he knew he needn't say anything.

The High King above all kings stooped towards him. Its mane, and some strange and solemn perfume that hung about the mane, was all round him. It touched his forehead with its tongue. He lifted his face and their eyes met. Then instantly the pale brightness of the mist and the fiery brightness of the Lion rolled themselves together into a swirling glory and gathered themselves up and disappeared. He was alone with the horse on a grassy hillside under a blue sky. And there were birds singing.

и Лесном царе, но, лишь взглянув на него, соскользнул на землю и низко поклонился. Он ничего не сказал, и сказать не мог, и знал, что говорить не нужно.

Царь зверей коснулся носом его лба. Шаста посмотрел на него, и глаза их встретились. Тогда прозрачное сияние воздуха и золотое сияние льва слились воедино и ослепили Шасту, а когда он прозрел, на зелёном склоне, под синим небом, никого не было: только он, да конь, да птицы на деревьях.

Chapter 12

SHASTA IN NARNIA

'Was it all a dream?' wondered Shasta. But it couldn't have been a dream for there in the grass before him he saw the deep, large print of the Lion's front right paw. It took one's breath away to think of the weight that could make a footprint like that. But there was something more remarkable than the size about it. As he looked at it, water had already filled the bottom of it. Soon it was full to the brim, and then overflowing, and a little stream was running downhill, past him, over the grass.

Shasta stooped and drank — a very long drink — and then dipped his face in and splashed his head. It was extremely cold, and clear as glass, and refreshed him very much. After that he stood up, shaking the water out of his ears and flinging the wet hair back from his forehead, and began to take stock of his surroundings.

Apparently it was still very early morning. The sun had only just risen, and it had risen out of the forests which he saw low down and far away on his right. The country which he was looking at was absolutely new to him. It was a green valley-land dotted with trees through which he caught the gleam of a river that wound away roughly to the North-West. On the far side of the valley there were high and even rocky hills, but they were lower than the mountains he had seen yesterday. Then he began to guess where he was. He turned and looked behind him and saw that the slope on which he was standing belonged to a range of far higher mountains.

Глава 12

ШАСТА В НАРНИИ

«Снилось мне это или нет?» — думал Шаста, когда увидел на дороге глубокий след львиной лапы (это была правая лапа, передняя). Ему стало страшно при мысли о том, какой надо обладать силой, чтобы оставить столь огромный и глубокий след. Но тут же он заметил ещё более удивительную вещь: след у него на глазах наполнился водой, она перелилась через край, и резвый ручеёк побежал вниз по склону, петляя по траве.

Шаста слез с коня, напился вволю, окунул в ручей лицо и побрызгал водой на голову. Вода была очень холодная и чистая, как стекло. Потом, поднявшись с колен, вытряхнув воду из ушей, мальчик убрал со лба мокрые волосы и огляделся.

По-видимому, было очень рано: солнце едва взошло; далеко внизу, справа, зеленел лес. Впереди и слева лежала страна, каких он до сих пор не видел: зелёные долины, редкие деревья, мерцание серебристой реки. По ту сторону долины виднелись горы, невысокие, но совсем непохожие на те, которые Шаста только что одолел. И тут он внезапно понял, что это за страна.

'I see,' said Shasta to himself. 'Those are the big mountains between Archenland and Narnia. I was on the other side of them yesterday. I must have come through the pass in the night. What luck that I hit it! — at least it wasn't luck at all really, it was *Him*. And now I'm in Narnia.'

He turned and unsaddled his horse and took off its bridle — 'Though you are a perfectly horrid horse,' he said. It took no notice of this remark and immediately began eating grass. That horse had a very low opinion of Shasta.

'I wish I could eat grass!' thought Shasta. 'It's no good going back to Anvard, it'll all be besieged. I'd better get lower down into the valley and see if I can get anything to eat.'

So he went on downhill (the thick dew was cruelly cold to his bare feet) till he came into a wood. There was a kind of track running through it and he had not followed this for many minutes when he heard a thick and rather wheezy voice saying to him,

'Good morning, neighbour.'

Shasta looked round eagerly to find the speaker and presently saw a small, prickly person with a dark face who had just come out from among the trees. At least, it

«Вон что! Я перевалил через хребет, отделяющий Орландию от Нарнии. И ночью... Как мне повезло, однако! Нет, при чём тут «повезло», это всё *он*! Теперь я в Нарнии».

Шаста расседлал коня, и тот тут же принялся щипать траву.

— Ты *очень* плохой конь, — сказал ему Шаста, но тот и ухом не повёл, поскольку тоже был о нём невысокого мнения.

«Ах если бы я мог есть траву! — подумал Шаста. — В Анвард идти нельзя, он осаждён. Надо спуститься в долину — может, кто-нибудь меня накормит».

И он побежал вниз по холодной мокрой траве, а добежав до рощи, услышал низкий, глуховатый голос:

— Доброе утро, сосед.

Шаста огляделся и увидел небольшое существо, которое вылезло из-за деревьев. То есть оно было небольшим для человека, но для ежа — просто огромным.

was small for a person but very big indeed for a hedgehog, which was what it was.

'Good morning,' said Shasta. 'But I'm not a neighbour. In fact I'm a stranger in these parts.'

'Ah?' said the Hedgehog inquiringly.

'I've come over the mountains — from Archenland, you know.'

'Ha, Archenland,' said the Hedgehog. 'That's a terrible long way. Never been there myself.'

'And I think, perhaps,' said Shasta, 'someone ought to be told that there's an army of savage Calormenes attacking Anvard at this very moment.'

'You don't say so!' answered the Hedgehog. 'Well, think of that. And they do say that Calormen is hundreds and thousands of miles away, right at the world's end, across a great sea of sand.'

'It's not nearly as far as you think,' said Shasta. 'And oughtn't something to be done about this attack on Anvard? Oughtn't your High King to be told?'

'Certain sure, something ought to be done about it,' said the Hedgehog. 'But you see I'm just on my way to bed for a good day's sleep. Hullo, neighbour!'

The last words were addressed to an immense biscuit-coloured rabbit whose head had just popped up from somewhere beside the path. The Hedgehog immediately told the Rabbit what it had just learned from Shasta. The Rabbit agreed that this was very remarkable news and that somebody ought to tell someone about it with a view to doing something.

And so it went on. Every few minutes they were joined by other creatures, some from the branches overhead and some from little underground houses at their feet, till the party consisted of five rabbits, a squirrel, two magpies, a goat-foot faun, and a mouse, who all talked at

— Доброе утро, — ответил мальчик. — Только я не сосед, я нездешний.

— Да? Откуда же ты?

— Вчера я был в Орландии, а ещё раньше...

— Орландия — это далеко, — перебил его ёж. — Я там не бывал.

— Понимаешь, злые тархистанцы хотят захватить Анвард, — сказал Шаста. — Надо предупредить вашего короля.

— Ну что ты! — воскликнул ёж. — Эти тархистанцы очень далеко, на краю света, за песчаным морем.

— Не так они и далеко, — возразил Шаста. — Что-то надо делать.

— Да, делать надо, — согласился ёж. — Но сейчас я занят, иду спать. Здравствуй, сосед!

Слова эти относились к огромному желтоватому кролику, которому ёж немедленно рассказал новость. Кролик согласился, что делать что-то надо, и так пошло: каждые несколько минут то с ветки, то из норы появлялось какое-нибудь существо, пока, наконец, не собрался отрядец из пяти кроликов, белки, двух галок, козлоногого фавна и мыши, причём все они говорили одновременно, соглашаясь с ежом. В то золотое время, когда, победив колдунью, Нарнией правил король Питер с братом и двумя сёстрами, мелкие лесные твари жили так счастливо, что распустились.

the same time and all agreed with the Hedgehog. For the truth was that in that golden age when the Witch and the Winter had gone and Peter the High King ruled at Cair Paravel, the smaller woodland people of Narnia were so safe and happy that they were getting a little careless.

Presently, however, two more practical people arrived in the little wood. One was a Red Dwarf whose name appeared to be Duffle. The other was a stag, a beautiful lordly creature with wide liquid eyes, dappled flanks and legs so thin and graceful that they looked as if you could break them with two fingers.

'Lion alive!' roared the Dwarf as soon as he had heard the news. 'And if that's so, why are we all standing still, chattering? Enemies at Anvard! News must be sent to Cair Paravel at once. The army must be called out. Narnia must go to the aid of King Lune.'

'Ah!' said the Hedgehog. 'But you won't find the High King at the Cair. He's away to the North trouncing those giants. And talking of giants, neighbours, that puts me in mind — '

'Who'll take our message?' interrupted the Dwarf. 'Anyone here got more speed than me?'

'I've got speed,' said the Stag. 'What's my message? How many Calormenes?'

'Two hundred: under Prince Rabadash. And — ' But the Stag was already away — all four legs off the ground at once, and in a moment its white stern had disappeared among the remoter trees.

'Wonder where he's going,' said a Rabbit. 'He won't find the High King at Cair Paravel, you know.'

'He'll find Queen Lucy,' said Duffle. 'And then — hullo! What's wrong with the Human? It looks pretty green. Why, I do believe it's quite faint. Perhaps it's mortal hungry. When did you last have a meal, youngster?'

Вскоре пришли два существа поразумней: гном по имени Даффл и прекрасный олень с такими тонкими красивыми ногами, что их, казалось, можно переломить двумя пальцами.

— Клянусь Асланом! — проревел гном, услышав новость. — Что же мы стоим и болтаем? Враг в Орландии! Скорее в Кэр-Параваль! Нарния поможет доброму королю Луму.

— Ф-фух! — сказал ёж. — Король Питер не в Кэр-Паравале, а на севере, где великаны. Кстати о великанах, я вспомнил...

— Кто же туда побежит? — перебил его Даффл. — Я не умею быстро бегать.

— А я умею, — сказал олень. — Что передать? Сколько там тархистанцев?

— Двести, — едва успел ответить Шаста, а олень уже нёсся стрелой к Кэр-Паравалю.

— Куда это он? — удивился кролик. — Короля Питера там нет...

— Королева Люси в замке, — сказал гном. — Человечек, что это с тобой? Ты совсем зелёный. Когда ты ел в последний раз?

'Yesterday morning,' said Shasta weakly.

'Come on, then, come on,' said the Dwarf, at once throwing his thick little arms round Shasta's waist to support him. 'Why, neighbours, we ought all to be ashamed of ourselves! You come with me, lad. Breakfast! Better than talking.'

With a great deal of bustle, muttering reproaches to itself, the Dwarf half led and half supported Shasta at a great speed further into the wood and a little downhill. It was a longer walk than Shasta wanted at that moment and his legs had begun to feel very shaky before they came out from the trees on to bare hillside. There they found a little house with a smoking chimney and an open door, and as they came to the doorway Duffle called out,

'Hey, brothers! A visitor for breakfast.'

And immediately, mixed with a sizzling sound, there came to Shasta a simply delightful smell. It was one he had never smelled in his life before, but I hope you have. It was, in fact, the smell of bacon and eggs and mushrooms all frying in a pan.

'Mind your head, lad,' said Duffle a moment too late, for Shasta had already bashed his forehead against the low lintel of the door. 'Now,' continued the Dwarf, 'sit you down. The table's a bit low for you, but then the stool's low too. That's right. And here's porridge — and here's a jug of cream — and here's a spoon.'

By the time Shasta had finished his porridge, the Dwarf's two brothers (whose names were Rogin and Bricklethumb) were putting the dish of bacon and eggs and mushrooms, and the coffee pot and the hot milk, and the toast, on the table.

It was all new and wonderful to Shasta for Calormene food is quite different. He didn't even know what the slices of brown stuff were, for he had never seen toast

— Вчера утром, — вздохнул Шаста.

Гном сразу же обнял его своей крошечной ручкой и воскликнул:

— Идём же, идём! Ах, друзья мои, как стыдно! Сейчас мы тебя накормим. А то стоим, болтаем...

Даффл быстро повёл путника в небольшой лесок. Шаста едва мог сделать и несколько шагов: ноги дрожали, — но тут они вышли на лужайку, где стоял домик, из трубы которого шёл дым, а дверь была открыта.

— Братцы, а у нас гость! — крикнул Даффл.

В тот же миг Шаста почуял дивный запах, неведомый ему, но хорошо известный нам с вами, яичницы с ветчиной и жарящихся грибов.

— Смотри не ушибись, — предупредил гном, но поздно: Шаста стукнулся головой о притолоку. — Теперь садись к столу. Он низковат, но и стул маленький. Вот так.

Перед Шастой поставили миску овсянки и кружку сливок. Мальчик ещё не доел кашу, а братья Даффл, Роджин и Брикл уже несли сковороду с яичницей, грибы и кофейник.

Шаста в жизни не ел и не пил ничего подобного, даже не знал, что за ноздреватые прямоугольники лежат в особой корзинке и почему карлики покры-

before. He didn't know what the yellow soft thing they smeared on the toast was, because in Calormen you nearly always get oil instead of butter. And the house itself was quite different from the dark, frowsty, fish-smelling hut of Arsheesh and from the pillared and carpeted halls in the palaces of Tashbaan. The roof was very low, and everything was made of wood, and there was a cuckoo-clock and a red-and-white checked tablecloth and a bowl of wild flowers and little curtains on the thick-paned windows. It was also rather troublesome having to use dwarf cups and plates and knives and forks. This meant that helpings were very small, but then there were a great many helpings, so that Shasta's plate or cup was being filled every moment, and every moment the Dwarfs themselves were saying, 'Butter please', or 'Another cup of coffee,' or 'I'd like a few more mushrooms,' or 'What about frying another egg or so?' And when at last they had all eaten as much as they possibly could the three Dwarfs drew lots for who would do the washing-up, and Rogin was the unlucky one. Then Duffle and Bricklethumb took Shasta outside to a bench which ran against the cottage wall, and they all stretched out their legs and gave a great sigh of contentment and the two Dwarfs lit their pipes. The dew was off the grass now and the sun was warm; indeed, if there hadn't been a light breeze, it would have been too hot.

'Now, Stranger,' said Duffle, 'I'll show you the lie of the land. You can see nearly all South Narnia from here, and we're rather proud of the view. Right away on your left, beyond those near hills, you can just see the Western Mountains. And that round hill away on your right is called the Hill of the Stone Table. Just beyond — '

But at that moment he was interrupted by a snore from Shasta who, what with his night's journey and his

вают их чем-то мягким и жёлтым (в Тархистане есть только оливковое масло).

Домик был совершенно не похож ни на тёмную, пропахшую рыбой хижину, ни на роскошный дворец в Ташбаане. Здесь всё ему нравилось — и низкий потолок, и деревянная мебель, и часы с кукушкой, и букет полевых цветов, и скатерть в красную клетку, и белые занавески. Одно было плохо: посуда оказалась слишком маленькой, — но справились и с этим — и миску, и чашку вновь и вновь наполняли, приговаривая: «Кофейку?», «Грибочков?», «Может, ещё яичницы?». Когда пришла пора мыть посуду, братья бросили жребий. Роджин остался убирать, а Даффл и Брикл вышли из домика, сели на скамейку и, с облегчением вздохнув, закурили трубки. Роса уже высохла, солнце припекало, и, если бы не ветерок, было бы жарко.

— Чужеземец, — сказал Даффл, — смотри, вот наша Нарния. Отсюда видно всё до южной границы, и мы этим очень гордимся. По правую руку — Западные горы. Именно там — Каменный Стол. За ними...

И тут раздался лёгкий храп — сытый и усталый Шаста заснул. Добрые гномы стали общаться же-

excellent breakfast, had gone fast asleep. The kindly Dwarfs, as soon as they noticed this, began making signs to each other not to wake him, and indeed did so much whispering and nodding and getting up and tiptoeing away that they certainly would have waked him if he had been less tired.

He slept pretty well nearly all day but woke up in time for supper. The beds in that house were all too small for him but they made him a fine bed of heather on the floor, and he never stirred nor dreamed all night. Next morning they had just finished breakfast when they heard a shrill, exciting sound from outside.

'Trumpets!' said all the Dwarfs, as they and Shasta all came running out.

The trumpets sounded again: a new noise to Shasta, not huge and solemn like the horns of Tashbaan nor gay and merry like King Lune's hunting horn, but clear and sharp and valiant. The noise was coming from the woods to the East, and soon there was a noise of horse-hoofs mixed with it. A moment later the head of the column came into sight.

First came the Lord Peridan on a bay horse carrying the great banner of Narnia — a red lion on a green ground. Shasta knew him at once. Then came three people riding abreast, two on great chargers and one on a pony. The two on the chargers were King Edmund and a fair-haired lady with a very merry face who wore a helmet and a mail shirt and carried a bow across her shoulder and a quiver full of arrows at her side. ('The Queen Lucy,' whispered Duffle.) But the one on the pony was Corin. After that came the main body of the army: men on ordinary horses, men on Talking Horses (who didn't mind being ridden on proper occasions, as when Narnia went to war), centaurs, stern, hard-bitten bears,

стами и говорить шёпотом, но так суетились, что он проснулся бы, если бы мог.

Ближе к ужину мальчик всё же проснулся, ещё раз поел и лёг в удобную постель, которую соорудили для него на полу из вереска, потому что в их деревянные кроватки он бы не влез. Шаста спал как убитый — даже сны не снились, — а утром лесок огласили звуки труб.

Гномы и Шаста выбежали из домика. Трубы затрубили снова — не грозные, как в Ташбаане, и не весёлые, как в Орландии, а чистые, звонкие и смелые. Вскоре зацокали копыта и из лесу выехал отряд.

Первым ехал лорд Перидан на гнедом коне, и в руке у него было знамя — алый лев на зелёном поле. Шаста сразу узнал этого льва. За ним следовал король Эдмунд и светловолосая девушка с очень весёлым лицом; на плече у неё был лук, на голове — шлем, у пояса — колчан, полный стрел («Королева Люси», — прошептал Даффл). Дальше на пони ехал принц Корин, а потом — и весь отряд, в котором, кроме людей и говорящих коней, были говорящие псы, кентавры, медведи и шестеро великанов. Да, в Нарнии есть и добрые великаны, только их меньше, чем злых. Шаста понял, что они не враги, но смотреть на них не решился, тут надо привыкнуть.

great Talking Dogs, and last of all six giants. For there are good giants in Narnia. But though he knew they were on the right side Shasta at first could hardly bear to look at them; there are some things that take a lot of getting used to.

Just as the King and Queen reached the cottage and the Dwarfs began making low bows to them, King Edmund called out,

'Now, friends! Time for a halt and a morsel!' and at once there was a great bustle of people dismounting and haversacks being opened and conversation beginning when Corin came running up to Shasta and seized both his hands and cried,

'What! *You* here! So you got through all right? I *am* glad. Now we shall have some sport. And isn't it luck! We only got into harbour at Cair Paravel yesterday morning and the very first person who met us was Chervy the Stag with all this news of an attack on Anvard. Don't you think — '

'Who is your Highness's friend?' said King Edmund who had just got off his horse.

'Don't you see, Sire?' said Corin. 'It's my double: the boy you mistook me for at Tashbaan.'

'Why, so he is your double,' exclaimed Queen Lucy. 'As like as two twins. This is a marvellous thing.'

'Please, your Majesty,' said Shasta to King Edmund, 'I was no traitor, really I wasn't. And I couldn't help hearing your plans. But I'd never have dreamed of telling them to your enemies.'

'I know now that you were no traitor, boy,' said King Edmund, laying his hand on Shasta's head. 'But if you would not be taken for one, another time try not to hear what's meant for other ears. But all's well.'

Поравнявшись с домиком (гномы стали кланяться), король крикнул:

— Друзья, не пора ли нам отдохнуть и подкрепиться?

Все шумно спешились, а принц Корин стрелой кинулся к Шасте, обнял его и воскликнул:

— Вот здорово! Ты здесь! А мы только высадились в Паравале, как прибежал Черво, олень, и всё нам рассказал. Как ты думаешь...

— Не представишь ли нам своего друга? — предложил король Эдмунд.

— Вы разве не помните, ваше величество? — удивился Корин. — Это же его вы приняли за меня в Ташбаане.

— Как они похожи! — вскричала королева. — Просто близнецы! Вот чудеса-то!

— Ваше величество, — сказал Шаста, — я вас не предал, не думайте. Хоть я и всё слышал, но никому не сказал!

— Я знаю, что ты не предатель, друг мой, — сказал король Эдмунд и положил ему руку на голову. — А вообще-то лучше не слушать то, что не предназначено для твоих ушей. Постарайся уж!

After that there was so much bustle and talk and coming and going that Shasta for a few minutes lost sight of Corin and Edmund and Lucy. But Corin was the sort of boy whom one is sure to hear of pretty soon and it wasn't very long before Shasta heard King Edmund saying in a loud voice:

'By the Lion's Mane, prince, this is too much! Will your Highness never be better? You are more of a heart's-scald than our whole army together! I'd as lief have a regiment of hornets in my command as you.'

Shasta wormed his way through the crowd and there saw Edmund, looking very angry indeed, Corin looking a little ashamed of himself, and a strange Dwarf sitting on the ground making faces. A couple of fauns had apparently just been helping it out of its armour.

'If I had but my cordial with me,' Queen Lucy was saying, 'I could soon mend this. But the High King has so strictly charged me not to carry it commonly to the wars and to keep it only for great extremities!'

What had happened was this. As soon as Corin had spoken to Shasta, Corin's elbow had been plucked by a Dwarf in the army called Thornbut.

'What is it, Thornbut?' Corin had said.

'Your Royal Highness,' said Thornbut, drawing him aside, 'our march today will bring us through the pass and right to your royal father's castle. We may be in battle before night.'

'I know,' said Corin. 'Isn't it splendid?'

'Splendid or not,' said Thornbut, 'I have the strictest orders from King Edmund to see to it that your Highness is not in the fight. You will be allowed to see it, and that's treat enough for your Highness's little years.'

'Oh, what nonsense!' Corin burst out. 'Of course I'm going to fight. Why, the Queen Lucy's going to be with the archers.'

Тут поднялся невообразимый шум и звон — ведь все были в кольчугах, — и Шаста минут на пять потерял из виду и Корина, и Эдмунда, и Люси. Но принц был не из тех, кого можно не заметить, и вскоре он в этом убедился.

— Ну что это, клянусь львом?! — раздался громкий голос короля. — С тобой, принц, больше хлопот, чем со всем войском.

Шаста пробился через толпу и увидел, что король разгневан, Корин немножко смущён, а незнакомый гном сидит на земле и чуть не плачет. Два фавна помогали ему снять кольчугу.

— Ах, будь у меня с собой лекарство! — посетовала королева Люси. — Король Питер строго-настрого запретил мне брать его в сражения.

А случилось вот что. Когда Корин поговорил с Шастой, его гном Торн взял принца за локоть и, отводя в сторонку, сказал:

— Ваше высочество, надеюсь, к ночи мы прибудем в замок вашего отца. Возможно, тогда и будет битва.

— Знаю. Вот здорово!

— Это дело вкуса, — уклончиво ответил гном. — Дело в том, что король Эдмунд наказал мне не пускать ваше высочество в битву. Вы можете смотреть — и на том спасибо, в ваши-то годы!

— Какая чепуха! — рассердился Корин. — Я обязательно буду сражаться! Королева Люси возглавит лучников, а я...

'The Queen's grace will do as she pleases,' said Thornbut. 'But you are in my charge. Either I must have your solemn and princely word that you'll keep your pony beside mine — not half a neck ahead — till I give your Highness leave to depart: or else — it is his Majesty's word — we must go with our wrists tied together like two prisoners.'

'I'll knock you down if you try to bind me,' said Corm.

'I'd like to see your Highness do it,' said the Dwarf.

That was quite enough for a boy like Corin and in a second he and the Dwarf were at it hammer and tongs. It would have been an even match for, though Corin had longer arms and more height, the Dwarf was older and tougher. But it was never fought out (that's the worst of fights on a rough hillside) for by very bad luck Thornbut trod on a loose stone, came flat down on his nose, and found when he tried to get up that he had sprained his ankle: a real excruciating sprain which would keep him from walking or riding for at least a fortnight.

'See what your Highness has done,' said King Edmund. 'Deprived us of a proved warrior on the very edge of battle.'

'I'll take his place, Sire,' said Corin.

'Pshaw,' said Edmund. 'No one doubts your courage. But a boy in battle is a danger only to his own side.'

At that moment the King was called away to attend to something else, and Corin, after apologizing handsomely to the Dwarf, rushed up to Shasta and whispered,

'Quick. There's a spare pony now, and the Dwarf's armour. Put it on before anyone notices.'

'What for?' said Shasta.

'Why, so that you and I can fight in the battle of course! Don't you want to?'

— Её величество вольны решать сами, — оборвал его Торн, — но вас его величество поручил мне. Дайте слово, что ваш пони не отойдёт от моего, или, по приказу короля, нас обоих свяжут.

— Да я им!.. — возмутился Корин.

— Хотел бы я на это взглянуть.

Вот этого Корин уже вынести не мог. Принц был выше, Торн — крепче и старше, и неизвестно, чем кончилась бы драка, если бы началась, но гном поскользнулся (вот почему не стоит драться на склоне), упал и сильно ушиб ногу — так сильно, что провалялся в постели две недели.

— Смотри, принц, что ты натворил! — попенял ему король Эдмунд. — Один из лучших наших воинов выбыл из строя.

— Я его заменю, сир!

— Ты храбр, сомнений нет, но в битве мальчик может ненароком нанести урон своим.

Тут короля кто-то позвал, и Корин, очень учтиво попросив прощения у гнома, зашептал Шасте на ухо:

— Скорее садись на его пони, бери его щит!

— Зачем?

— Да чтобы сражаться вместе со мной! — воскликнул Корин. — Ты что, не хочешь?

'Oh — ah, yes, of course,' said Shasta. But he hadn't been thinking of doing so at all, and began to get a most uncomfortable prickly feeling in his spine.

'That's right,' said Corin. 'Over your head. Now the sword-belt. But we must ride near the tail of the column and keep as quiet as mice. Once the battle begins every-one will be far too busy to notice us.'

— Ах да, конечно... — растерянно пробормотал Шаста, в то время как Корин уже натягивал на него кольчугу (с гнома её сняли, прежде чем внести его в домик), комментируя свои действия:

— Так. Через голову. Теперь меч. Поедем в хвосте, тихо, как мыши. Когда начнётся сражение, всем будет не до нас.

Chapter 13

THE FIGHT AT ANVARD

By about eleven o'clock the whole company was once more on the march, riding westward with the mountains on their left. Corin and Shasta rode right at the rear with the Giants immediately in front of them. Lucy and Edmund and Peridan were busy with their plans for the battle and though Lucy once said, 'But where is his goosecap Highness?' Edmund only replied, 'Not in the front, and that's good news enough. Leave well alone.'

Shasta told Corin most of his adventures and explained that he had learned all his riding from a horse and didn't really know how to use the reins. Corin instructed him in this, besides telling him all about their secret sailing from Tashbaan.

'And where is the Queen Susan?'

'At Cair Paravel,' said Corin. 'She's not like Lucy, you know, who's as good as a man, or at any rate as good as a boy. Queen Susan is more like an ordinary grown-up lady. She doesn't ride to the wars, though she is an excellent archer.'

The hillside path which they were following became narrower all the time and the drop on their right hand became steeper. At last they were going in single file along the edge of a precipice and Shasta shuddered to think that he had done the same last night without knowing it. 'But of course,' he thought, 'I was quite safe. That is why the Lion kept on my left. He was between me and the edge all the time.'

Глава 13

БИТВА

Часам к одиннадцати отряд двинулся к западу (горы были от него слева). Корин и Шаста ехали сзади, прямо за великанами. Люси, Эдмунд и Перидан были заняты предстоящей битвой, и хотя Люси спросила: «А где этот зверюга принц?» Эдмунд ответил: «Впереди его нет, и на том спасибо».

Шаста тем временем рассказывал принцу, что научился ездить верхом у коня и не умеет пользоваться уздечкой. Корин показал ему, потом описал, как они отплывали из Ташбаана.

— Где королева Сьюзен? — спросил Шаста.

— В Кэр-Паравале, — ответил Корин. — Люси у нас не хуже мужчины, то есть мальчика, а Сьюзен больше похожа на взрослую. Правда, Люси здорово стреляет из лука.

Тропа стала уже, и справа открылась пропасть. Теперь они ехали гуськом, по одному. «А я тут ехал, — подумал Шаста и вздрогнул. — Вот почему лев был по левую руку — шёл между мной и пропастью».

Then the path went left and south away from the cliff and there were thick woods on both sides of it and they went steeply up and up into the pass. There would have been a splendid view from the top if it were open ground but among all those trees you could see nothing — only, every now and then, some huge pinnacle of rock above the tree-tops, and an eagle or two wheeling high up in the blue air.

'They smell battle,' said Corin, pointing at the birds. 'They know we're preparing a feed for them.'

Shasta didn't like this at all.

When they had crossed the neck of the pass and come a good deal lower they reached more open ground and from here Shasta could see all Archenland, blue and hazy, spread out below him and even (he thought) a hint of the desert beyond it. But the sun, which had perhaps two hours or so to go before it set, was in his eyes and he couldn't make things out distinctly.

Here the army halted and spread out in a line, and there was a great deal of rearranging. A whole detachment of very dangerous-looking Talking Beasts whom Shasta had not noticed before and who were mostly of the cat kind (leopards, panthers, and the like) went padding and growling to take up their positions on the left. The giants were ordered to the right, and before going there they all took off something they had been carrying on their backs and sat down for a moment. Then Shasta saw that what they had been carrying and were now putting on were pairs of boots: horrid, heavy, spiked boots which came up to their knees. Then they sloped their huge clubs over their shoulders and marched to their battle position. The archers, with Queen Lucy, fell to the rear and you could first see them bending their bows and then hear the twang-twang as they tested the strings. And wherever

Тропа свернула влево, к югу, по сторонам теперь стоял густой лес. Отряд поднимался всё выше. Если бы здесь была поляна, вид открылся бы прекрасный, а так — иногда над деревьями мелькали скалы, в небе летали орлы.

— Чуют добычу, — сказал Корин.

Шасте это не понравилось.

Когда одолели перевал, спустились пониже и лес стал пореже, перед ними открылась Орландия в голубой дымке, а за нею, вдалеке, — жёлтая полоска пустыни. Отряд, который мы можем назвать и войском, остановился ненадолго, и Шаста только теперь увидел, сколько в нём говорящих зверей, большей частью похожих на огромных кошек. Они расположились слева, великаны — справа. Шаста обратил внимание, что они всё время несли на спине, а сейчас надели огромные сапоги, высокие, до самых колен, потом положили на плечи тяжёлые дубинки и вернулись на своё место. В арьергарде были лучники, среди них — королева Люси. Стоял звон — все рыцари надевали шлемы, обнажали мечи, поправляли кольчуги, сбросив плащи на землю. Никто не разговаривал. Это было очень торжественно и страшно, и Шаста подумал: «Ну я и попался...» Издалека донеслись какие-то тяжкие удары.

you looked you could see people tightening girths, putting on helmets, drawing swords, and throwing cloaks to the ground. There was hardly any talking now. It was very solemn and very dreadful. 'I'm in for it now — I really am in for it now,' thought Shasta. Then there came noises far ahead: the sound of many men shouting and a steady thud-thud-thud.

'Battering ram,' whispered Corin. 'They're battering the gate.'

Even Corin looked quite serious now.

'Why doesn't King Edmund get *on*?' he said. 'I can't stand this waiting about. Chilly too.'

Shasta nodded: hoping he didn't look as frightened as felt.

The trumpet at last! On the move now — now trotting — the banner streaming out in the wind. They had topped low ridge now, and below them the whole scene suddenly opened out; a little, many-towered castle with its gate towards them. No moat, unfortunately, but of course the gate shut and the portcullis down. On the walls they could see, like little white dots, the faces of the defenders. Down below, about fifty of the Calormenes, dismounted, were steadily swinging a great tree trunk against the gate. But at once the scene changed. The main bulk of Rabadash's men had been on foot ready to assault the gate. But now he had seen the Narnians sweeping down from the ridge. There is no doubt those Calormenes are wonderfully trained. It seemed to Shasta only a second before a whole line of the enemy were on horseback again, wheeling round to meet them, swinging towards them.

And now a gallop. The ground between the two armies grew less every moment. Faster, faster. All swords out now, all shields up to the nose, all prayers said, all teeth clenched. Shasta was dreadfully frightened. But it

— Таран, — сказал принц. — Таранят ворота. Почему король Эдмунд так тянет? Поскорей бы уже! И холодно...

Шаста кивнул, надеясь, что не очень заметно, как он испуган.

И тут пропели трубы! Отряд тронулся рысью, и очень скоро показался небольшой замок с множеством башен. Ворота были закрыты, мост поднят. Над стенами, словно белые точки, виднелись лица орландцев. Человек пятьдесят били стену большим бревном. Завидев отряд, они мгновенно вскочили в сёдла (клеветать не буду, тархистанцы прекрасно обучены).

Нарнийцы понеслись вскачь. Все выхватили мечи, все прикрылись щитами, все сжали зубы, все помолились льву. Два воинства сближались. Шаста себя не помнил от страха, но вдруг по-

suddenly came into his head, 'If you funk this, you'll funk every battle all your life. Now or never.'

But when at last the two lines met he had really very little idea of what happened. There was a frightful confusion; and an appalling noise. His sword was knocked clean out of his hand pretty soon. And he'd got the reins tangled somehow. Then he found himself slipping. Then a spear came straight at him and as he ducked to avoid it he rolled right off his horse, bashed his left knuckles terribly against someone else's armour, and then — But it is no use trying to describe the battle from Shasta's point of view; he understood too little of the fight in general and even of his own part in it. The best way I can tell you what really happened is to take you some miles away to where the Hermit of the Southern March sat gazing into the smooth pool beneath the spreading tree, with Bree and Hwin and Aravis beside him.

For it was in this pool that the Hermit looked when he wanted to know what was going on in the world outside the green walls of his hermitage. There, as in a mirror, he could see, at certain times, what was going on in the streets of cities far farther south than Tashbaan, or what ships were putting into Redhaven in the remote Seven Isles, or what robbers or wild beasts stirred in the great Western forests between Lantern Waste and Telmar. And all this day he had hardly left his pool, even to eat or drink, for he knew that great events were on foot in Archenland. Aravis and the Horses gazed into it too. They could see it was a magic pool: instead of reflecting the tree and the sky it revealed cloudy and coloured shapes moving, always moving, in its depths. But they could see nothing clearly. The Hermit could and from time to time he told them what he saw. A little while before Shasta rode into his first battle, the Hermit had begun speaking like this:

думал: «Если струсишь теперь, будешь трусить всю жизнь».

Когда отряды встретились, он перестал понимать что бы то ни было. Всё смешалось, стоял страшный грохот. Меч у него очень скоро выбили, а уздечку он сам выпустил из рук. Увидев, что в него летит копьё, он наклонился вбок, и соскользнул с коня, и ударился о чей-то доспех, и... Но мы расскажем не о том, что видел Шаста, а о том, что видел в пруду отшельник, рядом с которым стояли лошади и Аравита.

Именно в этом пруду он видел как в зеркале, что творится много южнее Ташбаана, какие корабли входят в Алую гавань на далёких островах, какие разбойники или звери рыщут в лесах Тельмара. Сегодня он от пруда не отходил, даже не ел, ибо знал, что происходит в Орландии. Аравита и лошади тоже смотрели. Они понимали, что пруд волшебный — в нём отражались не деревья и не облака, а странные туманные картины. Отшельник видел лучше, чётче и пересказывал им. Незадолго до того как Шаста принял участие в своей первой битве, он сказал:

'I see one — two — three eagles wheeling in the gap by Stormness Head. One is the oldest of all the eagles. He would not be out unless battle was at hand. I see him wheel to and fro, peering down sometimes at Anvard and sometimes to the east, behind Stormness. Ah — I see now what Rabadash and his men have been so busy at all day. They have felled and lopped a great tree and they are now coming out of the woods carrying it as a ram. They have learned something from the failure of last night's assault. He would have been wiser if he had set his men to making ladders: but it takes too long and he is impatient. Fool that he is! He ought to have ridden back to Tashbaan as soon as the first attack failed, for his whole plan depended on speed and surprise. Now they are bringing their ram into position. King Lune's men are shooting hard from the walls. Five Calormenes have fallen: but not many will. They have their shields above their heads. Rabadash is giving his orders now. With him are his most trusted lords, fierce Tarkaans from the eastern provinces.

— Я вижу орла... двух орлов... трёх... над пиком Бурь. Самый большой из них — самый старый из всех здешних орлов. Они чуют битву. А, вот почему люди Рабадаша так трудились весь день!.. Они тащат огромное дерево. Вчерашняя неудача чему-то их да научила. Лучше бы им сделать лестницы, но это долго, а Рабадаш нетерпелив. Какой, однако, глупец!.. Он должен был вчера уйти подобру-поздорову. Не удалась атака — и всё, ведь он мог рассчитывать только на внезапность. Нацелили бревно... Орландцы осыпают их стрелами... Они закрывают головы щитами... Рабадаш что-то кричит. Рядом с ним его приближённые. Вот Корадин из Тормунга, вот Азрох, Кламаш, Илгамут и какой-то тархан с красной бородой...

I can see their faces. There is Corradin of Castle Tormunt, and Azrooh, and Chlamash, and Ilgamuth of the twisted lip, and a tall Tarkaan with a crimson beard — '

'By the Mane, my old master Anradin!' said Bree.

'S-s-sh,' said Aravis.

'Now the ram has started. If I could hear as well as see, what a noise that would make! Stroke after stroke: and no gate can stand it for ever. But wait! Something up by Stormness has scared the birds. They're coming out in masses. And wait again... I can't see yet... ah! Now I can. The whole ridge, up on the east, is black with horsemen. If only the wind would catch that standard and spread it out. They're over the ridge now, whoever they are. Aha! I've seen the banner now. Narnia, Narnia! It's the red lion. They're in full career down the hill now. I can see King Edmund. There's a woman behind among the archers. Oh! — '

'What is it?' asked Hwin breathlessly.

'All his Cats are dashing out from the left of the line.'

'Cats?' said Aravis.

'Great cats, leopards and such,' said the Hermit impatiently. 'I see, I see. The Cats are coming round in a circle to get at the horses of the dismounted men. A good stroke. The Calormene horses are mad with terror already. Now the Cats are in among them. But Rabadash has reformed his line and has a hundred men in the saddle. They're riding to meet the Narnians. There's only a hundred yards between the two lines now. Only fifty. I can see King Edmund, I can see the Lord Peridan. There are two mere children in the Narnian line. What can the King be about to let them into battle? Only ten yards — the lines have met. The Giants on the Narnian right are doing wonders... but one's down... shot through

— Мой хозяин! — вскричал Игого. — Клянусь львом, это Анрадин.

— Тише!.. — сказала Аравита.

— Таранят ворота. Ну и грохот, я думаю! Таранят... ещё... ещё... ни одни ворота не выдержат. Кто же это скачет с горы? Спугнули орлов... Сколько воинов! А, вижу знамя с алым львом! Это Нарния. Вот и король Эдмунд. И королева Люси, и лучники... и коты!

— Коты? — переспросила Аравита.

— Да, боевые коты. Леопарды, барсы, пантеры. Они сейчас нападут на коней... Так! Тархистанские кони мечутся. Коты вцепились в них. Рабадаш посылает в бой ещё сотню всадников. Между отрядами сто ярдов... пятьдесят.. Вот король Эдмунд, вот лорд Перидан... И какие-то дети... Как же это король разрешил им сражаться? Десять ярдов... Встретились. Великаны творят чудеса... один упал... В середине ничего не разберёшь, слева яснее. Вот опять эти мальчики... Аслан милостивый! Это принц Корин и ваш друг Шаста. Они похожи как две капли воды. Корин сражается как истинный рыцарь... вот убил тархистанца. Теперь я вижу и середину... Ко-

the eye, I suppose. The centre's all in a muddle. I can see more on the left. There are the two boys again. Lion alive! one is Prince Corin. The other, like him as two peas. It's your little Shasta. Corin is fighting like a man. He's killed a Calormene. I can see a bit of the centre now. Rabadash and Edmund almost met then, but the press has separated them — '

'What about Shasta?' said Aravis.

'Oh, the fool!' groaned the Hermit. 'Poor, brave little fool. He knows nothing about this work. He's making no use at all of his shield. His whole side's exposed. He hasn't the faintest idea what to do with his sword. Oh, he's remembered it now. He's waving it wildly about... nearly cut his own pony's head off, and he will in a moment if he's not careful. It's been knocked out of his hand now. It's mere murder sending a child into the battle; he can't live five minutes. Duck, you fool — oh, he's down.'

'Killed?' asked three voices breathlessly.

'How can I tell?' said the Hermit. 'The Cats have done their work. All the riderless horses are dead or escaped now: no retreat for the Calormenes on them. Now the Cats are turning back into the main battle. They're leaping on the rams-men. The ram is down. Oh, good! good! The gates are opening from the inside: there's going to be a sortie. The first three are out. It's King Lune in the middle: the brothers Dar and Darrin on each side of him. Behind them are Tran and Shar and Cole with his brother Colin. There are ten — twenty — nearly thirty of them out by now. The Calormen line is being forced back upon them. King Edmund is dealing marvellous strokes. He's just slashed Corradin's head off. Lots of Calormenes have thrown down their arms and are running for the woods. Those that remain are

роль и царевич вот-вот встретятся... Нет, их разделили...

— А как там Шаста? — спросила Аравита.

— О бедный, глупый, храбрый мальчик! — воскликнул старец. — Он ничего не умеет, не знает, что делать со щитом. А уж с мечом... Нет, вспомнил! Размахивает во все стороны... чуть не отрубил голову своей лошадке... Ну, меч выбили. Как же его пустили в битву?! Он и пяти минут не продержится. Ах ты, бедняга! Упал.

— Убит? — хором воскликнули все трое.

— Не знаю. Коты своё дело сделали. Коней у тархистанцев теперь нет — кто погиб, кто убежал. А коты опять бросаются в бой! Вот прыгнули на спину этим, с тараном. Таран лежит на земле... Ах, хорошо! Ворота открываются, сейчас выйдут орландцы. Вот и король Лум! Слева от него — Дар, справа — Дарин. За ними Тари, и Зар, и Коль, и брат его Колин. Десять... двадцать... тридцать рыцарей. Тархистанцы кинулись на них. Король Эдмунд бьётся на славу. Отрубил Корадину голову. Тархистанцы бросают оружие, бегут в лес... А вот этим бежать некуда — слева коты, справа великаны, сзади Лум, твой тархан упал... Лум и Азрох бьются врукопашную... Лум побеждает... так-так... победил. Азрох — на земле. О, Эдмунд упал! Нет, поднялся. Бьется с Рабадашем

hard pressed. The Giants are closing in on the right — Cats on the left — King Lune from their rear. The Calormenes are a little knot now, fighting back to back. Your Tarkaan's down, Bree. Lune and Azrooh are fighting hand to hand; the King looks like winning — the King is keeping it up well — the King has won. Azrooh's down. King Edmund's down — no, he's up again: he's at it with Rabadash. They're fighting in the very gate of the castle. Several Calormenes have surrendered. Darrin has killed Ilgamuth. I can't see what's happened to Rabadash. I think he's dead, leaning against the castle wall, but I don't know. Chlamash and King Edmund are still fighting but the battle is over everywhere else. Chlamash has surrendered. The battle *is* over. The Calormenes are utterly defeated.'

When Shasta fell off his horse he gave himself up for lost. But horses, even in battle, tread on human beings very much less than you would suppose. After a very horrible ten minutes or so Shasta realized suddenly that there were no longer any horses stamping about in the immediate neighbourhood and that the noise (for there were still a good many noises going on) was no longer that of a battle. He sat up and stared about him. Even he, little as he knew of battles, could soon see that the Archenlanders and Narnians had won. The only living Calormenes he could see were prisoners, the castle gates were wide open, and King Lune and King Edmund were shaking hands across the battering ram. From the circle of lords and warriors around them there arose a sound of breathless and excited, but obviously cheerful conversation. And then, suddenly, it all united and swelled into a great roar of laughter.

Shasta picked himself up, feeling uncommonly stiff, and ran towards the sound to see what the joke was.

в воротах замка. Тархистанцы сдаются, Дарин убил Илгамута. Не вижу, что с Рабадашем. Наверное, убит. Кламаш и Эдмунд дерутся, но битва кончилась. Кламаш сдался. Ну, теперь всё.

Как раз в эту минуту Шаста приподнялся и сел. Ударился он не очень сильно, но лежал тихо и лошади его не растоптали, потому что, как это ни странно, ступают осторожно даже в битве. Итак, он приподнялся и, хотя понимал мало, догадался, что битва кончилась и победили Орландия и Нарния. Ворота стояли широко открытыми, тархистанцы — их осталось не много — явно были пленными, король Эдмунд и король Лум пожимали друг другу руки поверх упавшего тарана. Лорды взволнованно и радостно беседовали о чём-то, и вдруг все засмеялись.

Шаста вскочил, хотя рука у него сильно болела, и побежал посмотреть, что их рассмешило. Увидел

A very curious sight met his eyes. The unfortunate Rabadash appeared to be suspended from the castle walls. His feet, which were about two feet from the ground, were kicking wildly. His chain-shirt was somehow hitched up so that it was horribly tight under the arms and came half way over his face. In fact he looked just as a man looks if you catch him in the very act of getting into a stiff shirt that is a little too small for him. As far as could be made out afterwards (and you may be sure the story was well talked over for many a day) what happened was something like this. Early in the battle one of the Giants had made an unsuccessful stamp at Rabadash with his spiked boot: unsuccessful because it didn't crush Rabadash, which was what the Giant had intended, but not quite useless because one of the spikes tore the chain mail, just as you or I might tear an ordinary shirt. So Rabadash, by the time he encountered Edmund at the gate, had a hole in the back of his hauberk. And when Edmund pressed him back nearer and nearer to the wall, he jumped up on a mounting block and stood there raining down blows on Edmund from above. But then, finding that this position, by raising him above the heads of everyone else, made him a mark for every arrow from the Narnian bows, he decided to jump down again. And he meant to look and sound — no doubt for a moment he *did* look and sound — very grand and very dreadful as he jumped, crying, 'The bolt of Tash falls from above.' But he had to jump sideways because the crowd in front of him left him no landing place in that direction. And then, in the neatest way you could wish, the tear in the back of his hauberk caught on a hook in the wall. (Ages ago this hook had had a ring in it for tying horses to.) And there he found himself, like a piece of washing hung up to dry, with everyone laughing at him.

он нечто весьма странное: царевич Рабадаш висел на стене замка, яростно дрыгая ногами. Кольчуга закрывала ему половину лица, и казалось, что он с трудом надевает тесную рубаху. На самом деле случилось вот что: в самый разгар битвы один из великанов наступил на Рабадаша, но не раздавил (к чему стремился), а разорвал на нём кольчугу шипами своего сапога. Таким образом, когда Рабадаш встретился с Эдмундом в воротах, на спине в кольчуге у злосчастного царевича была дыра. Эдмунд теснил его к стене, и он вспрыгнул на выступы, чтобы поразить врага сверху. Рабадашу казалось, что он грозен и велик, так казалось и другим — но лишь одно мгновение. Он крикнул: «Таш разит метко!» — тут же отпрыгнул в сторону, испугавшись летящих в него стрел, и повис на крюке, который за много лет до того вбили в стену, чтобы привязывать лошадей.

'Let me down, Edmund,' howled Rabadash. 'Let me down and fight me like a king and a man; or if you are too great a coward to do that, kill me at once.'

'Certainly,' began King Edmund, but King Lune interrupted.

'By your Majesty's good leave,' said King Lune to Edmund. 'Not so.' Then turning to Rabadash he said, 'Your royal Highness, if you had given that challenge a week ago, I'll answer for it there was no one in King Edmund's dominion, from the High King down to the smallest Talking Mouse, who would have refused it. But by attacking our castle of Anvard in time of peace without defiance sent, you have proved yourself no knight, but a traitor, and one rather to be whipped by the hangman than to be suffered to cross swords with any person of honour. Take him down, bind him, and carry him within till our pleasure is further known.'

Strong hands wrenched Rabadash's sword from him and he was carried away into the castle, shouting, threatening, cursing, and even crying. For though he could have faced torture he couldn't bear being made ridiculous. In Tashbaan everyone had always taken him seriously.

At that moment Corin ran up to Shasta, seized his hand and started dragging him towards King Lune. 'Here he is, Father, here he is,' cried Corin.

'Aye, and here *thou* art, at last,' said the King in a very gruff voice. 'And hast been in the battle, clean contrary to your obedience. A boy to break a father's heart! At your age a rod to your breech were fitter than a sword in your fist, ha!' But everyone, including Corin, could see that the King was very proud of him.

— Вели меня снять, Эдмунд! — ревел Рабадаш, болтавшийся на крюке словно вещь, которую вывесили на просушку. — Сразись со мной как мужчина и король, а если ты слишком труслив, вели меня прикончить!

Король Эдмунд шагнул было к стене, чтобы снять его, но король Лум встал между ними и обратился к Рабадашу:

— Если бы вы, ваше высочество, бросили этот вызов неделю назад, ни в Нарнии, ни в Орландии не отказался бы никто, от короля Питера до говорящей мыши. Но вы доказали, что вам неведомы законы чести, и рыцарь не может скрестить с вами меч. Друзья мои, снимите его, свяжите и унесите в замок.

Не буду описывать, как бранился, кричал и даже плакал царевич Рабадаш. Он не боялся пытки, но боялся смеха. До сих пор ни один человек не смеялся над ним.

Корин тем временем подтащил к королю Луму упирающегося Шасту и сказал:

— Вот и он, отец.

— А, и ты здесь? — воскликнул король, обернувшись к принцу Корину. — Кто тебе разрешил сражаться? Ну что у меня за сын!

Но все, в том числе Корин, восприняли эти слова скорее как похвалу, чем жалобу, а лорд Дарин сказал:

'Chide him no more, Sire, if it please you,' said Lord Darrin. 'His Highness would not be your son if he did not inherit your conditions. It would grieve your Majesty more if he had to be reproved for the opposite fault.'

'Well, well,' grumbled the King. 'We'll pass it over for this time. And now — '

What came next surprised Shasta as much as anything that had ever happened to him in his life. He found himself suddenly embraced in a bear-like hug by King Lune and kissed on both cheeks. Then the King set him down again and said, 'Stand here together, boys, and let all the court see you. Hold up your heads. Now, gentlemen, look on them both. Has any man any doubts?'

And still Shasta could not understand why everyone stared at him and at Corin nor what all the cheering was about.

— Не браните его, государь. Он просто похож на вас. Да вы и сами бы огорчились, если бы принц...

— Ладно, ладно, — проворчал Лум, — на сей раз прощаю. А теперь...

И тут, к вящему удивлению Шасты, король Лум склонился к нему, крепко, по-медвежьи, обнял, расцеловал и, поставив рядом с Корином, крикнул своим рыцарям:

— Смотрите, друзья мои! Кто из вас ещё сомневается?

Но Шаста и теперь не понимал, почему все так пристально смотрят на них и так радостно кричат:

— Да здравствует наследный принц!

Chapter 14

HOW BREE BECAME A WISER HORSE

We must now return to Aravis and the Horses. The Hermit, watching his pool, was able to tell them that Shasta was not killed or even seriously wounded, for he saw him get up and saw how affectionately he was greeted by King Lune. But as he could only see, not hear, he did not know what anyone was saying and, once the fighting had stopped and the talking had begun, it was not worth while looking in the pool any longer.

Next morning, while the Hermit was indoors, the three of them discussed what they should do next.

'I've had enough of this,' said Hwin. 'The Hermit has been very good to us and I'm very much obliged to him I'm sure. But I'm getting as fat as a pet pony, eating all day and getting no exercise. Let's go on to Narnia.'

'Oh not today, Ma'am,' said Bree. 'I wouldn't hurry things. Some other day, don't you think?'

'We must see Shasta first and say goodbye to him — and — and apologize,' said Aravis.

'Exactly!' said Bree with great enthusiasm. 'Just what I was going to say.'

'Oh, of course,' said Hwin. 'I expect he is in Anvard. Naturally we'd look in on him and say goodbye. But that's on our way. And why shouldn't we start at once? After all, I thought it was Narnia we all wanted to get to?'

Глава 14

О ТОМ, КАК ИГОГО СТАЛ УМНЕЕ

Теперь мы должны вернуться к лошадям и Аравите. Отшельник сказал им, что Шаста жив и даже не очень серьёзно ранен, поскольку поднялся, а король Лум с необычайной радостью обнял его. Но отшельник только видел, а не слышал, потому не мог знать, о чём говорили у замка.

Наутро лошади и Аравита заспорили, что делать дальше.

— Я больше так не могу, — сказала Уинни. — Я растолстела, как домашняя лошадка, потому что всё время ем и не двигаюсь. Идёмте в Нарнию.

— Только не сейчас, госпожа моя, — возразил Игого. — Спешить никогда не стоит.

— Самое главное, — сказала Аравита, — попросить прощения у Шасты.

— Вот именно! — обрадовался Игого. — Я как раз хотел это сказать.

— Ну конечно, — поддержала Уинни. — А он в Анварде. Это ведь по дороге. Почему бы нам не выйти сейчас? Мы же шли из Тархистана в Нарнию!

'I suppose so,' said Aravis. She was beginning to wonder what exactly she would do when she got there and was feeling a little lonely.

'Of course, of course,' said Bree hastily. 'But there's no need to rush things, if you know what I mean.'

'No, I don't know what you mean,' said Hwin. 'Why don't you want to go?'

'M-m-m, broo-hoo,' muttered Bree. 'Well, don't you see, Ma'am — it's an important occasion — returning to one's country — entering society — the best society — it is so essential to make a good impression — not perhaps looking quite ourselves, yet, eh?'

Hwin broke out into a horse-laugh. 'It's your tail, Bree! I see it all now. You want to wait till your tail's grown again! And we don't even know if tails are worn long in Narnia. Really, Bree, you're as vain as that Tarkheena in Tashbaan!'

'You *are* silly, Bree,' said Aravis.

'By the Lion's Mane, Tarkheena, I'm nothing of the sort,' said Bree indignantly. 'I have a proper respect for myself and for my fellow horses, that's all.'

'Bree,' said Aravis, who was not very interested in the cut of his tail, 'I've been wanting to ask you something for

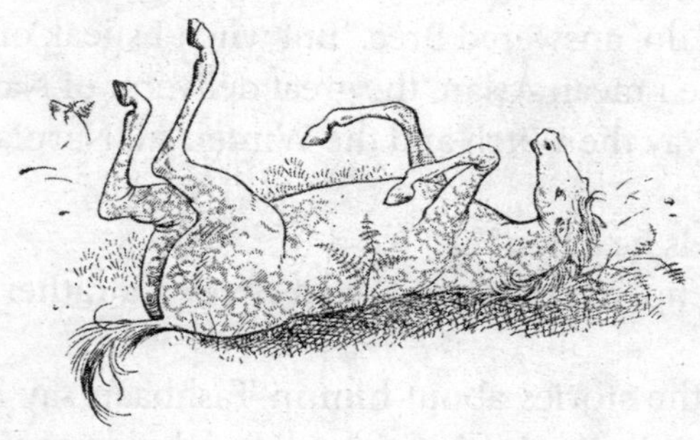

— Да... — медленно проговорила Аравита, думая о том, что же она будет делать в чужой стране.

— Конечно, конечно, — сказал Игого. — И всё-таки спешить нам некуда, если вы меня понимаете.

— Я не понимаю, — сказала Уинни.

— Как бы это объяснить? — замялся конь. — Когда возвращаешься на родину... в обществе... в лучшее общество... надо бы поприличней выглядеть...

— Ах, это из-за хвоста! — воскликнула Уинни. — Ты хочешь, чтобы он отрос. Честное слово, ты тщеславен, как ташбаанская тархина.

— И глуп, — прибавила Аравита.

— Лев свидетель, это не так! — вскричал Игого. — Просто я уважаю и себя, и своих собратьев.

— Скажи, Игого, — спросила Аравита, — почему ты часто поминаешь льва? Я думала, ты их не любишь.

a long time. Why do you keep on swearing *By the Lion* and *By the Lion's Mane*? I thought you hated lions.'

'So I do,' answered Bree. 'But when I speak of *the* Lion of course I mean Aslan, the great deliverer of Narnia who drove away the Witch and the Winter. All Narnians swear by *him*.'

'But is he a lion?'

'No, no, of course not,' said Bree in a rather shocked voice.

'All the stories about him in Tashbaan say he is,' replied Aravis. 'And if he isn't a lion why do you call him a lion?'

'Well, you'd hardly understand that at your age,' said Bree. 'And I was only a little foal when I left so I don't quite fully understand it myself.'

(Bree was standing with his back to the green wall while he said this, and the other two were facing him. He was talking in rather a superior tone with his eyes half shut; that was why he didn't see the changed expression in the faces of Hwin and Aravis. They had good reason to have open mouths and staring eyes; because while Bree spoke they saw an enormous lion leap up from outside and balance itself on the top of the green wall; only it was a brighter yellow and it was bigger and more beautiful and more alarming than any lion they had ever seen. And at once it jumped down inside the wall and began approaching Bree from behind. It made no noise at all. And Hwin and Aravis couldn't make any noise themselves, no more than if they were frozen.)

'No doubt,' continued Bree, 'when they speak of him as a Lion they only mean he's as strong as a lion or (to our enemies, of course) as fierce as a lion. Or something of that kind. Even a little girl like you, Aravis, must see that it would be quite absurd to suppose he is a real lion. In-

— Да, не люблю, но поминаю не каких-то львов, а самого Аслана, освободившего Нарнию от злой колдуньи. Здесь все так клянутся.

— А он лев? — спросила Аравита.

— Конечно, нет, — возмутился Игого.

— В Ташбаане говорят, что лев, — упорствовала девочка. — Но если не лев, почему ты зовёшь его львом?

— Тебе ещё этого не понять, да и сам я был жеребёнком, когда покинул Нарнию, поэтому тоже не совсем хорошо понимаю.

Пока они говорили, Игого стоял задом к зелёной стене, а Уинни и Аравита — лицом. Для пущей важности он прикрыл глаза, поэтому не заметил, как изменились вдруг и девочка, и лошадь: просто окаменели и разинули рты, — потому что на стене появился преогромный ослепительно золотистый лев и, мягко спрыгнув на траву, стал приближаться сзади к коню, беззвучно ступая. Уинни и Аравита не могли издать ни звука от ужаса и удивления.

— Несомненно, — продолжал тем временем вещать Игого, — называя его львом, хотят сказать, что он силён, как лев, или жесток, как лев, — конечно, к своим врагам. Даже в твои годы, Аравита, можно понять, как нелепо считать его *настоящим* львом.

deed it would be disrespectful. If he was a lion he'd have to be a Beast just like the rest of us. Why!' (and here Bree began to laugh) 'If he was a lion he'd have four paws, and a tail, and *Whiskers*! . . . Aie, ooh, hoo-hoo! Help!'

For just as he said the word *Whiskers* one of Aslan's had actually tickled his ear. Bree shot away like an arrow to the other side of the enclosure and there turned; the wall was too high for him to jump and he could fly no farther. Aravis and Hwin both started back. There was about a second of intense silence.

Then Hwin, though shaking all over, gave a strange little neigh, and trotted across to the Lion.

'Please,' she said, 'you're so beautiful. You may eat me if you like. I'd sooner be eaten by you than fed by anyone else.'

'Dearest daughter,' said Aslan, planting a lion's kiss on her twitching, velvet nose, 'I knew you would not be long in coming to me. Joy shall be yours.'

Then he lifted his head and spoke in a louder voice.

'Now, Bree,' he said, 'you poor, proud frightened Horse, draw near. Nearer still, my son. Do not dare not to dare. Touch me. Smell me. Here are my paws, here is my tail, these are my whiskers. I am a true Beast.'

'Aslan,' said Bree in a shaken voice, 'I'm afraid I must be rather a fool.'

'Happy the Horse who knows that while he is still young. Or the Human either. Draw near, Aravis my daughter. See! My paws are velveted. You will not be torn this time.'

'This time, sir?' said Aravis.

'It was I who wounded you,' said Aslan. 'I am the only lion you met in all your journeyings. Do you know why I tore you?'

'No, sir.'

Более того, это непочтительно. Ведь, будь он львом, то есть животным, как мы, у него было бы четыре лапы, и хвост, и усы...

И вдруг конь ойкнул от неожиданности: это ус Аслана коснулся его уха. Игого отскочил в сторону и обернулся. Примерно с секунду все четверо стояли неподвижно. Потом Уинни робкой рысью подбежала ко льву.

— Дорогая моя дочь, — сказал Аслан, касаясь носом её бархатистой морды. — Я знал, что тебя мне ждать недолго. Радуйся.

Он поднял голову и заговорил громче.

— А ты, Игого, бедный и гордый конь, подойди ближе. Потрогай меня. Понюхай. Вот мои лапы, вот хвост, вот усы. Я, как и ты, животное.

— Аслан, — потупился Игого, — прости мне мою глупость.

— Счастлив тот зверь, который может сознаться в глупости, пока ещё молод, как, впрочем, и человек. Подойди, дочь моя Аравита. Я втянул когти, не бойся: на сей раз не поцарапаю.

— На сей раз?..

— Это я тебя ударил, — сказал Аслан. — Только меня ты и встречала, больше львов не было. Да, поцарапал тебя я. А знаешь почему?

— Нет, мой господин, — ответила девочка.

'The scratches on your back, tear for tear, throb for throb, blood for blood, were equal to the stripes laid on the back of your stepmother's slave because of the drugged sleep you cast upon her. You needed to know what it felt like.'

'Yes, sir. Please — '

'Ask on, my dear,' said Aslan.

'Will any more harm come to her by what I did?'

'Child,' said the Lion, 'I am telling you your story, not hers. No one is told any story but their own.' Then he shook his head and spoke in a lighter voice.

'Be merry, little ones,' he said. 'We shall meet soon again. But before that you will have another visitor.' Then in one bound he reached the top of the wall and vanished from their sight.

Strange to say, they felt no inclination to talk to one another about him after he had gone. They all moved slowly away to different parts of the quiet grass and there paced to and fro, each alone, thinking.

About half an hour later the two Horses were summoned to the back of the house to eat something nice that the Hermit had got ready for them and Aravis, still walking and thinking, was startled by the harsh sound of a trumpet outside the gate.

'Who is there?' asked Aravis.

'His Royal Highness Prince Cor of Archenland,' said a voice from outside.

Aravis undid the door and opened it, drawing back a little way to let the strangers in.

Two soldiers with halberds came first and took their stand at each side of the entry. Then followed a herald, and the trumpeter.

— Я нанёс тебе ровно столько ран, сколько мачеха твоя нанесла бедной служанке, которую ты опоила сонным зельем, чтобы ты узнала, каково ей было.

— Скажи, пожалуйста... — начала Аравита, но замолкла.

— Говори, дорогая дочь, — сказал Аслан.

— Ей больше ничего из-за меня не будет?

— Я рассказываю каждому только его историю.

Тряхнув головой, лев произнёс чётко и громко:

— Радуйтесь, дети мои: скоро мы встретимся снова, — но раньше к вам придёт другой.

Одним прыжком он взлетел на стену и исчез за нею.

Как это ни странно, все долго молчали, медленно гуляя по зелёной траве. Примерно через полчаса отшельник позвал лошадей к заднему крыльцу, намереваясь покормить, и они ушли, и тут у ворот раздались звуки труб.

— Кто там? — спросила Аравита.

— Его королевское высочество принц Кор Орландский, — объявил глашатай.

Аравита открыла ворота и посторонилась, пропуская двух воинов с алебардами, герольда и трубача.

'His Royal Highness Prince Cor of Archenland desires an audience of the Lady Aravis,' said the Herald. Then he and the trumpeter drew aside and bowed and the soldiers saluted and the Prince himself came in. All his attendants withdrew and closed the gate behind them.

The Prince bowed, and a very clumsy bow for a Prince it was. Aravis curtsied in the Calormene style (which is not at all like ours) and did it very well because, of course, she had been taught how. Then she looked up and saw what sort of person this Prince was.

She saw a mere boy. He was bare-headed and his fair hair was encircled with a very thin band of gold, hardly thicker than a wire. His upper tunic was of white cambric, as fine as a handkerchief, so that the bright red tunic beneath it showed through. His left hand, which rested on his enamelled sword hilt, was bandaged.

Aravis looked twice at his face before she gasped and said, 'Why! It's Shasta!'

Shasta all at once turned very red and began speaking very quickly. 'Look here, Aravis,' he said, 'I do hope you won't think I'm got up like this (and the trumpeter and all) to try to impress you or make out that I'm different or any rot of that sort. Because I'd far rather have come in my old clothes, but they're burnt now, and my father said — '

'Your father?' said Aravis.

'Apparently King Lune is my father,' said Shasta. 'I might really have guessed it. Corin being so like me. We were twins, you see. Oh, and my name isn't Shasta, it's Cor.'

'Cor is a nicer name than Shasta,' said Aravis.

'Brothers' names run like that in Archenland,' said Shasta (or Prince Cor as we must now call him). 'Like Dar and Darrin, Cole and Colin and so on.'

— Его королевское высочество принц Кор Орландский просит аудиенции у высокородной Аравиты, — объявил герольд и склонился в поклоне.

Солдаты подняли алебарды. Когда принц вошёл, остальные шагнули обратно за ворота и закрыли их за собой.

Принц поклонился (довольно неуклюже для высокой особы), Аравита тоже склонилась перед ним (очень изящно, хотя и на тархистанский манер) и только потом взглянула на него.

Мальчик как мальчик, без шляпы и без короны, только очень тонкий золотой обруч обхватывал голову. Сквозь короткую белую тунику не толще носового платка пламенел алый камзол. Левая рука, лежавшая на эфесе шпаги, была перевязана.

— Ой, да это же Шаста! — присмотревшись повнимательнее, воскликнула Аравита.

Мальчик сильно покраснел и быстро заговорил:

— Ты не думай, я не хотел перед тобой выставляться!.. У меня нет другой одежды, прежнюю сожгли, а отец сказал...

— Отец? — переспросила Аравита.

— Король Лум. Я мог бы и раньше догадаться. Понимаешь, мы с Корином близнецы. Да, я не Шаста, а Кор!

— Очень красивое имя, — сказала Аравита.

— У нас в Орландии, — пояснил Кор (теперь мы будем звать его только так), — близнецов называют Дар и Дарин, Коль и Колин и тому подобное.

'Shasta — I mean Cor,' said Aravis. 'No, shut up. There's something I've got to say at once. I'm sorry I've been such a pig. But I did change before I knew you were a Prince, honestly I did: when you went back, and faced the Lion.'

'It wasn't really going to kill you at all, that Lion,' said Cor.

'I know,' said Aravis, nodding. Both were still and solemn for a moment as each saw that the other knew about Aslan.

Suddenly Aravis remembered Cor's bandaged hand. 'I say!' she cried, 'I forgot! You've been in a battle. Is that a wound?'

'A mere scratch,' said Cor, using for the first time a rather lordly tone. But a moment later he burst out laughing and said, 'If you want to know the truth, it isn't a proper wound at all. I only took the skin off my knuckles just as any clumsy fool might do without going near a battle.'

'Still you were in the battle,' said Aravis. 'It must have been wonderful.'

'It wasn't at all like what I thought,' said Cor.

'But Sha — Cor, I mean — you haven't told me anything yet about King Lune and how he found out who you were.'

'Well, let's sit down,' said Cor. 'For it's rather a long story. And by the way, Father's an absolute brick. I'd be just as pleased — or very nearly — at finding he's my father even if he wasn't a king. Even though Education and all sorts of horrible things are going to happen to me. But you want the story. Well, Corin and I were twins. And about a week after we were both born, apparently, they took us to a wise old Centaur in Narnia to be blessed or

— Шаста... то есть Кор, позволь сказать. Мне очень стыдно за своё поведение, я изменилась, хотя и не знала, что ты принц. Честное слово! Это произошло, когда ты вернулся, чтобы спасти нас от льва.

— Он не собирался вас убивать, — сказал Кор.

— Я знаю, — кивнула Аравита, и они помолчали, поняв, что оба беседовали с Асланом.

Наконец Аравита вспомнила, что у Кора перевязана рука, и воскликнула:

— Ах, я и забыла! Ты был в бою, и тебя ранили?

— Так, царапина, — произнёс Кор с той самой интонацией, с какой говорят вельможи, но тут же фыркнул: — Да нет, это не рана, а ссадина.

— И всё-таки ты сражался! Наверное, это очень интересно.

— Всё совсем не так, как я думал, — покачал головой Кор.

— Ах, Ша... Кор! Расскажи, как король узнал, кто ты.

— Давай присядем. Это долгая история. Кстати, отец у меня — лучше некуда. Я бы любил его точно так же... почти так же, если бы он не был королём. Конечно, меня будут учить и всё прочее, но ничего, потерплю. А история самая простая. Когда нам с Корином исполнилась неделя, нас повезли к старому доброму кентавру — благословить или что-то в этом роде. Он был пророк, кентавры часто бывают проро-

something. Now this Centaur was a prophet as a good many Centaurs are. Perhaps you haven't seen any Centaurs yet? There were some in the battle yesterday. Most remarkable people, but I can't say I feel quite at home with them yet. I say, Aravis, there are going to be a lot of things to get used to in these Northern countries.'

'Yes, there are,' said Aravis. 'But get on with the story.'

'Well, as soon as he saw Corin and me, it seems this Centaur looked at me and said, "A day will come when that boy will save Archenland from the deadliest danger in which ever she lay". So of course my Father and Mother were very pleased. But there was someone present who wasn't. This was a chap called the Lord Bar who had been Father's Lord Chancellor. And apparently he'd done something wrong — *bezzling* or some word like that — I didn't understand that part very well — and Father had had to dismiss him. But nothing else was done to him and he was allowed to go on living in Archenland. But he must have been as bad as he could be, for it came out afterwards he had been in the pay of the Tisroc and had sent a lot of secret information to Tashbaan. So as soon as he heard I was going to save Archenland from a great danger he decided I must be put out of the way. Well, he succeeded in kidnapping me (I don't exactly know how) and rode away down the Winding Arrow to the coast. He'd had everything prepared and there was a ship manned with his own followers lying ready for him and he put out to sea with me on board. But Father got wind of it, though not quite in time, and was after him as quickly as he could. The Lord Bar was already at sea when Father reached the coast, but not out of sight. And Father was embarked in one of his own warships within twenty minutes.

ками. Ты их не видела? Ну и дяди! Если честно, я их немножко боюсь. Тут ко многому надо привыкнуть...

— Да уж... — согласилась Аравита. — Но давай же рассказывай, рассказывай!

— Так вот, когда ему нас показали, он взглянул на меня и сказал: «Этот мальчик спасёт Орландию от великой опасности». Его услышал один придворный, лорд Бар, который раньше служил у отца лорд-канцлером и совершил какой-то проступок (не знаю, в чём там дело), за что был разжалован, хотя придворным остался. Вообще он был предателем — потом оказалось, что за деньги он посылал секретные сведения в Ташбаан. Так вот: услышав это предсказание, он решил меня уничтожить и похитил — не знаю как. Когда лорд Бар уже вышел в море на корабле, отец за ним погнался, на седьмой день нагнал, и у них был морской бой с десяти часов утра до самой ночи. Предателя убили, но он успел спустить на воду шлюпку, посадив туда одного рыцаря и меня. Лодка эта пропала. Как недавно выяснилось, это Аслан пригнал её к берегу, туда, где жил Аршиш. Хотел бы я знать, как звали того рыцаря! Он меня кормил, а сам умер от голода.

'It must have been a wonderful chase. They were six days following Bar's galleon and brought her to battle on the seventh. It was a great sea-fight (I heard a lot about it yesterday evening) from ten o'clock in the morning till sunset. Our people took the ship in the end. But I wasn't there. The Lord Bar himself had been killed in the battle. But one of his men said that, early that morning, as soon as he saw he was certain to be overhauled, Bar had given me to one of his knights and sent us both away in the ship's boat. And that boat was never seen again. But of course that was the same boat that Aslan (he seems to be at the back of all the stories) pushed ashore at the right place for Arsheesh to pick me up. I wish I knew that knight's name, for he must have kept me alive and starved himself to do it.'

'I suppose Aslan would say that was part of someone else's story,' said Aravis.

'I was forgetting that,' said Cor.

'And I wonder how the prophecy will work out,' said Aravis, 'and what the great danger is that you're to save Archenland from.'

'Well,' said Cor rather awkwardly, 'they seem to think I've done it already.'

Aravis clapped her hands. 'Why, of course!' she said. 'How stupid I am. And how wonderful! Archenland can never be in much greater danger than it was when Rabadash had crossed the Arrow with his two hundred horse and you hadn't yet got through with your message. Don't you feel proud?'

'I think I feel a bit scared,' said Cor.

'And you'll be living at Anvard now,' said Aravis rather wistfully.

'Oh!' said Cor, 'I'd nearly forgotten what I came about. Father wants you to come and live with us. He says there's

— Аслан сказал бы тебе лишь то, что ты должен знать о себе, — заметила Аравита.

— Да, ты права, я забыл, — согласился Кор.

— Интересно, как именно ты спасёшь Орландию.

— Я уже спас, — скромно сказал Кор.

Аравита всплеснула руками.

— Ах, конечно! Какая же я глупая! Рабадаш уничтожил бы её, если бы не ты. Где же ты будешь теперь жить? В Анварде?

— Ой, чуть не забыл, зачем пришёл к тебе. Отец хочет, чтобы ты жила с нами. У нас при дворе (они говорят «двор» — не знаю уж почему). Так вот, у нас нет хозяйки с той поры, как умерла моя мать. Пожалуйста, согласись. Тебе понравятся

been no lady in the court (they call it the court, I don't know why) since Mother died. Do, Aravis. You'll like Father — and Corin. They're not like me; they've been properly brought up. You needn't be afraid that — '

'Oh, stop it,' said Aravis, 'or we'll have a real fight. Of course I'll come.'

'Now let's go and see the Horses,' said Cor.

There was a great and joyous meeting between Bree and Cor, and Bree, who was still in a rather subdued frame of mind, agreed to set out for Anvard at once: he and Hwin would cross into Narnia on the following day. All four bade an affectionate farewell to the Hermit and promised that they would soon visit him again. By about the middle of the morning they were on their way. The Horses had expected that Aravis and Cor would ride, but Cor explained that except in war, where everyone must do what he can do best, no one in Narnia or Archenland ever dreamed of mounting a Talking Horse.

This reminded poor Bree again of how little he knew about Narnian customs and what dreadful mistakes he might make. So while Hwin strolled along in a happy dream, Bree got more nervous and more self-conscious with every step he took.

'Buck up, Bree,' said Cor. 'It's far worse for me than for you. You aren't going to be *educated*. I shall be learning reading and writing and heraldry and dancing and history and music while you'll be galloping and rolling on the hills of Narnia to your heart's content.'

'But that's just the point,' groaned Bree. 'Do Talking Horses roll? Supposing they don't? I can't bear to give it up. What do you think, Hwin?'

'I'm going to roll anyway,' said Hwin. 'I don't suppose any of them will care two lumps of sugar whether you roll or not.'

отец... и Корин. Они не такие, как я, они воспитанные...

— Прекрати! — воскликнула Аравита. — Конечно, я согласна.

— Тогда пойдём к лошадям.

Кор обнял Игого и Уинни, всё им рассказал, а потом все четверо простились с отшельником, пообещав не забывать. Дети не сели в седла — Кор объяснил, что ни в Орландии, ни в Нарнии никто не ездит верхом на говорящих лошадях, разве что в бою.

Услышав это, бедный конь вспомнил снова, как мало знает о здешних обычаях и как много ошибок может сделать. И если Уинни предалась сладостным мечтам, то он становился мрачнее и беспокойнее с каждым шагом.

— Ну что ты, — попытался успокоить его Кор. — Подумай, каково мне: меня будут *воспитывать*, учить грамоте, и танцам, и музыке, и геральдике, — а ты знай скачи по холмам сколько хочешь.

— В том-то и дело, — вздохнул Игого, — скачут ли говорящие лошади, а главное — катаются ли по земле...

— Как бы то ни было, я кататься буду, — сказала Уинни. — Думаю, они и внимания не обратят.

'Are we near that castle?' said Bree to Cor.

'Round the next bend,' said the Prince.

'Well,' said Bree, 'I'm going to have a good one now: it may be the last. Wait for me a minute.'

It was five minutes before he rose again, blowing hard and covered with bits of bracken.

'Now I'm ready,' he said in a voice of profound gloom. 'Lead on, Prince Cor, Narnia and the North.'

But he looked more like a horse going to a funeral than a long-lost captive returning to home and freedom.

— Замок ещё далеко? — спросил конь у принца.

— За тем холмом.

— Тогда я покатаюсь, пусть даже и в последний раз!

Покатавшись минут пять, он угрюмо сказал:

— Что же, пойдём. Веди нас, Кор Орландский.

Но вид у него был такой, словно он везёт погребальную колесницу, а не возвращается домой, к свободе, после долгого плена.

Chapter 15
RABADASH THE RIDICULOUS

The next turn of the road brought them out from among the trees and there, across green lawns, sheltered from the north wind by the high wooded ridge at its back, they saw the castle of Anvard. It was very old and built of a warm, reddish-brown stone.

Before they had reached the gate King Lune came out to meet them, not looking at all like Aravis's idea of a king and wearing the oldest of old clothes; for he had just come from making a round of the kennels with his Huntsman and had only stopped for a moment to wash his doggy hands. But the bow with which he greeted Aravis as he took her hand would have been stately enough for an Emperor.

'Little lady,' he said, 'we bid you very heartily welcome. If my dear wife were still alive we could make you better cheer but could not do it with a better will. And I am sorry that you have had misfortunes and been driven from your father's house, which cannot but be a grief to you. My son Cor has told me about your adventures together and all your valour.'

'It was he who did all that, Sir,' said Aravis. 'Why, he rushed at a lion to save me.'

'Eh, what's that?' said King Lune, his face brightening. 'I haven't heard that part of the story.'

Then Aravis told it. And Cor, who had very much wanted the story to be known, though he felt he couldn't

Глава 15

РАБАДАШ ВИСЛОУХИЙ

Когда они наконец вышли из-под деревьев, то увидели зелёный луг, прикрытый с севера лесистой грядой, и королевский замок, очень старый, сложенный из тёмно-розового камня.

Король уже шёл им навстречу по высокой траве. Аравита совсем не так представляла себе королей — на нём был потёртый камзол, ибо он только что обходил псарню и едва успел вымыть руки, но поклонился с такой учтивостью и таким величием, каких не увидишь в Ташбаане.

— Добро пожаловать, маленькая госпожа! Будь моя дорогая супруга королева жива, тебе было бы здесь лучше, но мы сделаем для тебя всё, что можем. Сын мой Кор рассказал о твоих злоключениях и твоём мужестве.

— Это он был мужественным, государь, — возразила Аравита. — Кинулся на льва, чтобы спасти нас с Уинни.

Король просиял:

— Вот как? Этого я не слышал.

Аравита поведала историю, а Кор, который очень хотел, чтобы отец об этом узнал, совсем не обрадо-

tell it himself, didn't enjoy it so much as he had expected, and indeed felt rather foolish. But his father enjoyed it very much indeed and in the course of the next few weeks told it to so many people that Cor wished it had never happened.

Then the King turned to Hwin and Bree and was just as polite to them as to Aravis, and asked them a lot of questions about their families and where they had lived in Narnia before they had been captured. The Horses were rather tongue-tied for they weren't yet used to being talked to as equals by Humans — grown-up Humans, that is. They didn't mind Aravis and Cor.

Presently Queen Lucy came out from the castle and joined them and King Lune said to Aravis, 'My dear, here is a loving friend of our house, and she has been seeing that your apartments are put to rights for you better than I could have done it.'

'You'd like to come and see them, wouldn't you?' said Lucy, kissing Aravis. They liked each other at once and soon went away together to talk about Aravis's bedroom and Aravis's boudoir and about getting clothes for her, and all the sort of things girls do talk about on such an occasion.

After lunch, which they had on the terrace (it was cold birds and cold game pie and wine and bread and cheese), King Lune ruffled up his brow and heaved a sigh and said, 'Heigh-ho! We have still that sorry creature Rabadash on our hands, my friends, and must needs resolve what to do with him.'

Lucy was sitting on the King's right and Aravis on his left. King Edmund sat at one end of the table and the Lord Darrin faced him at the other. Dar and Peridan and Cor and Corin were on the same side as the King.

вался, как думал прежде: скорее ему было неловко, — зато король прямо светился от гордости за сына и раз за разом пересказывал придворным эту историю, отчего принц совсем уж смутился.

С Игого и Уинни король тоже был учтив и подолгу беседовал. Лошади отвечали нескладно, поскольку ещё не привыкли говорить со взрослыми людьми. К их облегчению, из замка вышла королева Люси, и король сказал Аравите:

— Дорогая моя, вот наш большой друг, королева Нарнии. Не хочешь ли с нею отдохнуть?

Люси поцеловала Аравиту, они сразу прониклись симпатией друг к другу и отправились в замок, весело болтая о том о сём.

Завтрак подали на террасе (холодную дичь, пирог, вино и сыр), и когда все ещё ели, король Лум, нахмурившись, сказал:

— Ох-ох-ох! Нам надо ещё что-то сделать с беднягой Рабадашем.

Люси сидела по правую руку от короля, Аравита — по левую. Во главе стола сидел король Эдмунд, напротив него — лорды Дарин, Дар, Перидан. Корин и Кор заняли места напротив дам и короля Лума.

'Your Majesty would have a perfect right to strike off his head,' said Peridan. 'Such an assault as he made puts him on a level with assassins.'

'It is very true,' said Edmund. 'But even a traitor may mend. I have known one that did.' And he looked very thoughtful.

'To kill this Rabadash would go near to raising war with the Tisroc,' said Darrin.

'A fig for the Tisroc,' said King Lune. 'His strength is in numbers and numbers will never cross the desert. But I have no stomach for killing men (even traitors) in cold blood. To have cut his throat in the battle would have eased my heart mightily, but this is a different thing.'

'By my counsel,' said Lucy, 'your Majesty shall give him another trial. Let him go free on strait promise of fair dealing in the future. It may be that he will keep his word.'

'Maybe Apes will grow honest, Sister,' said Edmund. 'But, by the Lion, if he breaks it again, may it be in such time and place that any of us could swap off his head in clean battle.'

'It shall be tried,' said the King: and then to one of the attendants, 'Send for the prisoner, friend.'

Rabadash was brought before them in chains. To look at him anyone would have supposed that he had passed the night in a noisome dungeon without food or water; but in reality he had been shut up in quite a comfortable room and provided with an excellent supper. But as he was sulking far too furiously to touch the supper and had spent the whole night stamping and roaring and cursing, he naturally did not now look his best.

'Your royal Highness needs not to be told,' said King Lune, 'that by the law of nations as well as by all reasons of prudent policy, we have as good right to your head as

— Отрубите ему голову, ваше величество, — сказал Перидан. — Кто он, как не убийца?

— Спору нет, он негодяй, — сказал Эдмунд. — Но и негодяй может исправиться. Я знал такой случай...

— Если мы убьём Рабадаша, на нас нападёт Тисрок, — сказал Дарин.

— Ну что ты! — возразил король Орландии. — Сила его в многочисленном войске, а такому огромному войску не перейти пустыню. Но я не люблю убивать беззащитных. В бою — дело другое, а так, хладнокровно...

— Возьми с него слово, что он больше не будет, — предложила Люси. — Может, он его и сдержит.

— Скорее обезьяна сдержит, — заметил Эдмунд. — И ладно бы он проявил своё вероломство в таком месте, где возможен честный бой.

— Попробуем, — принял наконец решение король Лум. — Приведите пленника, друзья мои.

Рабадаш выглядел так, словно его морили голодом: и действительно за эти сутки от злости и ярости он не притронулся ни к пище, ни к питью, — хотя жаловаться ему было не на что.

— Вы знаете сами, ваше высочество, — сказал король, — что и по справедливости, и по закону мы вправе лишить вас жизни. Однако, снисходя к вашей

ever one mortal man had against another. Nevertheless, in consideration of your youth and the ill nurture, devoid of all *gentilesse* and courtesy, which you have doubtless had in the land of slaves and tyrants, we are disposed to set you free, unharmed, on these conditions: first, that — '

'Curse you for a barbarian dog!' spluttered Rabadash. 'Do you think I will even hear your conditions? Faugh! You talk very largely of nurture and I know not what. It's easy, to a man in chains, ha! Take off these vile bonds, give me a sword, and let any of you who dares then debate with me.'

Nearly all the lords sprang to their feet, and Corin shouted:

'Father! Can I *box* him? Please.'

'Peace! Your Majesties! My Lords!' said King Lune. 'Have we no more gravity among us than to be so chafed by the taunt of a pajock? Sit down, Corin, or shalt leave the table. I ask your Highness again, to hear our conditions.'

'I hear no conditions from barbarians and sorcerers,' said Rabadash. 'Not one of you dare touch a hair of my head. Every insult you have heaped on me shall be paid with oceans of Narnian and Archenlandish blood. Terrible shall the vengeance of the Tisroc be: even now. But kill me, and the burnings and torturings in these northern lands shall become a tale to frighten the world a thousand years hence. Beware! Beware! Beware! The bolt of Tash falls from above!'

'Does it ever get caught on a hook half-way?' asked Corin.

'Shame, Corin,' said the King. 'Never taunt a man save when he is stronger than you: then, as you please.'

'Oh you foolish Rabadash,' sighed Lucy.

молодости, а также к тому, что вы выросли, не ведая ни милости, ни чести, среди рабов и тиранов, мы решили отпустить вас на следующих условиях: во-первых...

— Нечестивый пёс! — выкрикнул Рабадаш. — Легко болтать со связанным пленником! Дай мне меч, и я тебе покажу, каковы *мои* условия!

Мужчины вскочили, а Корин воскликнул, сжимая кулаки:

— Отец! Дозволь, я его поколочу!

— Друзья мои, успокойтесь, — сказал король Лум. — Сядь, Корин, или я тебя выгоню из-за стола. Итак, ваше высочество, условия мои...

— Я не обсуждаю ничего с дикарями и чародеями! — опять оборвал его Рабадаш. — Если вы оскорбите меня, отец мой Тисрок потопит ваши страны в крови. Убейте — и костры, казни, пытки тысячу лет не забудут в этих землях. Берегитесь! Богиня Таш всё видит...

— Куда же она смотрела, когда ты висел на крюке? — усмехнулся Корин.

— Стыдись! — попенял ему король. — Нехорошо издеваться над теми, кто слабее.

— Ах, Рабадаш! — вздохнула Люси. — Какой же ты глупый!..

Next moment Cor wondered why everyone at the table had risen and was standing perfectly still. Of course he did the same himself. And then he saw the reason. Aslan was among them though no one had seen him coming. Rabadash started as the immense shape of the Lion paced softly in between him and his accusers.

'Rabadash,' said Aslan. 'Take heed. Your doom is very near, but you may still avoid it. Forget your pride (what have you to be proud of?) and your anger (who has done you wrong?) and accept the mercy of these good kings.'

Then Rabadash rolled his eyes and spread out his mouth into a horrible, long mirthless grin like a shark, and wagged his ears up and down (anyone can learn how to do this if they take the trouble). He had always found this very effective in Calormen. The bravest had trembled when he made these faces, and ordinary people had fallen to the floor, and sensitive people had often fainted. But what Rabadash hadn't realized is that it is very easy to frighten people who know you can have them boiled alive the moment you give the word. The grimaces didn't look at all alarming in Archenland; indeed Lucy only thought Rabadash was going to be sick.

'Demon! Demon! Demon!' shrieked the Prince. 'I know you. You are the foul fiend of Narnia. You are the enemy of the gods. Learn who *I* am, horrible phantasm. I am descended from Tash, the inexorable, the irresistible. The curse of Tash is upon you. Lightning in the shape of scorpions shall be rained on you. The mountains of Narnia shall be ground into dust. The — '

'Have a care, Rabadash,' said Aslan quietly. 'The doom is nearer now: it is at the door: it has lifted the latch.'

Не успела она закончить фразу, как — к удивлению Кора — его отец, дамы и двое мужчин молча поднялись со своих мест, повернув головы в одну сторону. Встал и он и увидел, как между столом и пленником, мягко ступая, прошёл огромный лев.

— Рабадаш, — раздался в тишине голос Аслана, — поспеши. Судьба твоя ещё не решена. Забудь о своей гордыне (чем тебе гордиться?), злобе (кто тебя обидел?) и прими по собственной воле милость добрых людей.

Рабадаш выкатил глаза, жутко ухмыльнулся и (что совсем не трудно) зашевелил ушами. На тархистанцев всё это действовало безотказно: самые смелые просто тряслись, а кто послабей — падали в обморок. Он не знал, однако, что дело тут было не столько в самих гримасах, сколько в том, что по его слову любого могли немедленно сварить живьём в кипящем масле. Здесь же это эффекта не возымело — только сердобольная Люси испугалась, что ему плохо.

— Прочь! — закричал Рабадаш. — Я тебя знаю! Ты гнусный демон, мерзкий северный бес, враг богов. Узнай, низменный призрак, что я потомок великой богини, Таш неумолимой! Она разит метко. Проклятие её — на тебе. Тебя поразит молния... искусают скорпионы... здешние горы обратятся в прах...

— Тише, Рабадаш, — сказал лев совершенно спокойно. — Судьба твоя вот-вот свершится, она у дверей, сейчас их откроет.

'Let the skies fall,' shrieked Rabadash. 'Let the earth gape! Let blood and fire obliterate the world! But be sure I will never desist till I have dragged to my palace by her hair the barbarian queen, the daughter of dogs, the — '

'The hour has struck,' said Aslan: and Rabadash saw, to his supreme horror, that everyone had begun to laugh.

They couldn't help it. Rabadash had been wagging his ears all the time and as soon as Aslan said, 'The hour has struck!' the ears began to change. They grew longer and more pointed and soon were covered with grey hair. And while everyone was wondering where they had seen ears like that before, Rabadash's face began to change too. It grew longer, and thicker at the top and larger eyed, and the nose sank back into the face (or else the face swelled out and became all nose) and there was hair all over it. And his arms grew longer and came down in front of him till his hands were resting on the ground: only they weren't hands, now, they were hoofs. And he was standing on all fours, and his clothes disappeared, and everyone laughed louder and louder (because they couldn't help it) for now what had been Rabadash was, simply and unmistakably, a donkey. The terrible thing was that his human speech lasted just a moment longer than his human shape, so that when he realized the change that was coming over him, he screamed out:

'Oh, not a Donkey! Mercy! If it were even a horse — e'en — a hor — eeh — auh, eeh-auh.' And so the words died away into a donkey's bray.

'Now hear me, Rabadash,' said Aslan. 'Justice shall be mixed with mercy. You shall not always be an Ass.'

At this of course the Donkey twitched its ears forward and that also was so funny that everybody

— Ну и пусть! — выкрикнул Рабадаш. — Пусть упадут небеса, разверзнется земля! Пусть кровь зальёт эти страны, поглотит огонь — я не сдамся, пока не притащу к себе во дворец за косы эту дочь гнусных псов, эту...

— Час пробил, — проговорил лев, и Рабадаш, к своему ужасу, увидел, что все смеются.

Да и как удержаться от смеха, если уши у пленника, которыми он всё ещё шевелил, стали расти и покрываться серой шёрсткой. Пока все думали, где видели такие уши, Рабадаш уже обзавёлся копытами — и на ногах, и на руках, — а затем хвостом. Глаза стали больше, лицо превратилось в нечто наподобие носа. Он опустился на четвереньки, одежда исчезла, а смешнее (и страшнее) всего было то, что последним его покинул дар речи и он успел лишь отчаянно прокричать:

— Только не в осла! Хоть в коня... в коня-а-э-а-ио-о-о!

— Слушай меня, Рабадаш, — проговорил Аслан. — Справедливость смягчится милостью. Ты не всегда будешь ослом.

Осёл задвигал ушами, и все, как ни старались сдержаться, захохотали снова.

laughed all the more. They tried not to, but they tried in vain.

'You have appealed to Tash,' said Aslan. 'And in the temple of Tash you shall be healed. You must stand before the altar of Tash in Tashbaan at the great Autumn Feast this year and there, in the sight of all Tashbaan, your ass's shape will fall from you and all men will know you for Prince Rabadash. But as long as you live, if ever you go more than ten miles away from the great temple in Tashbaan you shall instantly become again as you now are. And from that second change there will be no return.'

There was a short silence and then they all stirred and looked at one another as if they were waking from sleep. Aslan was gone. But there was a brightness in the air and on the grass, and a joy in their hearts, which assured them that he had been no dream: and anyway, there was the donkey in front of them.

King Lune was the kindest-hearted of men and on seeing his enemy in this regrettable condition he forgot all his anger.

'Your royal Highness,' he said. 'I am most truly sorry that things have come to this extremity. Your Highness will bear witness that it was none of our doing. And of course we shall be delighted to provide your Highness with shipping back to Tashbaan for the — er — treatment which Aslan has prescribed. You shall have every comfort which your Highness's situation allows: the best of the cattleboats — the freshest carrots and thistles — '

But a deafening bray from the Donkey and a well-aimed kick at one of the guards made it clear that these kindly offers were ungratefully received.

And here, to get him out of the way, I'd better finish off the story of Rabadash. He (or it) was duly sent back by boat to Tashbaan and brought into the temple of

— Ты поминал богиню Таш, — продолжил лев. — В её храме и обретёшь человеческий облик. На осеннем празднике в этом году ты встанешь перед её алтарем, и при всём народе с тебя спадёт ослиное обличье, но если когда-нибудь удалишься от храма дальше чем на десять миль, то опять станешь ослом, уже навсегда.

И, тихо ступая, Аслан удалился. Все будто бы очнулись, но сияние зелени, и свежесть воздуха, и радость в сердце доказывали, что это был не сон. Кроме того, осёл стоял перед ними.

Король Лум по доброте своей, увидев врага в столь плачевном положении, сразу позабыл про гнев и сказал:

— Ваше высочество, мне очень жаль, что дошло до этого. Вы сами знаете, что мы тут ни при чём. Не сомневайтесь, мы переправим вас в Ташбаан, чтобы вас там... э-э... вылечили. Сейчас вам дадут самых свежих репейников и морковки...

Неблагодарный осёл дико взревел, лягнул одного из лордов...

На этом можно было закончить рассказ о царевиче Рабадаше, но мне хочется добавить, что его со всей почтительностью отвезли в Ташбаан и привели

Tash at the great Autumn Festival, and then he became a man again. But of course four or five thousand people had seen the transformation and the affair could not possibly be hushed up. And after the old Tisroc's death when Rabadash became Tisroc in his place he turned out the most peaceable Tisroc Calormen had ever known. This was because, not daring to go more than ten miles from Tashbaan, he could never go on a war himself: and he didn't want his Tarkaans to win fame in the wars at his expense, for that is the way Tisrocs get overthrown. But though his reasons were selfish, it made things much more comfortable for all the smaller countries round Calormen. His own people never forgot that he had been a donkey. During his reign, and to his face, he was called Rabadash the Peacemaker, but after his death and behind his back he was called Rabadash the Ridiculous, and if you look him up in a good History of Calormen (try the local library) you will find him under that name. And to this day in Calormene schools, if you do anything unusually stupid, you are very likely to be called 'a second Rabadash'.

Meanwhile at Anvard everyone was very glad that he had been disposed of before the real fun began, which was a grand feast held that evening on the lawn before the castle, with dozens of lanterns to help the moonlight. And the wine flowed and tales were told and jokes were cracked, and then silence was made and the King's poet with two fiddlers stepped out into the middle of the circle. Aravis and Cor prepared themselves to be bored, for the only poetry they knew was the Calormene kind, and you know now what that was like. But at the very first scrape of the fiddles a rocket seemed to go up inside their heads, and the poet sang the great old lay of Fair Olvin and how he fought the Giant Pire and turned him

в храм богини на осенний праздник, где он снова обрёл человеческий облик. Множество народу — тысяч пять — видело это, но что поделаешь... А когда умер Тисрок, в стране наступила вполне сносная жизнь. Произошло это по двум причинам: Рабадаш не вёл никаких войн, потому что сам возглавить войско не мог, а полководцы нередко свергают царей. Кроме того, народ помнил, что он некогда был ослом. В лицо его называли Рабадашем Миротворцем, а за глаза — Рабадашем Вислоухим. И если вы заглянете в историю его страны (спросите её в городской библиотеке), он значится там именно так. Даже теперь в тархистанских школах говорят про глупого ученика: «Второй Рабадаш!»

Когда осла увезли, в замке Лума начался пир. Вино лилось рекой, сверкали огни, звенел смех, а потом наступила тишина и на середину луга вышел певец с двумя музыкантами. Кор и Аравита приготовились скучать, ибо не знали других стихов, кроме тархистанских, но певец запел о том, как светловолосый Олвин победил двухголового великана, и обратил его в гору, и взял в жены прекрасную Лили, и песня эта — или сказка — им очень понравилась. Игого петь не умел, но рассказал о битве при Зулиндрехе, а королева Люси — о злой колдунье, льве и платяном шкафе (историю эту знали все, кроме наших четырёх героев).

into stone (and that is the origin of Mount Pire — it was a two-headed Giant) and won the Lady Liln for his bride; and when it was over they wished it was going to begin again. And though Bree couldn't sing he told the story of the fight at Zalindreh. And Lucy told again (they had all, except Aravis and Cor, heard it many times but they all wanted it again) the tale of the Wardrobe and how she and King Edmund and Queen Susan and Peter the High King had first come into Narnia.

And presently, as was certain to happen sooner or later, King Lune said if was time for young people to be in bed. 'And tomorrow, Cor,' he added, 'shalt come over all the castle with me and see the estate, and mark all its strength and weakness: for it will be thine to guard when I'm gone.'

'But Corin will be the King then, Father,' said Cor.

'Nay, lad,' said King Lune, 'thou art my heir. The crown comes to thee.'

'But I don't want it,' said Cor. 'I'd far rather — '

''Tis no question what thou wantest, Cor, nor I either. 'Tis in the course of law.'

'But if we're twins we must be the same age.'

'Nay,' said the King with a laugh. 'One must come first. Art Corin's elder by full twenty minutes. And his better too, let's hope, though that's no great mastery.' And he looked at Corin with a twinkle in his eyes.

'But, Father, couldn't you make whichever you like to be the next King?'

'No. The king's under the law, for it's the law makes him a king. Hast no more power to start away from thy crown than any sentry from his post.'

'Oh dear,' said Cor. 'I don't want to at all. And Corin — I am most dreadfully sorry. I never dreamed my turning up was going to chisel you out of your kingdom.'

Наконец король Лум послал младших спать и прибавил на прощание:

— А завтра, Кор, мы осмотрим с тобой замок и земли, которые, когда я умру, будут твоими.

— Отец, — возразил Кор, — править будет Корин.

— Нет, — твёрдо сказал Лум, — мой наследник — ты!

— Но я не хочу! Мне бы лучше...

— Дело не в том, кто чего хочет, — таков закон.

— Но мы ведь близнецы!

Король засмеялся:

— Ты старше его на двадцать минут и, надеюсь, лучше, хотя это не обязательно.

Странно, но младший сын нимало не обиделся.

— Разве ты не можешь сам назначить наследника? — удивился Кор.

— Нет. Мы, короли, подчиняемся закону, так что я не свободнее, чем часовой на посту.

— Это мне совсем не нравится. А Корин... я и не знал, что подкладываю ему такую свинью.

'Hurray! Hurray!' said Corin. 'I shan't have to be King. I shan't have to be King. I'll always be a prince. It's princes have all the fun.'

'And that's truer than thy brother knows, Cor,' said King Lune. 'For this is what it means to be a king: to be first in every desperate attack and last in every desperate retreat, and when there's hunger in the land (as must be now and then in bad years) to wear finer clothes and laugh louder over a scantier meal than any man in your land.'

When the two boys were going upstairs to bed Cor again asked Corin if nothing could be done about it. And Corin said:

'If you say another word about it, I'll — I'll knock you down.'

It would be nice to end the story by saying that after that the two brothers never disagreed about anything again, but I am afraid it would not be true. In reality they quarrelled and fought just about as often as any other two boys would, and all their fights ended (if they didn't begin) with Cor getting knocked down. For though, when they had both grown up and become swordsmen, Cor was the more dangerous man in battle, neither he nor anyone else in the North Countries could ever equal Corin as a boxer. That was how he got his name of Corin Thunder-Fist; and how he performed his great exploit against the Lapsed Bear of Stormness, which was really a Talking Bear but had gone back to Wild Bear habits. Corin climbed up to its lair on the Narnian side of Stormness one winter day when the snow was on the hills and boxed it without a time-keeper for thirty-three rounds. And at the end it couldn't see out of its eyes and became a reformed character.

— Ура! — воскликнул братец. — Я не буду королём и навсегда останусь принцем, что куда веселее.

— Ты даже не представляешь, Кор, как твой брат прав, — заметил король Лум. — Быть королём — это значит в самый страшный бой идти первым, а отступать последним; в годы неурожая облачаться в праздничные одежды и принимать за пир самую скудную трапезу.

Подходя к опочивальне, Кор ещё раз спросил, нельзя ли всё изменить, и Корин сказал:

— Вот стукну, тогда узнаешь!

Я был бы рад завершить повесть словами, что больше братья никогда не спорили, но мне не хочется лгать. Они ссорились и дрались ровно столько, сколько ссорятся и дерутся все мальчишки их лет, и побеждал обычно Корин. Когда же они выросли, Кор лучше владел мечом, но Корин дрался врукопашную лучше всех в обоих королевствах, потому его и прозвали Железным Кулаком и потому он победил страшного медведя, который был говорящим, но сбежал к немым, а это очень плохо. Корин пошёл на него один зимой и победил на тридцать третьем раунде, после чего медведь исправился.

Aravis also had many quarrels (and, I'm afraid, even fights) with Cor, but they always made it up again: so that years later, when they were grown up, they were so used to quarrelling and making it up again that they got married so as to go on doing it more conveniently. And after King Lune's death they made a good King and Queen of Archenland and Ram the Great, the most famous of all the kings of Archenland, was their son. Bree and Hwin lived happily to a great age in Narnia and both got married but not to one another. And there weren't many months in which one or both of them didn't come trotting over the pass to visit their friends at Anvard.

Аравита тоже часто ссорилась с Кором (боюсь — иногда и дралась), но всегда мирилась, а когда они выросли и поженились, всё это было им не в новинку. После смерти своего короля они долго и мирно правили Орландией, а их сменил сын — Рам Великий. Игого и Уинни в Нарнии прожили очень долго, но не поженились: каждый завёл собственную семью. Почти каждый месяц они преодолевали рысью перевал, чтобы навестить в Анварде своих венценосных друзей.

ACTIVITIES

Chapter 1–3

1. Translate into English the words and expressions from the text.

уделять внимание; пребывать в миролюбивом настроении; грива; преступление и наказание; поручиться; спрятать за пазухой; непреклонный; приданое; выдать свое невежество

2. Translate into Russian the words and expressions from the text.

southward, to find fault with somebody, to box the ears, indigence, to demand hospitality, to deprive somebody of something, to befriend the destitute, to urge, disguise, inexorable

3. A) Match the verbs with their definitions in Russian.

to set out	разразиться, вспыхивать
to put on	смотреть
to go out	отправляться, выходить, выезжать
to point out	ладить
to break out	поддерживать, соблюдать
to keep up	устанавливать, надевать
to look at	покидать, выходить
to get on	указывать

B) Fill in the sentences with the verbs in the right form.

1. This is how Shasta ____________ *(отправляться)* on his travels.
2. For the roar ______________ *(разразиться)* again, this time on their left from the direction of the forest.
3. And now tell me at once what price you ________ *(устанавливать)* him, for I am wearied with your loquacity.
4. On most days Arsheesh ____________ *(выходить)* in his boat to fish in the morning, and in the afternoon he harnessed his donkey to a cart and loaded the cart with fish and went a mile or so southward to the village to sell it.
5. The roaring of the brutes on each side was horribly close and they seemed to be ______________ *(поддерживать)* with the galloping horses quite easily.
6. He did not even ____________________ *(смотреть)* Shasta but seemed anxious to urge his horse straight on.
7. During these discussions Aravis became a little, a very little, less unfriendly to Shasta; one usually ____________ *(ладить)* better with people when one is making plans than when one is talking about nothing in particular.
8. So it was settled that the Tombs should be their assembly place on the other side of Tashbaan, and everyone felt they were ____________ *(ладить)* very well till Hwin humbly ____________ *(указать)* that the real problem was not where they should go when they had got through Tashbaan but how they were to get through it.

4. Fill in the sentences with the right prepositions.

1. But __ that same year in which the Tisroc (may he live ___ ever) began his august and beneficent reign, ___ a night when the moon was ___ her full, it pleased the gods to deprive me ___ my sleep.
2. And now tell me __ once what price you put ___ him, for I am wearied ____ your loquacity.
3. Twilight was coming ____ apace and a star or two was already out, but the remains ___ the sunset could still be seen ___ the west.
4. ____ the other hand, you can't get very far on those two silly legs ___ yours (what absurd legs humans have!) without being overtaken.
5. And ____ the way, what about starting?
6. I'll vouch ____ the boy, Tarkheena.

5. A) Match the expressions with their Russian equivalents.

to come on apace	не мочь не делать чего-либо
to find fault with somebody	лишить чего-либо
to be moved by something	идти быстро, не отставать; идти нога в ногу
to deprive of something	принять во внимание
to take into account	придираться
at dead of night	да будет тебе известно
be it known to you	глухой ночью
can't help doing something	быть тронутым чем-либо

B) Fill in the sentences with the expressions in the right form.

1. If it had sold well he would come home in a moderately good temper and say nothing to Shasta, but if it

had sold badly he would ______________ (*придираться)* him and perhaps beat him.

2. But in that same year in which the Tisroc (may he live for ever) began his august and beneficent reign, on a night when the moon was at her full, it pleased the gods to __________ *(лишить)* my sleep.
3. Twilight was ______________ *(идти быстро, не отставать)* and a star or two was already out, but the remains of the sunset could still be seen in the west.
4. Accordingly, remembering how the gods never fail to reward those who befriend the destitute, and being ___________ *(быть тронутым чем-либо)* compassion (for your servant is a man of tender heart)...
5. This must be ___________ *(принять во внимание)* in fixing the price.
6. A little boy in rags riding (or trying to ride) a war-horse ______________ *(глухой ночью)* couldn't mean anything but an escape of some sort.
7. ______________ *(да будет тебе известно)* that as I made my journey towards your house to perform the contract of marriage between me and your daughter Aravis Tarkheena...
8. People who know a lot of the same things ______ ________ *(не мочь не)* talking about them, and if you're there you ______________ *(не мочь не)* feeling that you're out of it.

6. Form adjectives with the help of the suffix table.

Suffix	Parts of speech	Meaning
-ful	adjective	full of, characterized by
-able	adjective	capable of, tending to
-ous	adjective	having the quality or nature of, full of

1. full of delight;
2. tending to peace;
3. full of dread;
4. full of anxiety;
5. having the quality of judiciousness;
6. tending to give comfort;

7. Fill in the sentences using the words from Exercise 6.

1. Shasta thought that beyond the hill there must be some ______________ *(восхитительный)* secret which his father wished to hide from him.
2. 'But another poet has likewise said, "He who attempts to deceive the ______________ *(разумный)* is already baring his own back for the scourge."'
3. I should feel much more ______________ *(удобный)*.
4. Or if he was in a ______________ *(миролюбивый)* mood he would say, 'O my son, do not allow your mind to be distracted by idle questions.'
5. He did not even look at Shasta but seemed ______________ *(беспокойный)* to urge his horse straight on.
6. It would be ______________ *(ужасный, отвратительный)* to find, when I get back to Narnia, that I've picked up a lot of low, bad habits.

Chapter 4–6

1. Translate into English the words and expressions from the text.

оскорблять, обзывать кого-либо; дружить с незапамятных времен; поговорка; намекать; угрожать; скрывать, маскировать, прятать; ручаться, давать слово; рыцарский поединок, турнир, самообладание, спокойствие

2. **Translate into Russian the words and expressions from the text.**

innumerable, do not give a fig for something, scapegrace, naughty, naught, to diminish one's hope, outrage, to and fro, to contrive, to be dazed with sunstroke, to mistake somebody for somebody.

3. **A) Match the verbs with their Russian equivalents.**

to keep on	взбираться
to blot out	поглощать, подчинять
to gobble up	торчать острием вверх, навострить
to prick up	выходить
to bring up	продолжать
to come out	сбивать, опрокидывать
to knock down	продолжать, поддерживать
to climb up	заслонять, уничтожать
to keep up	растить, воспитывать

B) Fill in the sentences with the verbs in the right form.

1. The Narnian King — for Shasta began to see by the way the rest spoke to him that he must be a king — ____________ (*продолжать что-либо*) asking him questions.
2. And little lands on the borders of a great empire were always hateful to the lords of the great empire. He longs to __________ them _______ (*заслонять; уничтожать*), __________ them _______ (*поглощать, подчинять*).
3. 'For I have flown above it far and wide in my younger days,' (you may be sure that Shasta _______________ ____________ (*торчать острием вверх; навострить*) his ears at this point).

4. Having been ________________(*растить, воспитывать*) by a hard, close-fisted man like Arsheesh, he had a fixed habit of never telling grown-ups anything if he could help it.
5. He ran howling into a house and his big brother ____________(*выходить*). So I __________ the big brother __________(*сбивать*).
6. After that I ______________(*взбираться*) a pipe on to the roof of a house and lay quiet till it began to get light this morning.
7. He had been trying his hardest for a long time not to think of ghouls: but he couldn't _______ it _____ (*продолжать, поддерживать*) any longer.

4. Fill in the sentences with the right prepositions, where necessary.

1. You could see that they were ready to be friends with anyone who was friendly and didn't *give a fig* _______ *anyone* who wasn't.
2. Would have been a *cause* almost _____ *war* between Archenland and Narnia which are friends *time out* _____ *mind*.
3. There was *a sort* ____ *threatening*, though still veiled under *a show* _____ *courtesy*, in every word he spoke.
4. And little lands on the borders of a great empire were always *hateful* _____ *the lords* of the great empire. He longs to *blot* them _____, *gobble* them _____.
5. For the Faun was *holding* both his horns _______ *his hands* as if he were trying to keep his head on by them and writhing to and fro as if he had a *pain* _____ *his inside*.
6. *Having been brought* _____ by a hard, closefisted man like Arsheesh, he had a fixed *habit* _____ *never telling* grown-ups anything if he could *help* ______ it.

7. King Edmund caught me ______ *the street* and *mistook me* ______ *you*.
8. He looked round; and his heart almost *burst* ______ *relief*.

5. A) Match the expressions with their Russian equivalents.

I don't give a fig for something	с незапамятных времен
to mistake someone for someone	ручаться, давать слово
as true as steel	сердце дрогнуло, ёкнуло
to pledge one's honour	меня не волнует...
time out of mind	преданный и верный
heart gives a great leap	перепутать кого-либо с кем-либо

B) Fill in the sentences with the expressions in the right form.

1. You could see that they were ready to be friends with anyone who was friendly and ______________ *(их не волновал)* anyone who wasn't.
2. Would have been a cause almost of war between Archenland and Narnia which are friends __________ __________ *(с незапамятных времен)*.
3. She was proud and could be hard enough but she was __________________ *(преданный и верный)* and would never have deserted a companion, whether she liked him or not.
4. King Edmund caught me in the street and ________ me ______ you *(перепутал нас с тобой)*.
5. And let the message be worded as graciously as the Queen can contrive without _____________ her _____________ *(ручаться, давать слово)*: so as to give the Prince a hope that she is weakening.

6. Then his ____________________ *(сердце дрогнуло, ёкнуло)*, for he recognized them as Bree and Hwin. But the next moment his heart went down into his toes again.

Chapters 7–9

1. Translate into English the words and expressions from the text.

помолвить, обручить; разумный, здравомыслящий; погрузиться в думы; осмотрительность; стремительность, импульсивность; соловей; благословение

2. Translate into Russian the words and expressions from the text.

absentmindedly, to go back on arrangement, conspicuous, extinguish, exasperate, to desist from doing something, to learn a sharp lesson, loquacious, incantation, weathercock, nuisance

3. A) Match the verbs with their Russian equivalents.

to keep on	держать в удалении
to cut off	испортить, напортачить
to keep off	усмирять
to shout out	вставать
to screw up	изолировать, прекращать
to get up	продолжать
to put down	выкрикивать

B) Fill in the sentences with the verbs in the right form.

1. But the next day passed very slowly. Lasaraleen wanted to go back on the whole arrangement and ________________ *(продолжать)* telling Aravis that

Narnia was a country of perpetual snow and ice inhabited by demons and sorcerers, and she was mad to think of going there.

2. He must ____________ them ____*(испортить, напортачить)* and ____________ *(продолжать)* looking ahead at Mount Pire and ____________ *(выкрикивать)* directions.
3. Yet as the irrefutable and sapient Tisroc has said it is very grievous to be constrained to ________ our hands _______ *(держать в удалении)* such a dainty dish as Narnia.
4. When she stepped ashore she found herself in darkness for the rise of the ground, and the trees, ____________ *(изолировать, прерывать)* the moonlight.
5. In fact he decided that he would ____________ *(вставать)* and persuade them to go on.
6. To this Hwin made no answer, being, like most highly bred mares, a very nervous and gentle person who was easily ____________ *(усмирять)*.

4. Fill in the sentences with the right prepositions, where necessary.

1. But ______ *the next day* passed very slowly. Lasaraleen wanted to go *back* ________ *the whole arrangement* and *kept* ________ *telling* Aravis that Narnia was a country of perpetual snow and ice inhabited by demons and sorcerers, and she was mad *to think* _____ *going* there.
2. Last of all came a little hump-backed, wizened old *man* ______ *whom* she recognized ______ *a shudder* the new Grand Vizier and her own betrothed husband, Ahoshta Tarkaan himself.
3. This seemed to *exasperate* ______ *the Prince*.

4. The Tisroc was apparently *sunk* _____ *thought*, but when, after a long pause, he noticed what was happening, he said tranquilly...
5. My son, _____ *all means desist* _____ *kicking* the venerable and enlightened Vizier.
6. When she *stepped* _____ *ashore* she found herself _____ *darkness* for the rise of the ground, and the trees, *cut* ______ the moonlight.
7. _______ *fact* he decided that he would *get* _____ and persuade them to *go* _______.

5. A) Match the expressions with their Russian equivalents.

to desist from doing something	быть сдерживаемым чем-либо
before you can say knife	проявлять благоразумие и вежливость
to exercise prudence and courtesy	даровать благоразумие и осмотрительность
to be constrained by something	переставать, воздерживаться
to make blood run cold	леденить кровь
as changeable as weathercocks	непостоянный, подобный флюгеру
to bestow prudence and circumspection	моментально, не успеть и глазом моргнуть

B) Fill in the sentences with the expressions in the right form.

1. My son, by all means ______________ *(переставать, воздерживаться)* kicking the venerable and enlightened Vizier.
2. You shall say that I did it without your knowledge and against your will, and without your blessing, ________________ *(быть сдерживаемым)* the violence of my love and the impetuosity of youth.

3. For it is well known that women are as ______________________________.
4. The cool, placid voice in which he spoke these words __________ Aravis's ____________________ *(леденить кровь)*.
5. But the third time, as his bare feet touched the sand he screamed with pain and got one foot back in the stirrup and the other half over Bree's back ______________ you ______________________ *(моментально, не успеть и глазом моргнуть)*.
6. I shall ___________________________________ *(проявлять благоразумие и вежливость)* and spill as little Narnian blood as I can.
7. 'How blessed is Calormen,' said the Vizier, popping up his face again, 'on whose ruler the gods have been pleased to ____________________________ *(даровать благоразумие и осмотрительность)*!'

Chapter 10–12

1. Translate into English the words and expressions from the text.

перейти вброд; позорить, дискредитировать; самодовольство, заносчивость; рвануться, броситься; быстроногий; бодрствующий, бессонный

2. Translate into Russian the words and expressions from the text.

dragonfly, to hesitate, for one hideous hundredth of a second, on the edge of something, to have insurance of something, to have wits, to lose sight of something, to take stock, abreast, to seize, as life

3. A) Match the verbs with their Russian equivalents.

to catch up	вставать, подниматься
to pick up	быть привыкшим
to be used to	оказаться
to give up	догнать
to stand up	поднимать, собирать
to turn out	бросить, прекратить

B) Fill in the sentences with the verbs in the right form.

1. And certainly both Horses were doing, if not all they could, all they thought they could; which is not quite the same thing. Bree had __________________ *(догнать)* with Hwin and they thundered side by side over the turf.
2. After that he ________________ *(вставать, подниматься)*, shaking the water out of his ears and flinging the wet hair back from his forehead, and began to take stock of his surroundings.
3. Then, to his utter astonishment, the lion, still on its hind legs, checked itself suddenly, turned head over heels, _____________ itself _________ *(поднимать, собирать)*, and rushed away.
4. Aravis couldn't help making a face when she tasted it, for goats' milk is rather a shock when you ________ not ___________ *(быть привыкшим)* it.
5. And now it was quite dark and they seemed to have ________________ *(бросить, прекратить)* blowing that horn.

4. Fill in the sentences with the right prepositions, where necessary.

1. Thornbut trod on a loose stone, came flat *down* ____ *his nose*, and found when he tried to *get* _____ that he had sprained his ankle: a real excruciating sprain

which would *keep* him ______ walking or riding for ______ *least* a fortnight.

2. 'See what your Highness has done,' said King Edmund. '*Deprived* us _____ a proved warrior _____ the very *edge* of battle.'
3. The weather had changed and the *whole* ___ that green enclosure was *filled*, like a great green cup, ______ sunlight.
4. I've been snubbing him and *looking down* ______ *him* ever since you met us and now he *turns* _____ to be the best of us all.
5. He *spread* _____________ his arms to Shasta, his face lit up, and he *cried* _____________ in a great, deep voice that seemed to come __________ *the bottom* of his chest.

5. Form adjectives with the help of the suffix table.

Suffix	Parts of speech	Meaning
-ful	adjective	full of, characterized by
-able	adjective	capable of, tending to

1. full of peace;
2. characterized by grace;
3. full of beauty;
4. full of mourning;
5. tending to be remarked.

6. Fill in the sentences using the words from Exercise 5.

1. Bree turned round at last, his face _______________ *(траурный)* as only a horse's can be.
2. It was a very _____________ *(мирный)* place, lonely and quiet.

3. The other was a stag, a _____________ *(красивый)* lordly creature with wide liquid eyes, dappled flanks and legs so thin and _____________ *(изящный)* that they looked as if you could break them with two fingers.
4. But there was something more _____________ *(замечательный, отличающийся)* than the size about it.
5. At one end of the pool, completely overshadowing it with its branches, there grew the hugest and most _____________ *(красивый)* tree that Shasta had ever seen.
6. The Rabbit agreed that this was very _____________ *(замечательный, отличающийся)* news and that somebody ought to tell someone about it with a view to doing something

Chapter 13–15

1. Translate into English the words and expressions from the text.

поставить на ком-либо крест, считать погибшим; узнать, пронюхать, своевременно разгадать что-либо; дойти до крайности; свергать

2. Translate into Russian the words and expressions from the text.

to funk, to be as like as two peas, stepmother, inclination, to overhaul, to one's heart content, to put on a level with something or somebody, in consideration of, to be disposed to do something, to be graved at, gravity, to bear witness of

3. A) Match the verbs with their Russian equivalents.

to spread out	участвовать
to look in	помириться
to get on	продолжать
to be in	выгонять, убирать, удалять
to burst out	зайти, заглянуть
to go on	рассредоточиваться
to put out	искать, наводить справку
to look up	продвигаться, идти вперёд
to make up	вспыхнуть, разразиться

B) Fill in the sentences with the verbs in the right form.

1. Here the army halted and ___________ *(рассредоточиваться)* in a line, and there was a great deal of rearranging.
2. 'I ___________ *(принимать участие)* for it now — I really ___________ *(принимать участие)* for it now,' thought Shasta.
3. I expect he is in Anvard. Naturally we'd ___________ *(зайти, заглянуть)* on him and say goodbye.
4. But a moment later he ___________ *(вспыхнуть, разразиться)* laughing and said, 'If you want to know the truth, it isn't a proper wound at all.'
5. 'Yes, there are,' said Aravis. 'But ___________ *(идти вперёд)* with the story.'
6. So as soon as he heard I was going to save Archenland from a great danger he decided I must be ___________ *(убирать, выгонять)* of the way.
7. During his reign, and to his face, he was called Rabadash the Peacemaker, but after his death and behind his back he was called Rabadash the Ridiculous, and if you ___________ him ______ *(искать, наводить*

справку) in a good History of Calormen (try the local library) you will find him under that name.

8. Aravis also had many quarrels (and, I'm afraid, even fights) with Cor, but they always ______ it ______ *(помириться)* again: so that years later, when they were grown up, they were so used to quarrelling and __________ it _____ *(помириться)* again that they got married so as to ______________ *(продолжать)* doing it more conveniently.

4. Fill in the sentences with the right preposition, where necessary.

1. He ought to have ridden back to Tashbaan as soon as the first attack failed, for his whole plan *depended* _____ speed and surprise.
2. When Shasta fell off his horse he gave himself up ______ *lost*.
3. 'Your Majesty would have a perfect right to *strike* ______ his head,' said Peridan. 'Such an assault as he made *puts him* _____ *a level* _____ *assassins*.'
4. Nevertheless, _____ *consideration* _____ your youth and the ill nurture, devoid of all *gentilesse* and courtesy, which you have doubtless had in the land of slaves and tyrants, we are disposed to set you free, unharmed, _____ *these conditions*: first, that...
5. _____ *this* of course the Donkey twitched its ears forward and that also was so funny that everybody laughed all the more. They tried not to, but they tried _____ *vain*.
6. This was because, not daring to go more than ten miles from Tashbaan, he could never *go* ____ a war himself: and he didn't want his Tarkaans to win *fame* ____ *the wars* _____ his *expense*, for that is the way Tisrocs get overthrown.

5. A) Match the expressions with their Russian equivalents.

to get wind of something	вдоволь, сколько душе угодно
as like as two peas	дойти до крайности
to one's heart content	похожий как две капли воды
to give oneself up for lost	за чей-либо счёт
to come to extremity	почуять, разгадать заранее
at one's expense	поставить крест, считать погибшим

B) Fill in the sentences with expressions in the right form.

1. One is Prince Corin. The other, ________________ *(похожий как две капли воды)*. It's your little Shasta.
2. This was because, not daring to go more than ten miles from Tashbaan, he could never go on a war himself: and he didn't want his Tarkaans to win fame in the wars ____________________ *(за его счёт)*, for that is the way Tisrocs get overthrown.
3. When Shasta fell off his horse he ________________ *(поставил на себе крест)*.
4. 'Your royal Highness,' he said. 'I am most truly sorry that things have ____________________ *(дойти до крайности)*.'
5. But Father ________________ *(прознал заранее)*, though not quite in time, and was after him as quickly as he could.
6. I shall be learning reading and writing and heraldry and dancing and history and music while you'll be galloping and rolling on the hills of Narnia ______________________ *(сколько душе угодно)*.

Учебное издание

СОВРЕМЕННЫЙ БЕСТСЕЛЛЕР: БИЛИНГВА

Льюис Клайв Стейплз

ХРОНИКИ НАРНИИ. КОНЬ И ЕГО МАЛЬЧИК = THE CHRONICLES OF NARNIA. THE HORSE AND HIS BOY

(орыс тілінде)

Ответственный редактор *Н. Уварова*
Редакторы *Н. Хасаия, Е. Вьюницкая*
Младший редактор *О. Колышева*
Художественный редактор *В. Безкровный*
Технический редактор *Л. Зотова*
Компьютерная верстка *Н. Билюкина*
Корректор *Е. Савинова*

ООО «Издательство «Эксмо»
123308, Москва, ул. Зорге, д. 1. Тел. 8 (495) 411-68-86.
Home page: **www.eksmo.ru** E-mail: **info@eksmo.ru**

Өндіруші: «ЭКСМО» АҚБ Баспасы, 123308, Мәскеу, Ресей, Зорге көшесі, 1 үй.
Тел. 8 (495) 411-68-86.
Home page: www.eksmo.ru E-mail: info@eksmo.ru.
Тауар белгісі: «Эксмо»
Қазақстан Республикасында дистрибьютор және өнім бойынша арыз-талаптарды қабылдаушының өкілі «РДЦ-Алматы» ЖШС, Алматы қ., Домбровский көш., 3«а», литер Б, офис 1.
Тел.: 8(727) 2 51 59 89,90,91,92, факс: 8 (727) 251 58 12 вн. 107; E-mail: RDC-Almaty@eksmo.kz
Өнімнің жарамдылық мерзімі шектелмеген.
Сертификация туралы ақпарат сайтта: www.eksmo.ru/certification

Сведения о подтверждении соответствия издания согласно законодательству РФ о техническом регулировании можно получить на сайте Издательства «Эксмо»

Өндірген мемлекет: Ресей
Сертификация қарастырылмаған

Подписано в печать 13.02.2017. Формат 84x100$^1/_{32}$.
Гарнитура «Minion Pro». Печать офсетная. Усл. печ. л. 17,11.
Тираж 3000 экз. Заказ 7714/17.

Отпечатано в соответствии с предоставленными материалами в ООО "ИПК Парето-Принт", 170546, Тверская область Промышленная зона Боровлево-1, комплекс №3А
www.pareto-print.ru

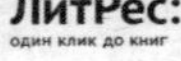

ISBN 978-5-699-84286-5